THE National SABR Pastime

Baseball in Texas and Beyond

Edited by Steve West and Cecilia M. Tan

 Published by The Society for American Baseball Research

THE NATIONAL PASTIME – 2025 EDITION

Copyright © 2025 The Society for American Baseball Research

Editor: Cecilia M. Tan
Design and production: Lisa Hochstein
Cover art: Courtesy of the Texas Rangers
Fact checker: Clifford Blau
Proofreader: Keith R.A. DeCandido

ISBN 978-1-960819-41-3 print edition
ISBN 978-1-960819-40-6 ebook edition

Society for American Baseball Research, Inc.
Cronkite School at ASU
555 N. Central Ave. #406C
Phoenix, AZ 85004

Web: www.sabr.org
Phone: (602) 496–1460

Contents

From the Editor

When I was asked to edit this book to accompany the SABR national convention in the Dallas-Fort Worth area, I thought about what to cover about baseball in Texas, and where it should focus. Naturally the Texas Rangers had to be a part of the story, but I wanted it to show so much more.

First, *Where*, exactly? When you think about the Rangers, you think about North Texas, but their reach goes far beyond. The Rangers Radio Network broadcasts from Arkansas in the east to New Mexico in the west, from Oklahoma in the north to San Antonio in the south. That made for a natural region to focus on, and I'm pleased to say we have articles from across the area.

Then we had to solve for which subjects to cover.

Texas has a long baseball history, which many people know. Sure, the major leagues arrived in the 1960s and 1970s, but there was already a deep tradition of baseball, from high schools to college to the minors. In the early days, Texas was perfect for spring training, and major league teams took advantage. The minors flourished, with teams in almost every town, at least until there weren't. Black teams and Negro League teams came and went. And of course, college ball thrives to this day in Texas and Oklahoma.

After some thought, we decided that we wanted to capture all of that.

We put out a call to Dallas-Fort Worth's Banks-Bragan chapter and several nearby SABR chapters, and received a very encouraging response. SABR members naturally wanted to write about their interests, which included the entire length and breadth of baseball in Texas and beyond. Our *What* and *When* questions quickly had their answers.

Reading through the articles as they were submitted, I ran across so much I did not know about Texas baseball history. Yes, I knew some of the names and some of the stories, but there is plenty here to grab your interest. You probably know nothing about high school baseball in San Antonio in the 1960s, for example, but we have a story about it. There are articles about college ball in both Texas and Oklahoma over the years (fun fact: Banks-Bragan chapter president Paul Rogers, who wrote two articles in this book, was once president of the Southwest Conference).

Back in the day there were dozens of minor league teams in Texas, but now there are just eight, in part due to economics, but also because of football. Former Rangers outfielder Josh Hamilton once said that Dallas-Fort Worth was not a baseball town, because football dominated the world of sports in Dallas. In some ways he was right, but that didn't stop me and tens of thousands of Rangers fans from chanting "Baseball Town" when he came back here to play.

Texas being Texas, you might be surprised to see how much history Black baseball has in the state. From early Black teams to Negro League players, we're pleased to bring some of these stories to light. There's even an article about wartime baseball at Camp Hood, which, although not focused on Black players, reminds us of Jackie Robinson, whose own inciting incident may have been in the very same place.

I thank every contributor to this book, all of whom are helping to keep baseball history alive in Texas and beyond. When asked, they stepped up to the plate and hit a home run, and this book is all the better for it. I especially want to thank my co-editor Cecilia Tan, who has guided me in so many ways through the book, and definitely helped make it as good as it is.

Baseball still thrives in Texas, with thousands of people every day watching games from local sandlots to the professional level. In the past decade both major league teams in Texas have won a World Series (and as a Rangers fan, I would be remiss if I didn't remind you that—sorry Astros fans—the Astros cheated!).

I'm also not ashamed to admit the Dallas Cowboys dominate the headlines here. Still, there are millions of Rangers fans for whom no moment was lower than when Nelson Cruz missed the catch which would have won the World Series in 2011, but no moment was greater than when we won it all in 2023.

I hope you enjoy this look at baseball across the region and throughout the history of Texas and beyond.

– Steve West
Carrollton, Texas
June 2025

Deadball Era Major League Baseball Comes to Waxahachie, Texas

Jim Chapman

Some might think that major league baseball debuted in the Dallas-Fort Worth Metroplex in 1972, with the Washington Senators' reincarnation as the Texas Rangers in Arlington, Texas, but major-league history in the area harkens back to the Deadball Era. Over a century ago, the major leagues flourished in Waxahachie, Texas, in the springtime.

The Detroit Tigers, featuring the legendary Ty Cobb, trained there from 1916 through 1918. The following year, the Cincinnati Reds encamped there before embarking on their 1919 campaign—the one that culminated in a World Series triumph over the infamous "Black Sox." Ironically, after a year off from hosting spring training, in 1921 Waxahachie switched from the Reds to hosting the Sox. The six-year stretch from 1916 through 1921 was a memorable period for Waxahachie, and today the principal sites utilized by the visiting major league teams still stand as iconic structures serving the community.

Texas hosted spring training for many major league teams from 1903 to 1941.[1] The relatively warm weather in March and the ready availability of rail travel were enticing to teams from colder climates. The peak years for spring training in Texas were 1904 through 1922. Thereafter, San Antonio was the only Texas city regularly utilized for spring training. From the 1920s on, the expansion of the railroad and the resulting development boom in Florida lured an increasing number of major league teams—still largely East-Coast-based—to the sunnier Florida climate, which could be reached by rail even more easily than Texas. The newspaper chart at right shows the locations of the major league spring training camps in 1916 when spring training at Texas was at its peak. Texas and Florida each hosted five teams, with the rest scattered across the southern states of Louisiana, Virginia, Georgia, and Arkansas.

In the first two decades of the 1900s, many Texas communities made pitches directly to major league teams to lure them to their towns for spring training. The competition to bring a big-league squad to town for a month or more fueled intense courting. Waxahachie, a small town located 25 miles south of Dallas, was one of the most successful suitors, ultimately enticing three different major league teams to town for a total of five training camps during the period.

Intrepid Waxahachie community leaders astutely took advantage of the surge of interest in Texas spring training sites by major league teams in the 1910s. Waxahachie's flirtation with the big leagues began in

(L to R): Harry Heilmann (HOF), George Burns (1926 AL MVP), Ty Cobb (HOF), Bobby Veach, and Sam Crawford (HOF) in front of the grandstand at Jungle Park, Waxahachie in March 1917. The ballpark site is still used by the local high school baseball team.

Los Angeles Express, March 10, 1916

New Rogers Hotel, Waxahachie, Texas

The Rogers Hotel as it appeared when the Detroit Tigers stayed there in 1916–18.

White Sox manager "Kid" Gleason (left), and Hall of Fame pitcher "Red" Faber (right) in front of the Jungle Park grandstand, 1921.

earnest in 1915 when representatives of the Waxahachie Chamber of Commerce reached out with a lucrative offer to the Detroit Tigers ownership about the possibility of hosting the team for spring training.[2] Texas intrigued the Tigers, and they also had offers from several other Texas communities. During the 1915 offseason, the Tigers dispatched their manager, Hall of Famer Hughie Jennings, and their groundskeeper to Texas to tour the vying towns in North Central Texas.[3] They were duly impressed with Waxahachie, which was ultimately the Tigers' choice. Several reasons, aside from just the warm weather and expansive transit network, lured them to Waxahachie.

Foremost was the luxurious Rogers Hotel, which had been completed several years prior in 1912 and was an ideal base for the team. The Rogers was a much nicer and more modern hotel than most communities of Waxahachie's size could boast, and was located next to a popular natural hot spring. In January 1916, to further entice the Tigers, a 20-square-foot, three- to five-foot-deep pool was installed in the hotel basement with water pumped in from the adjacent hot spring.[4] The basement also was modified to include a locker room with 33 lockers and billiard tables for the players. There was even a rooftop garden, visible on the postcard shown at left, available for the player's relaxation.

A newly constructed ballpark where the Tigers could train was also a key factor in their selection of Waxahachie. The Waxahachie Chamber of Commerce formed and capitalized a stock company, the Waxahachie Athletic Park Association, which in turn agreed to construct a stadium at a cost of $4,000, on vacant land across from the city cemetery.[5] The players could walk the three-quarter-mile trip to the stadium alongside the railroad tracks. The stadium was christened "Jungle Park" in honor of the new occupants, the Tigers. A covered grandstand was hastily constructed, and the entire field was enclosed within a wooden fence. A stadium is still located at this site, now known as Richards Park in honor of Waxahachie native Paul Richards, a former major league player and manager, and is the home of the Indians, the Waxahachie High School baseball team.

There was another major benefit of Waxahachie as far as the team owners, if not necessarily the players, were concerned. Waxahachie and its surroundings were "dry," meaning alcohol would not be a temptation for the players. Combined with the easy rail access to nearby training sites for other major league teams in Marlin Springs (New York Giants), Palestine (St. Louis Browns), and Mineral Wells (Chicago White Sox), Waxahachie's appeal becomes evident. A full-page article from the 1916 *Detroit Free Press* (as seen in the online appendix on SABR.org) extolls Waxahachie's virtues and compares it—in puffery the locals would be loath to believe—to New York and Paris.[6]

Waxahachie, in turn, was enamored with the major leaguers and their sojourn in town. Locals feted the players with numerous parties and banquets. Overflow crowds watched workouts and games against visiting teams such as the New York Giants. Many famous Hall of Fame players came to Waxahachie during those years. The 1916–18 Tigers teams that trained in Waxahachie were loaded with future Hall of Famers such as Ty Cobb, Sam Crawford, Harry Heilmann, and Hughie Jennings. The 1919 Reds fielded Hall of Famer Edd Roush. The 1921 White Sox team was also loaded with

Hall of Famers such as Eddie Collins, Harry Hooper, Ray Schalk, and Red Faber. Other Hall of Famers who passed through Waxahachie during those years included Tris Speaker, Rogers Hornsby, and Christy Mathewson.

After the 1918 season, the Tigers opted to move to Macon, Georgia, for spring training as flooding had heavily damaged the wooden Jungle Park.[7] After being spurned by the Tigers, local leaders quickly put the ballpark back in shape and enticed the Cincinnati Reds to switch to Waxahachie as their spring training site for 1919. But despite winning the World Series that year, the Reds opted for Miami, Florida, the following year, bypassing Waxahachie altogether. Texas papers suggested the move was made for a big pile of money and the preference for a locale where, even with the oncoming of Prohibition, booze and fast living thrived.[8] The Reds switched late enough in the year that Waxahachie was not able to attract another team in time for spring training in 1920. The White Sox trained in Waxahachie prior to the 1921 season and were the final major league team to do so.

By 1922, wooden Jungle Park was falling into disrepair once again and the White Sox opted to train in Seguin.[9] While minor league teams such as the Kansas City Blues trained in Waxahachie in the 1920s, the big-league squads never returned.

For a brief but glorious while over one hundred years ago, Waxahachie was a hotbed of major league baseball. It was quite an accomplishment for such a small city to host spring training for the major league teams. The memory of the baseball stars that passed through town has dimmed with the passage of time, but the structures that accommodated them are still part of the citizens' daily lives. When you visit the Globe Life Field environs in Arlington this year for SABR 53, remember, there was a time a little more than a century ago when the newest big-league ballpark was in Waxahachie, Texas. ∎

Notes

1. Frank Jackson, "Crossing Red River, Spring Training in Texas," *The National Pastime*, no. 26 (2006), 85–91.
2. "Notes," *Waxahachie Daily Light*, August 26, 1915.
3. "Waxahachie Looks Good to Jennings," *Waxahachie Daily Light*, November 15, 1915.
4. "New Camp is a Great One, Best Equipped Park," *Waxahachie Daily Light*, March 11, 1916.
5. "Stock Company Will Provide a Ball Park," *Waxahachie Daily Light*, December 4, 1915.
6. "Jungaleers's Training Camp Teeming with Hospitality," *Detroit Free Press*, February 6, 1916.
7. "Pallid Hose Will Train for Coming Pennant in Texas," *Moline Daily Dispatch*, December 8, 1919.
8. Molten Cobb, "The Stove League," *Austin American-Statesman*, December 7, 1919.
9. "Fans Favor the Texas Camping," *The Brookfield Argus and Linn County Farmer*, December 27, 1921.

Spring Training Ballparks at Marlin, Texas
Early Twentieth Century Major League Baseball in a Central Texas Town

Monte Cely

From 1900 to 1941 as many as seven major league teams held spring training in Texas. San Antonio was the preferred Texas locale. Marlin, in central Texas near Waco, was second. The Alamo City hosted for 29 seasons; Marlin for 16.[1]

For nearly 60 years, beginning in the 1890s, Marlin was a popular resort, known for its hot mineral baths. The natural waters were discovered accidentally in 1892 when sinking a new well for drinking water produced a gusher of 147-degree water containing large amounts of sodium, sulfur, magnesium, iron, and other minerals.[2]

Marlin already had two hospitals and was a regional medical center. The Marlin Sanitarium bathhouse was built in 1896. It and others built in that era attracted thousands of the afflicted, as well as health vacationers. To support these visitors, several first-class hotels were built, including the Arlington and the Falls (the eighth hotel in Conrad Hilton's chain).

Many patrons came by rail. The Houston and Texas Central Railway (H&TC) had completed its line through Marlin in 1872. A spur of the International-Great Northern (I&GN) came into town in 1900, followed by the Missouri Pacific in 1902.[3]

The same factors that made Marlin welcoming and accessible to tourists made it attractive to major league baseball clubs. Beginning in 1904, five different major league teams spent all or part of the pre-season in Marlin.

EARLY VISITORS: 1903 TO 1907

In February 1903, Ted Sullivan, representing Charles Comiskey, contacted Marlin about training there in March. Marlin responded favorably and committed to providing suitable grounds for the Chicagos.[4] But the window of opportunity was too narrow, as Comiskey wrote the following week that his team could not come in 1903. He did leave the door open for a Marlin visit the following year.

Sullivan returned in December 1903 to meet with locals at the Arlington Hotel, and subsequently the Sox arrived in Marlin on March 7, 1904. With the team were four Chicago newspapermen. The local *Marlin* *Democrat* reporter wrote that "a million people will... learn Marlin's location on the map."[5] The team trained at the "ballpark at the old fairgrounds."

EAST SIDE FIELDS AT THE FAIRGROUNDS

The "Fair Ground" was east of downtown. The Falls County Fair was held there and included harness racing. The race track had grandstands. The high school used the grounds for track meets. This ball field was called the "east side" field, the "old fairgrounds" field, or the "Comiskey" field, and was used exclusively by visiting teams until 1911.

In December 1904 Comiskey stated the club would not return to Texas, opting for New Orleans in 1905.[6] He wrote that he preferred to come back, but could not work out the scheduling with "...the St. Louis men, who had pre-empted training places in Texas..." and wanted a commitment that his club would spend the entire spring in Texas.[7]

In early February 1905, Arlington hotel management received a telegram from Cardinals manager Charles "Kid" Nichols requesting arrangements to train in Marlin. They responded that the same rates and grounds that Comiskey had used would be available to the St. Louis Nationals. The Cardinals committed the following week to train in Marlin for three weeks. Marlin also received a letter from the Browns expressing interest in training there.[8] This fell through, as the Browns trained in Dallas in 1905.

The Arlington Hotel, a spring training hotspot for two decades.

The Cardinals arrived in Marlin on Sunday, March 5, 1905. Their contingent of 27 arrived by private rail car on the I&GN tracks. After a Monday tour of the Arlington and the fairgrounds field, Nichols expressed his satisfaction.[9]

The Redbirds did not return in 1906, but the Cincinnati Reds arrived March 6. The Reds planned to train there for two weeks, spend a few days in San Antonio, and then take an exhibition tour around the state. The following week, Reds business manager F.C. Bancroft said that he loved Marlin as a training site and planned a three-year commitment to train there. The local news reported that the I&GN railroad offered a special price for Marlin fans to travel to Waco to see the Reds play: 75¢ round trip in coach![10]

With growing interest and the potential for multiple teams in Spring 1907, improvements were needed for the East Side Fairgrounds. In January 1907 the local *Daily Democrat* challenged: "Ball Grounds Must be Fixed Up—Great Opportunity for Publicity of Marlin's Health Resort." A second field and enclosed grounds were needed. $200 was being requested from local supporters. The Arlington committed $50. The Reds returned in 1907 and were joined by Connie Mack's Philadelphia Athletics.[11]

Mack, along with John Shibe, son of co-owner Ben Shibe, and the Athletics reached Marlin on March 3. They immediately went to work at the east-side grounds.[12] The Reds had their entire squad in Marlin by March 11. Upon arrival, Reds management expressed concern to the Arlington that both teams could not be properly accommodated. They were assured of a separate floor at the hotel, separate dining facilities, and the use of a second field at the east-side grounds. As Mack's men stayed as planned until March 15, things worked out.[13] The Reds left Marlin on March 25 for New Orleans. On the way, they stopped in College Station for a game with the Texas A&M squad.[14]

THE GIANTS COME TO MARLIN

In September 1907 Arlington management received a letter from Texas League representatives in Dallas asking whether Marlin could give the Giants exclusive accommodations for Spring 1908. The letter stated, "It would be much better for you to have the New York team…owing to the great amount of advertising you would get in the New York papers. McGraw would bring about 30 or 35 people with him, including the best sporting writers in the country."[15]

The Arlington responded and in late December McGraw announced to the Gotham media that he would take the Giants to Marlin for the 1908 preseason.[16] The Giants had trained in Los Angeles in 1907, and McGraw wanted a location with fewer distractions. In early February 1908 most of the Giants left New York City by steamship for New Orleans, then traveled by rail from there to Marlin.

Giants' groundskeeper John Murphy, head gardener at the Polo Grounds, was already in Marlin working the East Side Fairgrounds fields. Murphy said "…it is lucky they sent me ahead, as the grounds had been given up for steers, pigs, and horses…but the field is now in shape, with the infield grassy and the outfield as smooth as a billiard table."[17]

The first group of Giants, mostly "yannigans" trying to make the team, arrived in Marlin on February 19, 1908, led by veteran catcher Roger Bresnahan. With them were sportswriters Sam Crane of the *New York Journal & American* and Sid Mercer of the *New York Globe*. Crane also authored stories that ran in the local newspaper. Arriving from Los Angeles on Saturday, February 22, McGraw immediately fell in love with Marlin. Crane, writing in the *Marlin Democrat*, quoted McGraw as saying, "If we do win the flag this year, much of the credit will go to Marlin!" By March 4, McGraw reported that all 29 players were in Marlin, and that "real practice" would start the next day. "Mac" also noted with satisfaction that several members of the squad were much lighter than the previous spring.[18]

After a good experience at Marlin, the Giants returned in spring 1909. Arlington management was cabled that majority owner John T. Brush would accompany the club. Brush suffered from locomotor ataxia, a progressive disease of the nervous system, and hoped to improve his health by partaking of the curative waters. After just a few days in Marlin, Brush

The Giants at the East Side Fairgrounds, prior to their move to their new park.

AUTHOR'S COLLECTION

said he was "...deriving a world of benefit from the Marlin water...I will become a walking advertisement for Marlin." Likewise, sportswriter Crane, ill upon arriving in Marlin, said he was "100 percent better after my first two baths in the mineral water."[19]

The Giants continued to train at the East Side Fairgrounds during 1909 and 1910. However, Brush planned to purchase local land for a future permanent spring training facility.[20]

EMERSON PARK, THE GIANTS' PERMANENT FACILITY

Before leaving in late March 1910, McGraw "...took a ride to the outskirts of the town and selected the place for the new ball grounds which the people of Marlin are to present to the New York Giants. The site finally chosen will make a fine large field, being over 400 feet square." This was to become Emerson Park, the Giants' spring training home for the rest of the decade.[21]

On March 7, 1911, the site was deeded to the Giants. A ceremony was held preceding a Giants intra-squad game. Postmaster Dunn R. Emerson, a landowner in south Marlin and baseball booster, made the presentation. Mayor F.S. Heffner went to the pitcher's mound and pitched to Giants catcher Chief Meyers, with McGraw batting.[22]

The Giants built a large park, complete with grandstands and bleachers, on this property south of the business district. Fred Snodgrass claimed the park was about two miles (actually round trip) from the Arlington. Twice daily the Giants walked south to the ballpark along nearby railroad tracks.

During January 1912, groundskeeper Murphy warned McGraw of a meningitis outbreak in Texas, reporting cases statewide at 1300, with 518 deaths. After discussion with local health officials, McGraw was convinced that the danger was minimal.[23] Christy Mathewson was shortly in St. Louis, on February 28, in charge of 15 Giants players traveling by rail to Marlin. McGraw opened spring workouts on March 1.[24]

Early 1913 found groundskeeper Murphy back in Marlin. Livestock had grazed on the outfield grass and he again worked to make the field level. Murphy also advised that the Arlington was under new management.[25] That spring was rainy with up to three inches falling daily. The Giants resorted to other exercises, including running, handball, and throwing medicine balls.

Also early in 1913, Olympic hero and Native American Jim Thorpe negotiated with McGraw to play for the Giants. Sealing the deal "by long distance telephone," Mac ordered Thorpe to Marlin. He arrived shortly and impressed with his batting power. One clout landed "beyond the tennis courts in far left

The Giants walking the railroad tracks, 1913. This is a seldom seen wide-angle view of the team walking to Emerson Park.

field."[26] McGraw used Thorpe at first base and in the outfield"[27] Thorpe played parts of six seasons with the Giants.

New Giants' president H.N. "Harry" Hempstead made his first visit in 1913. He was John Brush's son-in-law, becoming club president upon Brush's death. Hempstead quickly signed McGraw to a five-year contract at a handsome $30,000 per year.[28]

In a unique Fall appearance, the Giants played the White Sox on November 3, 1913, at Emerson Park, part of an exhibition swing prior to the teams' World Tour. Marlin fans lobbied McGraw to put Mathewson in the pitcher's box, but Matty was ill. Jeff Tesreau pitched the "home team" to an 11–1 thrashing of Comiskey's men. The teams went on to Los Angeles, then sailed for Japan, India, Egypt, France, and England. Fortunately for the travelers, the Great War had not yet started. They sailed from England back to New York aboard the *Lusitania*—some 15 months before the ship would be sunk by a German U-boat.[29]

Baseball gossip in early 1914 concerned "raids" by the Federal League. The Feds claimed 175 players from major league rosters. Rumors swirled that Mathewson, Tesreau, and Snodgrass might jump. Once McGraw returned from the World Tour and was able to talk to his men (several of whom did not travel overseas) he was generally able to retain their services by inking multi-year contracts.[30]

New groundskeeper Henry Fabian made his first visit to Marlin in early 1914. John Murphy had passed away in September and Fabian was in his first year as the Polo Grounds head gardener. Fabian reported that Emerson Park's pitching rubber was twelve inches too far from home plate![31] The pitchers were grateful for this discovery. In December 1914, the Marlin ballpark was deeded to the Giants.[32] The property was controlled by the Giants organization until the 1970s.[33]

The local newspaper was now affiliated with the Associated Press, so World War reports dominated the news. But the Giants continued to be big local news. The Giants' party numbered 62 on the Arlington register by late February 1915.[34] Training was often interrupted during Spring 1915 due to cold weather. As a result, the Giants sent their "colts" on a 17-day barnstorming tour through Texas, Oklahoma, Arkansas, Tennessee, and Virginia, finally arriving at the Polo Grounds.[35]

Ted Sullivan returned to Marlin in early 1916. He was the featured speaker at the Orpheum Theater for "World Tour of the Giants and White Sox," a lecture and film about the recent global tour.[36] Deciding not to retire, Mathewson signed for another year and led the first contingent of Giants headed for Marlin. McGraw arrived from Havana with Crane, Mercer, and a "moving picture crew."[37]

The highlight of Spring 1916 was an exhibition game with the Tigers. Detroit trained in nearby Waxahachie and visited Marlin to close out training. Several Tigers, including manager and McGraw buddy Hughie Jennings, joined the Giants for their Farewell Ball held at the Arlington. The next day, Friday March 24, the Giants defeated the Tigers, 4–1. Over 2,000 fans from throughout Central Texas watched the game at Emerson Park.[38]

With the nation nearing war in early 1917, the Giants returned for their tenth spring in Marlin. Groundskeeper Fabian arrived early after visiting his son at Texas A&M. Improvements were underway at Emerson Park, including construction of batting cages, more grandstand seating, and piping of water to the field. The Marlin Commercial Club was funding some of this work, as Port Arthur and Corpus Christi attempted to lure McGraw to the Texas Gulf Coast.[39]

RIMES PARK

Needing more pitching for 1917, McGraw had nineteen hurlers in camp. To provide space for everyone, plus accommodate exhibition games, improvements were made to a semi-abandoned ballfield called Rimes Park.

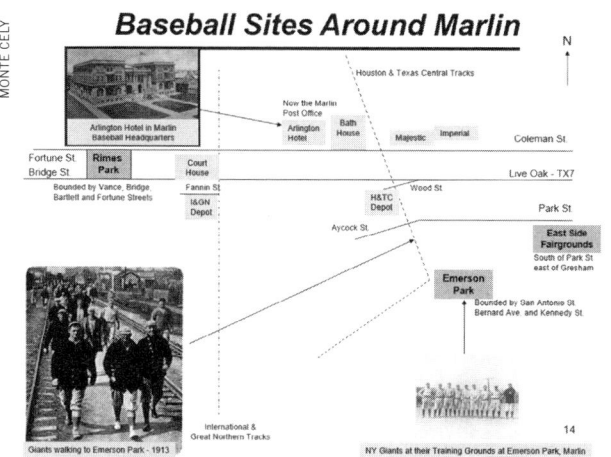

Baseball Sites Around Marlin

Giants walking to Emerson Park - 1913

NY Giants at their Training Grounds at Emerson Park, Marlin

Rimes was utilized briefly in 1915, and extensively in 1917 and 1918. It is described as the "west side field," "a few blocks west of the Giants' hotel." Originally used by the Marlin High baseball team, it was already partially enclosed. A plat map of Marlin shows a "Rimes Addition" that begins about four blocks west of the current post office. This location matches descriptions of Rimes Park, and places the field in the area bounded by Vance, Fortune, Bartlett, and Bridge Streets.

With America's full involvement in the Great War, questions arose about the status of professional baseball for 1918. Traveling to New York in January, Marlin's Dr. N.D. Buie visited McGraw and Giants secretary John Foster. Dr. Buie was assured the Giants would return to Marlin, although wartime considerations might dictate a later arrival and shorter stay.[40]

Consequently, the Giants arrived in Marlin on March 11, 1918. As in 1917, both Emerson and Rimes Parks were needed. Emerson was used for batting, fielding, and general workouts by the entire team, while Rimes was used by the pitchers and for exhibition games. A highlight of that Spring was a game with the Army Air Service aviators from Waco's Rich Field. After defeating the airmen 14–11 at Rimes, McGraw was flown back to Waco for dinner with the commanding officers.[41]

SPRING TRAINING MOVES AWAY

Spring training and the regular season were curtailed in 1919. "Giants not Coming Here" lamented the *Marlin Democrat* on February 3, 1919. The Marlin Commercial Club had received a letter from Foster that expressed the club's utmost regret that they would not return to Marlin that year. The 1919 major-league season was limited to 140 games, with spring training prohibited until March 22. Those restrictions, plus the lack of training opponents in Texas, forced the Giants to seek other arrangements.[42]

The Giants spent the spring of 1919 at the University of Florida campus. Although Foster's letter had said the Giants would only skip one year in Marlin, when they returned to Texas in 1920 it was to San Antonio. In December 1919 *The New York Times* reported, "For many years the Giants had a training camp at Marlin...McGraw has chosen San Antonio because it affords better hotel facilities and a better ballpark..."[43]

A contingent of Giants players returned briefly to Marlin in late February 1923. Pitchers and catchers reported early in the care of coaches Hughie Jennings and "Cozy" Dolan. The Kiwanis Club held a luncheon in the team's honor, and New York writer Crane waxed nostalgic about past days in Marlin. After two weeks, they joined the rest of the team in San Antonio. As the Giants were leaving the Arlington, a group of White Sox and manager Kid Gleason arrived in the hotel's lobby. The Chicago group planned to spend a week in Marlin and then travel to Seguin.[44]

The Giants batterymates left Marlin, this time for good, on March 2, 1923.[45] The Chicago group left on March 8. This marked the end of major league spring training in Marlin. Improved transportation and civic investments were drawing more teams to Florida. By 1941, only the St. Louis Browns and Boston Braves trained in Texas, spending their last spring at San Antonio.[46]

Today, nothing remains of Marlin's three early twentieth-century ballfields. The Emerson Park site was converted into a housing project, and the Fairgrounds and Rimes locations were redeveloped for other uses. However those railroad tracks still exist, and a visiting baseball fan can easily envision Giants players of the past century walking to spring training in Marlin, Texas. ∎

Acknowledgments

Many thanks to librarians Dale Kling and Gail Woodward at the Pauline & Jane Chilton Memorial Public Library in Marlin, Texas. Thanks also to librarians Alisha Bell and Hannah Kubacak at the Waco-McLennan County Library Genealogy Services department. All these librarians provided great assistance in locating and accessing primary source materials. Thanks to Mark Pelzel at the Marlin *Democrat* newspaper office for his advice as to sources. Finally, thanks to my wife Linda for her many hours in helping locate online resources, viewing microfilm, and reviewing drafts of this paper.

Notes

1. Jackson, Frank, "Crossing Red River—Spring Training in Texas," *The National Pastime* #26 (SABR, 2006): 85–91; A summation of the author's findings from *Daily Democrat* (Marlin, Texas) issues (1903–23) and from *The New York Times* issues (1907–23).
2. McLeod, Gerald, "Day Trips—Marlin," *Austin Chronicle*, February 18, 2005, www.austinchronicle.com accessed September 3, 2023.
3. "About Marlin, Texas," www.marlintx.net accessed September 4, 2023.
4. "Want to Come to Marlin—Chicago League Team Wants to Train Here," *Daily Democrat* (Marlin, Texas), February 9, 1903: 1.
5. "They Like Marlin Weather—A Fine Lot of Fellows are Comiskey's Men," *Daily Democrat* (Marlin, Texas), March 8, 1904: 1.
6. Chicago Tribune—December 31, 1904, *Chicago Tribune* archives, online at www.pqasb.pqarchiver.com/chicagotribune, accessed February 3, 2008.
7. "White Sox Not to Visit Marlin," *Daily Democrat* (Marlin, Texas), January 5, 1905: 1.
8. *Daily Democrat* (Marlin, Texas), February 13, 1905: 1.
9. "The Cardinals Arrive—Reach Marlin in Special Car, Twenty-seven Strong—Manager Nichols Sees Grounds and Likes Them," *Daily Democrat* (Marlin, Texas), March 6, 1905: 1.
10. "Bancroft in Love with Marlin—Best Training Ground He Ever Saw—Three-year Contract," *Daily Democrat* (Marlin, Texas), March 16, 1906: 1.
11. "Ball Grounds Must Be Fixed Up!," *Daily Democrat* (Marlin, Texas), January 5, 1907: 1.
12. "Athletics Are Here—Famous Quaker City Team in Training," *Daily Democrat* (Marlin, Texas), March 4, 1907:1.
13. "Connie Mack Says This Town Best Place On Map—Ganzel Is Better Pleased and Reds Will Stay," *Daily Democrat* (Marlin, Texas), March 6, 1907: 1.
14. "Reds Bid Good Bye to Marlin—Leave for New Orleans with Stop at A&M," *Daily Democrat* (Marlin, Texas), March 25, 1907: 1.
15. "New York Ball Team May Come—Dallas Manager Says They Can Be Secured for Marlin," *Daily Democrat* (Marlin, Texas), September 26, 1907: 1.
16. "Giants Plan for Spring Training—New York Nationals to Thaw Out Next March at Marlin Springs, Texas," *The New York Times*, December 22, 1907: 1S.
17. Morris, Peter, *Level Playing Fields: How the Groundskeeping Murphy Brothers Shaped Baseball* (University of Nebraska Press, 2007): 102.
18. "McGraw's Team Complete—More Players Report to Marlin Springs—Regulars Win Game," *The New York Times*, March 4, 1908: 3S.
19. "Giants Talk for Marlin," *Daily Democrat* (Marlin, Texas), February 26, 1909: 1.
20. "Eastern Newspapers Reflect Sentiment to Town's Great Advantage," *Daily Democrat* (Marlin, Texas), February 26, 1909: 1.
21. "Eastern Newspapers Reflect Sentiment to Town's Great Advantage," *Daily Democrat* (Marlin, Texas), February 26, 1909: 1.
22. "Marlin Presents Giants with Park," *The New York Times*, March 8, 1911: 8.
23. "The Meningitis Record—For State Since January 1," *Daily Democrat* (Marlin, Texas), February 14, 1912: 1.
24. "Giants All Report at Marlin Camp—38 Players Round Out Squad—Matty and Rube Look Good," *The New York Times*, March 2, 1912: 9.
25. "Sun Will Shine on Giants in South Land," *The New York Times*, January 21, 1913: 24.
26. "Wet Day Spoils Practice—Rain Follows One of Best All-around Days Yet," *Daily Democrat* (Marlin, Texas), March 12, 1913: 3.
27. "Giants Return Home: All Will Be Seen in Games with Yale at Polo Grounds To-day," *The New York Times*, April 9, 1913: 10.
28. Alexander, Charles, *John McGraw* (Viking, 1988): 167.
29. McGraw, John, *My Thirty Years in Baseball* (Boni & Liveright, 1923; Bison Press reprinting, 1995): 248.
30. "Mathewson Halting—Considering Federal's Boston Offer," *Daily Democrat* (Marlin, Texas), February 25, 1914: 1.
31. "Grounds Keeper for Giants Here—Much Work is Needed," *Daily Democrat* (Marlin, Texas), January 30, 1914: 2.
32. "Giants' Christmas Gift—Citizens of Marlin Present Deed in Training Park," *The New York Times*, December 20, 1914: 3S.
33. Jackson, Frank, "Crossing Red River—Spring Training in Texas," *The National Pastime* #26 (SABR, 2006): 88.
34. *Daily Democrat* (Marlin, Texas), February 27, 1915: 2.
35. "Colts Start Touring—Leave Marlin at Midnight on Exhibition Trip With Extra Strong Lineup," *Daily Democrat* (Marlin, Texas), March 24, 1915: 2.
36. "Giants vs. White Sox at the Orpheum Theater—Tomorrow," *Daily Democrat* (Marlin, Texas), February 1, 1916: 4.
37. "Giants Hold First Try-out—McGraw Puts Fledglings Thru Lively Paces While Old Players Limber Up," *Daily Democrat* (Marlin, Texas), February 28, 1916: 2.
38. "Giants vs. Tigers—Baseball Game at Emerson Park," *Daily Democrat* (Marlin, Texas), March 25, 1916: 4.
39. "Points on Building City—Ten Reasons Why Every Citizen Should be Member of Commercial Club," *Daily Democrat* (Marlin, Texas), March 6, 1917: 4.
40. "New York Giants Coming—National League Pennant Winners Will Reach Marlin Next Week," *Daily Democrat* (Marlin, Texas), January 3, 1918: 2.
41. "McGraw Takes Air Trip—Giants Defeat Aviators from Waco Before Many Spectators," *Daily Democrat* (Marlin, Texas), March 26, 1918: 2.
42. "Giants Not Coming Here—Secretary Writes That Team Will Have to Skip One Year," *Daily Democrat* (Marlin, Texas), February 3, 1919: 3.
43. "Pick Camp for Giants - N.Y. Nationals Will Train at San Antonio Next Spring," *The New York Times*, December 7, 1919: 3S.
44. "White Sox Reach Marlin—Chicago Players Mingle with Giants Here for Conditioning," *Daily Democrat* (Marlin, Texas), February 28, 1923: 3.
45. "Two Sessions at Marlin—Giants' Battery Men Helped by Ideal Weather," *The New York Times*, March 3, 1923: 12.
46. Jackson, Frank, "Crossing Red River—Spring Training in Texas," *The National Pastime* #26 (SABR, 2006): 91.

The 1919 Texas Negro Baseball League Championship

Dallas Black Giants vs. San Antonio Black Aces

Bill Staples Jr.

The Armistice of November 11, 1918, ended the fighting in World War I, but for Black soldiers like O'Neal Pullen—a professional baseball player from Texas who served in the segregated 509th Engineer unit in France—the fight for freedom continued at home.[1] Returning to a nation gripped by racial fear and hostility, he and other Black veterans faced threats of violence and exclusion despite their service.

This tension fueled the "Red Summer" of 1919, marked by riots and 77 lynchings, of which 11 were Black veterans.[2] Amid this turmoil, the Texas Negro Baseball League (TNBL) became a vital institution, providing hope and unity for Black communities across the Lone Star State.[3] Its legacy reflected the broader struggle for equality and set the stage for the formation of the Negro National League (NNL) in 1920.

1919 SEASON OPENER

The *Dallas Express* served as the voice of the Black community, prominently featuring a Frederick Douglass quotation—"The Republican Party is the ship, all else the sea"—under its masthead.[4] Its pages were filled with the latest civil rights concerns, local activities, and sporting news, including the pre-season meeting of TNBL officials in Dallas on February 11.[5]

Represented at the table were the leaders of the Austin Black Senators, Beaumont Black Oilers, Dallas Black Giants, Fort Worth Black Panthers, Galveston Black Pirates, Houston Black Buffaloes, San Antonio Black Broncos, and Waco Black Navigators. It was announced that many clubs expected to bolster their rosters with former players returning from military service.[6]

Dallas Black Giants manager, 41-year old R. Lee Jones, promised a "strongest and most formidable" lineup despite losing key players to Beaumont like second baseman Bob Bailey and pitcher William "Nacogdoches" Ross.[7] Jones had already secured signed contracts from 16 players, including star pitchers Dave "Lefty" Brown and Andrew Cooper, and catchers James Brown and Riley Mackey.[8]

The season opener at Gardner Park on Easter Sunday, April 20, featured a Dallas victory over Waco, 5–2.[9] "Before a crowd of fully 3,500 enthusiasts, the Dallas Black Giants copped the opening game of the Texas League season," reported the *Express*. "The big crowd that packed Gardner's stadium was thrilled with echoes of sweet music during the process of the game by Alexander's Jazz Band. Popular airs whiffed through the air to the delight of fandom."[10]

There's a saying in Texas, "If you don't like the weather, wait a minute, it'll change." It appears this was also true of team rosters for the 1919 TNBL season.

RUBE FOSTER SCOUTS IN DALLAS

Absent from the opening-day lineup were star pitcher "Lefty" Brown and catcher James Brown (no relation). In early April, Rube Foster, the Chicago American Giants manager, arrived in Dallas to scout prospects. He watched the Black Giants in action and afterward signed the Brown battery. The *Chicago Defender* enthusiastically covered the scouting declaring, "No one in the world knows better how to pick a player than 'Rube.'... ("Lefty") Brown looks a winning type of ball player and room just had to be made for him."[11]

It's uncertain if Foster was less impressed with future star Mackey or if Dallas management prevented him from advancing

Gardner Park, Dallas Texas

his career up north. Whatever dynamics unfolded, Mackey's time in Dallas ended abruptly. He left the Black Giants in early May and signed with the Waco Black Navigators.[12] Pitcher Andy Cooper would never appear in a Black Giants box score for the season. More changes were on the horizon for the TNBL.

HONORING THE TROOPS

That Spring, the White Texas League owners in Dallas and San Antonio announced a contest to rename the teams to honor returning troops. The Dallas Giants became the Dallas Marines, and the San Antonio Broncos became the San Antonio Aces, inspired by the famed flying aces of the war.[13] The Black teams followed suit, but by mid-season the Black Giants rejected the "Marines" name, calling it "jinxy" after experiencing bad luck, both on and off the field.[14]

DALLAS TEAM JAILED

In late May, the Black Giants faced racial injustice in San Marcos. While waiting at a train station for the arrival of the Waco Black Navigators, the entire team was arrested by Hays County Sheriff George M. Allen, who was known to have ties to the Ku Klux Klan. They were charged with vagrancy, a common pretext for targeting Blacks in the Jim Crow South.[15] Sheriff Allen's actions were typical of the systemic racism of the time and aligned with the Klan's statement published in the San Marcos Record just two years later, "We believe in White Supremacy and we believe that White men should keep White men's places."[16]

FIRE-SALE IN WACO

In early June, the financially struggling Waco team sold its top talent to San Antonio, including Mackey, Henry Blackmon, "Crush" Holloway, Robert "High-pockets" Hudspeth, Namon Washington, Walter "Steel Arm" Davis, and Morris Williams.[17] The Dallas Express would later select Blackmon (a 165th Regiment veteran) and Davis for their honorary All-Star team for the 1919 season.[18] Powered by their new talent, the Black Aces won 16 of their next 18 games and began to draw crowds larger than their White counterparts.[19] The San Antonio Evening News celebrated their skill: "It is a well known fact that the negro ball players play just as good if not better ball than some of the regular professional clubs which play through the country."[20]

REGULAR SEASON MATCH-UPS

Throughout the regular season, the Black Giants and Black Aces faced off 10 times, with San Antonio winning the series 7 games to 3.[21] Among those victories for

the Black Aces was the annual Juneteenth Celebration game at Gardner Park.[22] For the regular season, San Antonio outscored Dallas 29 to 19, averaging a score of roughly 3–2 per game.[23] With a stronger offense and consistent pitching, the Black Aces proved themselves the better team heading into the postseason. San Antonio manager L.W. Moore was also praised for his leadership and strategic baseball mind, earning him the nickname "the Black Connie Mack."[24]

This season also showcased future Hall of Fame catcher Riley Mackey's distinctive vocal catching style, which years later contributed to his nickname "Biz" for giving opposing batters "the business." The San Antonio Evening News noted, "Did you ever hear a magpie chattering and jabbering? Well, Riley Mackey (no, he is not Irish), is the epitome of 'jaberation.' There is not a second when he is behind the bag that he is not chattering and jabbering, exhorting his teammates to show a 'little pepah ou' dere.'"[25]

CHAMPIONSHIP SERIES

The standings published by the San Antonio Evening News on September 9 were used to select the top two teams for the TNBL championship series, though a few games remained. The Black Aces led with a commanding .818 winning average (45–10 record), followed by the Waco Black Navigators (.765, 13–4), who disbanded after 17 games, and the Dallas Black Giants (.750, 51–17).[26]

Table 1. Texas Negro Baseball League Standings, 1919 Season[27]

Team	Games	Won	Lost	Pct.
San Antonio Black Aces	55	45	10	.818
Waco Black Navigators*	17	13	4	.765
Dallas Black Giants	68	51	17	.750
Houston Black Buffaloes	37	25	12	.676
Austin Black Senators	49	28	21	.571
Beaumont Black Oilers	33	18	15	.545
Fort Worth Black Panthers*	23	4	19	.174
Galveston Black Pirates*	19	2	17	.105

*Disbanded before the end of the season.

League Park, located on the southside of San Antonio, hosted the five-game championship series a few weeks later.[28] The season-long rivalry intensified as Dallas bolstered its roster with Beaumont stars, including catcher O'Neal Pullen, pitcher Charlie Hunter, and two former Black Giants players—Bob Bailey and William Ross, a veteran with the 165th Regiment who played ball with the Camp Travis nine.[29]

The only roster change for the Black Aces was the absence of third-baseman Henry Blackmon. Despite receiving a lot of ink in the pre-series press, the all-star infielder did not appear in any postseason games. The reason for his absence was not reported. Namon Washington and Bob McClure filled in at the hot corner.[30]

The *San Antonio Evening News* captured the excitement building up to the series:

Fans who have watched the progress of the black aggregation (the Aces) assert that they have never seen the National game played in a more spectacular manner or with more pep and entertainment.

Mayor Bell, all the City Commissioners, Fire Chief Goetz, and Police Chief Mussey, accompanied by a platoon of San Antonio's "Finest," will head the parade. Flaring bands, highly decorated autos, and hundreds of fans on foot will march through the streets the day of the great game.

At League Park, there will be a Negro band, "jazzing it along," to keep up the spirits of the fans. But that is hardly needed when the Black Aces are in action.[31]

GAME 1: Thursday, September 25, 4:30PM

Under the warm Texas afternoon sun—82 degrees with light winds—the series began with a 1–0 victory for the Black Aces. Although game details weren't published, the score suggested a pitching duel and set a competitive tone for the series. According to the scant reports in the press, "several thousand fans, black and white" packed the ballpark.[32] Special trains brought in fans from Luling, Lockhart, and Austin.[33] The San Antonio stadium was ready for the crowd, as it seated 6,160 spectators in the grandstand, with an additional 600 in the bleachers. It was an intimate setting, as the ballpark featured the league's smallest outfield, measuring just 270 feet to left and 280 to right.[34]

GAME 2: Friday, September 26, 4:30PM

The Black Giants evened the series with a narrow 2–1 victory. Pitcher Ross, the ringer from the Black Oilers with a 14–6 season record (including a 19-strikeout game against Galveston), delivered a stellar performance. He outdueled the Black Aces' "Steel Arm" Davis, who boasted a 26–2 record with 10 shutouts for the season. Ross's veteran composure secured Dallas their first win, tying the series at 1–1.

GAME 3: Saturday, September 27, 3:30PM

The Black Aces took control of the series with a dominant 8–1 victory. Bob McClure delivered a stellar performance on the mound, allowing just four hits, while the San Antonio offense capitalized on Charlie Hunter, tallying 11 hits, including doubles by Johnny Jones and Andrew Wilson. Dallas's lone highlight came from Robert Sloan's triple. The decisive win put the Black Aces ahead in the series, 2–1. The score:

	R	H	E
Black Giants	1	4	2
Black Aces	8	11	1

Batteries: Hunter and Pullen; McClure and Mackey.[38]

GAME 4: Sunday, September 28, 3:00PM

A dramatic Sunday doubleheader closed the championship, with the Black Giants securing a 2–1 win in the first game. Connie Rector's stellar pitching stifled the Black Aces, while 31-year-old Morris Williams (veteran from the 370th Infantry) took the loss.[39] A decisive home run by Pullen in the 4th inning sealed the victory. Surprisingly, the Aces committed five errors. There were no grumblings in the press about the uncharacteristically sloppy defense, but it's not far-fetched to think that it occurred under the influence of San Antonio's management to ensure a game 5. Nonetheless, the win tied the series at 2–2, setting up an intense winner-take-all finale. The score:

	R	H	E
Black Giants	2	7	0
Black Aces	1	7	5

Batteries: Rector and Pullen; Williams and Mackey.[40]

GAME 5: Sunday, September 28, approx. 4:50PM

The series finale was an unforgettable offensive showdown, with the Black Aces rallying to claim a thrilling 7–5 victory. San Antonio's starter, "Steel Arm" Davis, struggled early, giving up a triple and two singles in the first inning that quickly put the Black Giants up, 2–0. With only one out, manager Moore pulled Davis and sent Mackey to the mound, resulting in a four-player defensive shuffle (reflected in the box score, see page 18). Davis moved to center field and later had his moment of redemption at the plate.

Dallas extended their lead with a run in the 3rd and two more in the top of the 5th, building what seemed like an insurmountable 5–0 advantage. Then, as the *San Antonio Evening News* aptly reported, "the Aces got really busy" in the bottom of the 5th.

Wilson and Davis started with singles, but Ross eliminated Wilson at third base on Washington's fielder's choice. After Washington stole second and Hudspeth was walked intentionally, McClure stunned the crowd and pitcher Ross with a clutch single that drove in Davis and Washington (Score: 5–2). Holloway followed with a booming double that brought Hudspeth and McClure home (Score: 5–4). When Mackey stepped up and singled, Holloway raced across the plate to tie the game at 5–5.

The drama reached its climax in the bottom of the 8th. With the score still tied, Davis came to bat with two on. According to the *Evening News*:

> There were two balls and two strikes on him. Davis was desperate for a hit, his determination practically crackling in the air. Crouching like a pup scratching a pot and wiping the perspiration from his awning, he took a bead on one of Ross' groovers. Crack! The ball soared into center field, as the crowd erupted in anticipation.[41]

Davis stood proudly on base while Dorn and Wilson scored the go-ahead runs. The *Evening News* described the electrifying scene: "The fans went wild…the shouts, yells, screams, and joyous laughter…shattered the air at the park when this event happened."

From there, Mackey shut the door on Dallas with dominant pitching, sealing the win and the championship for the Black Aces. The *San Antonio Evening News* declared, "Nothing could stop the Black Aces…Mackey put on the clamps and held (Dallas) at his mercy."[42]

With the 7–5 victory, the San Antonio Black Aces were crowned champions of the 1919 Texas Negro Baseball League season.[43] See the final-game box score at right.[44]

SERIES SUMMARY

The 5-game series at League Park was a fierce and tightly contested battle that showcased the spirit and talent of early Black baseball in Texas. The Black Aces outscored the Black Giants 18–10, but each game brought intense competition, from pitchers' duels to the explosive finale. Standout performances on both teams highlighted the grit and skill of these players.

Series standouts include (statistics based on three available box scores):

DALLAS BLACK GIANTS

• **O'Neal Pullen**: Dallas' offensive leader, hitting .500 (6-for-12) with one run scored and steady defensive work behind the plate, recording 21 putouts and one assist.

• **Robert Sloan**: A reliable hitter with a .417 average (5-for-12) and three runs, complemented by flawless fielding.
• **William "Bolegs" Curtis**: Anchored first base with 30 error-free putouts, boasting a 1.000 fielding percentage.
• **Bob Bailey**: Sparked the offense with a team-high four runs, adding four putouts and six assists at second base.
• **William "Nacogdoches" Ross**: Delivered a key pitching performance in Game 2, earning the win with a strong showing on the mound to help even the series at 1–1.
• **Connie Rector**: Pitched a crucial Game 4 victory, outdueling the Black Aces and securing a 2–1 win to tie the series 2–2, with sharp control and poise on the mound.

SAN ANTONIO BLACK ACES

• **Bob McClure**: Dominated at the plate with a .600 average (6-for-10), scoring once and delivering key defensive plays with six putouts and two assists. Also the winning pitcher of Game 3.
• **Robert "Highpockets" Hudspeth**: A defensive rock with 33 putouts and a perfect 1.000 fielding percentage, while hitting .364 (4-for-11) and scoring twice.
• **Christopher "Crush" Holloway**: Contributed consistently with a .333 average (4-for-12) and one run, adding three putouts and nine assists on defense.
• **Riley Mackey**: A pivotal player, batting .300 (3-for-10) with three runs scored. He excelled with 17 putouts, four assists, and strong relief pitching that secured the Aces' championship run.

TEXAS TURMOIL: THE 1920 EXODUS

The 1920 season brought upheaval for the champion Black Aces, marked by legal disputes and a significant loss of talent. Ownership of the franchise was contested,

September 28 Championship Game Box Score

BLACK GIANTS	AB	R	H	BLACK ACES	AB	R	H
Hamilton, ss	5	0	0	Washington, 3b-c	3	1	0
Bailey, 2b	3	2	1	Hudspeth, 1b	3	1	2
Sloan, cf	4	3	3	McClure, cf-3b	3	1	2
Pullen, c	4	0	2	Jones, ss	4	0	1
Williams, 3b	4	0	1	Holloway, 2b	4	1	1
Curtis, 1b	4	0	0	Mackey, c-p	3	0	2
Hunter, rf	4	0	0	Dorn, rf	3	1	0
Rector, lf	4	0	0	Wilson, lf	4	1	1
Ross, p	4	0	1	Davis, p-cf	4	1	1
TOTAL	36	5	8	TOTAL	31	7	10

SCORE BY INNINGS

	1	2	3	4	5	6	7	8	9	F
Black Giants	2	0	1	0	2	0	0	0	0	5
Black Aces	0	0	0	0	5	0	0	2	x	7

SUMMARY: Innings pitched by Davis: one-third. Runs allowed by Davis: 2. Hits off Davis: 3. Two-base hit: Pullen. Three-base hit: Sloan. Stolen bases: Washington, McClure, Holloway, Williams. Sacrifice hit: Dorn. Strikeouts: Ross 4, Mackey 5. Bases on balls: Ross 2, Mackey 1. Double play: Bailey to Curtis. Wild pitch: Ross. Time of game: 2 hours. Umpire: Taylor.

with S.C. Perkins and J.J. Maclin eventually prevailing over former owner L.W. Moore after a lengthy legal battle. However, this victory was quickly overshadowed by the departure of several star players, including Mackey, Hudspeth, Holloway, Williams, Washington, and Davis, who left to join the Indianapolis A.B.C.s.[46]

This exodus was reportedly facilitated by a connection between former Black Aces owner Charles Bellinger and C.I. Taylor, owner of the A.B.C.s, possibly as political payback against Perkins and Maclin for stealing the franchise from Moore. The departure of these key players not only weakened the Black Aces but also significantly bolstered the A.B.C.s as they prepared for the inaugural season of the NNL.[47]

CONCLUSION

Rube Foster's founding of the NNL in 1920 was a watershed moment in American history, offering Black ballplayers a premier stage to showcase their talents, resist segregation, and foster an independent baseball community. Drawing inspiration from abolitionist Frederick Douglass, much like the Dallas Express but adding his own flair, Foster famously declared the new league's motto: *"We are the ship, all else the sea."*

The creation of the NNL was both a response to the racial violence of the "Red Summer" of 1919 and a peaceful form of protest, providing financial independence and self-expression for Black Americans. Texas, home to the exceptional talent of the TNBL, played a vital role in this new era. The league elevated the game nationwide and ensured Texas's talent could no longer be ignored.

However, the NNL's success came at a cost to Texas baseball. Just as the integration of the American and National Leagues would later deplete the Negro Leagues, the national spotlight of the NNL drew Texas's best players. Of the 20 players associated with the 1919 TNBL championship, 17 eventually received offers to play in the Major Negro Leagues (See Table 2). Between 1920 and 1947, Texas lost much of its top-tier talent, and Black baseball in the state never returned to its pre-1920 caliber.

Despite this, Texas's legacy in Black baseball remains undeniable. As of 2025, 37 individuals have been inducted into the National Baseball Hall of Fame for their contributions in Negro Leagues baseball. Remark-

Table 2. 1919 Texas Negro Baseball League Player Profiles—Dallas and San Antonio

Dallas Black Giants

Name	Birth Date	Birthplace	Age	First Major Negro League Club
Robert "Bob" Clayton Bailey	Jan 17, 1895	Grand Cane, LA	24	None–Joined Fort Worth Black Panthers (declined NNL offers)
William "Bolegs" Curtis	Jan 13, 1892	Franklin, LA	27	1924 Indianapolis ABCs
John Hamilton	Jan 23, 1900	Greenwood, LA	19	Unknown
O'Neal Pullen	Sep 8, 1892	Beaumont, TX	27	1920 Brooklyn Royal Giants
Charles "Buber" Hunter	Jan 7, 1895	Louisiana	24	None– Returned to Beaumont Black Oilers
R. Lee Jones (mgr.)	Apr 23, 1878	Texas	41	None
Cornelius Rector	Jun 15, 1892	Arkadelphia, AR	27	1920 Hilldale Club
William "Nacogdoches" Ross	Oct 5, 1893	Corrigan, TX	26	1922 Indianapolis ABCs
Robert Sloan	Jan 1, 1889	Walnut Springs, TX	30	1920 Brooklyn Royal Giants
Adam "Black Cat" Williams	Jun 19, 1892	Columbus, TX	27	1924 Indianapolis ABCs

San Antonio Black Aces

Name	Birth Date	Birthplace	Age	First Major Negro League Club
Henry Blackmon	Sep 19, 1891	Hillsboro, TX	28	1920 Indianapolis ABCs
Walter "Steel Arm" Davis	Jun 22, 1896	Wortham, TX	23	1920 Chicago Giants
Grant "Ditty" Dorn	Sep 12, 1890	Luling, TX	29	None–Returned to San Antonio Black Broncos
Christopher "Crush" Holloway	Sep 15, 1896	Hillsboro, TX	23	1921 Indianapolis ABCs
Robert "Highpockets" Hudspeth	Apr 6, 1894	Luling, TX	25	1920 Indianapolis ABCs
Johnny Jones	Feb 7, 1896	Elgin, TX	23	1922 Detroit Stars
James Raleigh Mackey	Jul 27, 1897	Caldwell County, TX	22	1920 Indianapolis ABCs
Leonidas William "L.W." Moore (mgr.)	Jan 16, 1886	Luling, TX	33	None
Bob McClure	Mar 24, 1891	Egypt, TX	28	1920 Indianapolis ABCs
Namon Washington	Jun 20, 1894	Hallettsville, TX	25	1920 Indianapolis ABCs
Andrew "Big" Wilson	Mar 2, 1894	Luling, TX	25	Unknown
Morris Williams	Aug 15, 1888	Seguin, TX	31	1920 Indianapolis ABCs

ably, eight of them—22 percent—were born in Texas, including Andy Cooper, Rube and Willie Foster, Louis Santop, Hilton Smith, Willie Wells, "Cyclone" Joe Williams, and James Raleigh "Biz" Mackey—former star of both the Dallas Black Giants and the San Antonio Black Aces.

This proud Black baseball legacy stands as a powerful testament to Texas's enduring influence on the history of the National Pastime. ■

Notes

1. O'Neal Pullen's military service: Ancestry.com. "U.S., Army Transport Service, Passenger Lists, 1910–1939." Record No. 10142687, Neal Pullen, Private First Class, Company C, 509 Engineers (Colored), Service No. 282,426, https://www.ancestry.com/search/collections/61174/records/10142687.
2. David F. Krugler, *1919, The Year of Racial Violence: How African Americans Fought Back* (New York: Cambridge University Press, 2014), 42.
3. The term "Colored" was commonly used by the Texas press to describe the Black professional baseball league in 1919. At the time, influential national leaders, such as Booker T. Washington and W.E.B. Du Bois, advocated for "Negro" as a dignified and respectful term to describe Black Americans. It was seen as a step away from the derogatory implications of other terms, including "Colored." The word "Negro" gained widespread acceptance within the Black community, especially during the early 20th century, as leaders used it to foster unity, pride, and recognition of shared heritage. Therefore, the word "Negro" is used instead of "Colored" throughout this article to describe historical Black baseball in Texas.
4. *Dallas Express*, January 11, 1919, 1; The Republican Party was originally a progressive force, founded in 1854 to oppose slavery's expansion and champion equality. Under leaders like Abraham Lincoln, it advanced civil rights through the Emancipation Proclamation, the 13th, 14th, and 15th Amendments, and promoted infrastructure and educational reforms to modernize the nation.
5. "Base Ball," *Dallas Express*, February 15, 1919, 4.
6. "Base Ball."
7. Ancestry.com. "Lee R Jones in the 1920 United States Federal Census." Accessed February 10, 2025. https://www.ancestry.com/search/collections/6061/records/22295360.
8. Future Baseball Hall of Famer James Raleigh Mackey had not yet earned the famous moniker "Biz" and during his early career was known as "Riley," presumably a southern pronunciation of his legal middle name. One of the earliest, if not the first, references to the ballplayer "Biz" Mackey appeared in 1923. See: "Winters Sets Black Sox Down With Lone Bingle As Mates Bombard Sykes:…W Rollo Wilson," *Pittsburgh Courier*, June 2, 1923, 6.
9. Gardner Park, located south of the Trinity River on the northeast corner of Jefferson and Colorado Streets, opened on March 6, 1915, with an exhibition game between the Dallas Colts and New York Giants. Christy Mathewson threw out the ceremonial first pitch. Sources: Opening date: "METRO PAST," *Dallas Morning News*, March 6, 1990, 16A; Location: "Baseball Season Will Open here Wednesday," *Dallas Morning News*, February 20, 1916, 48.
10. "Base Ball," *Dallas Express*, April 26, 1919, 10.
11. "American Giants Open Sunday," *Chicago Defender*, April 12, 1919, 11.
12. "Diamond Flashes," *Dallas Express*, May 10, 1919, 5.
13. "How About That New Nickname?" *San Antonio Evening News*, April 23, 1919, 8; "'Aces' Gaining in Club Name Contest," *Dallas Morning News*, March 26, 1919, 19.
14. "Black Giants Here," *San Antonio Light*, July 3, 1919, 9. Author's note: Since the Dallas players rejected the "Marines" nickname and Black newspapers like the *Dallas Express* continued to use "Black Giants" while only the White press used "Black Marines," this article refers to the team as the "Black Giants" throughout.
15. "Baseball Team Jailed for Vagrancy," *Austin American-Statesman*, May 30, 1919, 2.
16. Texas Historical Commission. *Ulysses Cephas*. San Marcos, TX: Texas Historical Commission. Accessed Jan. 25, 2025. https://sanmarcostx.gov/DocumentCenter/View/18969/Ulysses-Cephas---Texas-Historical-Commission-PDF.
17. "Black Aces Sign Fast Players; Off to Dallas," *San Antonio Express*, June 8, 1919, 30.
18. "Suggestion of an All Star Team in Texas," *Dallas Express*, August 30, 1919, 8.; Henry Blackmon's service record retrieved from "United States, Veterans Administration Master Index, 1917–1940", FamilySearch (https://www.familysearch.org/ark:/61903/1:1:QPC3-KV6V : Wed Mar 06 18:11:11 UTC 2024), Entry for Henry Blackmon, 16 January 1919.
19. "Black Aces Book Three Games Here," *San Antonio Express*, July 3, 1919, 16.
20. "Black Aces are Ready for Dark Marines," *San Antonio Evening News*, July 2, 1919, 15.
21. Season stats compiled by author. See: https://bit.ly/1919_TNBL.
22. "Black Giants Drops Three in a Row," *Dallas Express*, June 21, 1919, 12.
23. Season stats compiled by author.
24. "A Dozen Black Aces Sure Make Winning Hand," *San Antonio Evening News*, September 12, 1919, 11.
25. "A Dozen Black Aces Sure Make Winning Hand."
26. "Standings in the Texas Colored League," *San Antonio Evening News*, September 9, 1919, 9.
27. Sharp-eyed readers may notices the number of wins and losses is not balanced. Unlike today, when each team in a league plays the same number of games, this was not the reality in 1919 Texas Black baseball. These numbers reflect what was reported on September 9, 1919 in the clipping that can be seen here: https://bit.ly/1919_TNBL.
28. League Park (formerly known as Block Stadium) was located on the southside of San Antonio, at the corner of South Presa, Carolina and Labor Streets. Source: "The day (March 31, 1922) that Babe Ruth knocked it out of the park in San Antonio," *Memories of San Antonio*, March 31, 2022. https://memoriesofsanantonio.com/2022/03/31/the-day-that-babe-ruth-knocked-it-out-of-the-park-in-san-antonio/.
29. "Mistah Steel Arm Davis HappySon of Ham, Loses Pitching Duel to Ross," *San Antonio Evening News*, September 27, 1919, 11; William Ross military record: FamilySearch. "William Ross, Military Service, 29 April 1918." *Texas, World War I Records, 1917-1920*. Accessed February 11, 2025. https://www.familysearch.org/ark:/61903/1:1:QV18-NQXJ.
30. "Mistah Steel Arm Davis Raps Out Double Which Wins Negro Ball Title," *San Antonio Evening News*, September 29, 1919, 9.
31. "A Dozen Black Aces Sure Make Winning Hand."
32. "Black Aces Take First Series Game," *San Antonio Evening News*, September 26, 1919, 11.
33. "State Baseball Bugs Entrain for 'Santone' for Negro Title Tilt," *San Antonio Evening News*, September 26, 1919, 11.
34. Field dimensions and seating capacity for League Park (originally called Block Stadium) in 1915: "Texas League Ball Parks," *The Houston Post*, September 5, 1915, 17.
35. "How the Black Oilers Have Set the Pace for 1919," *Dallas Express*, August 30, 1919, 8.
36. "A Dozen Black Aces Sure Make Winning Hand."
37. "Mistah Steel Arm Davis HappySon of Ham, Loses Pitching Duel to Ross."
38. "Black Aces Ready for Final Games," *San Antonio Express*, September 28, 1919, 27.
39. Morris Williams military service: Ancestry.com, "U.S., Army Transport Service Arriving and Departing Passenger Lists, 1910–1939, record for Morris Williams, 7 April 1918, Departure Place: Newport News, VA, Ship: President Grant, Residence: Seguin, Tex., Service Details: Corporal, Company, Lc 370th Infantry, U.S.N.G., 93rd Provisional Division," https://www.ancestry.com/search/collections/61174/records/4846249.
40. "Mistah Steel Arm Davis Raps Out Double Which Wins Negro Ball Title."
41. "Mistah Steel Arm Davis Raps Out Double Which Wins Negro Ball Title."
42. "Mistah Steel Arm Davis Raps Out Double Which Wins Negro Ball Title."
43. "Mistah Steel Arm Davis Raps Out Double Which Wins Negro Ball Title."
44. Adam "Black Cat" Williams, 3b, was incorrectly listed as "Adams, 3b" in the published box score. Since all other players are referenced by their last names, it's been corrected here for consistency. Also, the last name of San Antonio left fielder Grant Dorn was published as "Don" and has been corrected here for posterity.
45. Championship series stats compiled by author. See: https://bit.ly/1919_TNBL.
46. Bill Staples, Jr. "Black Giant: Biz Mackey's Texas Negro League Career." *Black Ball: A Negro Leagues Journal* 1, no. 1, Spring 2008 (McFarland, Jefferson, NC), 102–105.
47. Staples.

Nokona Baseball Gloves

America's Pastime, American Made

Joseph Wancho

"Everybody thinks it's just whatever glove you have on your
hand, but it becomes part of you, part of your body,"[1]

—*Craig Biggio*

The phrase "flashing the leather" is a common saying in baseball. These words are used to acknowledge an excellent play made in the field by a defensive player. Of course, the leather is symbolic of the players' baseball glove. While this catchphrase may reference a defensive play in baseball, "flashing the leather" is a way of life in Nocona, Texas.

Nocona is located approximately 88 miles northwest of Dallas and eight miles from the Oklahoma border. The city is named after Comanche Indian Chief Peta Nocona. It was founded in 1887 and incorporated in 1891.[2] Situated in Montague County, Nocona has a rich history in manufacturing; however, homemade products became a booming success in Nocona—in particular, leather goods.

The Nocona Boot Company was founded in 1925 by Enid Justin. The tradition of making legendary and stylish boots in Nocona is carried on today by Fenoglio Boots.[3] Enid was the daughter of H.J. Justin, who started making boots in Spanish Fort on the Red River in Montague County in 1878. After the elder Justin's death in 1918, Enid's brothers wanted to move the company to Fort Worth. However, Enid was against the relocation, but in 1925, the Justin Boot Company did move to Fort Worth. Enid then started the Nocona Boot Company.[4]

Nocona Leather Goods Company was founded in 1926 by Cadmus McCall and T.B. Wilkes. The company produced handbags, wallets, and various other leather goods. However, when the stock market crashed in 1929, demand for wallets and handbags plummeted. Bob Storey, who worked for an oil company, arrived in Nocona in 1931. McCall was also the president of the local bank that took control over the leather plant.[5] Storey fell in love with McCall's daughter, Mary. When the oil company that employed Storey wanted to relocate him to Louisiana, he did not want to end his relationship with the young lady, and McCall installed him as the manager of the leather factory.

Noting the change in the nation's demographics, the company correctly predicted that there would be a need for sporting goods out West. In 1932, they began to manufacture baseball gloves and footballs, and in 1934, when applying for a patent changed the branding on their gloves from Nocona to Nokona, spelled with a "k" because the patent office would not let a city's name be trademarked.[6] Today their line includes not only baseball gloves, but also softball gloves, uniform belts, and other accessories.[7]

Most Nokona gloves are made from cowhide or steerhide, but some are made from kangaroo leather, with other exotic leathers available in their catalog.[8] A tannery in Milwaukee sends the leather in smooth, butter-soft sheets. Another in South Dakota sends bison. The kangaroo skin is sent from Australia for their Nokonaroo model. The goal is a mitt or glove that is soft and pliable and needs no breaking in by the customer.[9]

The side of a cow measures approximately 25 square feet, enough for four or five gloves.[10] To manufacture one glove, it may take $4\frac{1}{2}$ to 5 feet of leather. For each glove, up to 25 pieces are cut by hand using a set of custom dies. Over 2000 cutting dies are in use in the factory.[11] One of the only automated parts of the process is the embroidery of the logo, which is done by machine, but all the rest of the stitching and welting is done individually by skilled sewers.

The most important step in producing a glove is stitching. It may take a worker up to two years to learn to sew a first-class glove. An experienced sewer can turn out a dozen gloves a day.[12] Two thirds of the cost for a Nokona baseball glove—typically $500 to $750, but ranging from $250 for a "My First Nokona" model up to $1,200 for some of the exotic leathers[13]—is labor. Each glove at Nokona must be hand-laced. Rob Storey—Bob's grandson, who is vice president of the company today—says that a machine has yet to be invented that can lace a glove.[14] Webs are also woven by hand.[15]

When the main part of the stitching is done, the glove is inside out. Each finger must be inverted, stretched onto a hot iron (shaped like a giant metal hand), have its lining fitted, and then be resewn. Next, the new gloves are pounded with a mallet until they are smooth. A petroleum jelly with the consistency of peanut butter is applied as an adhesive between the lining and the outer shell of the glove, and then the lacing is done, with over 120 holes for the tensile-strength leather cord to be stitched through.[16] The finished glove is then "broken in," pounded in the pocket and moisturized with lanolin. "Up to forty different labor operations go into making a glove," says Storey.[17]

Many of the gloves have a red label stitched to the wrist strap with the words "American Made" and "Nokona Since 1934." In 2014, the company switched from a logo depicting a Native American with two feathers in his hair to a modern, minimalist logo of square (or diamond) with two parallel lines, meant to invoke the original.[18] The "retro" logo is still available as a custom option.

One service that Nokona provides its customers is that they will rebuild and recondition their older gloves for a nominal fee. "It's the greatest thing I've ever heard, and I'm a dealer," said Randy Jatzlau of Budget Sporting Goods in Houston.[19]

While there are many stories and theories about how to break in a glove, Storey tells one interesting tale. A customer claimed a brand new mitt was defective and had returned it. Storey said that the customer had oiled the glove, wrapped it around a ball and put it in the microwave to dry. As a result, the material in the laces turned to plastic.[20]

During World War II, through a government grant, Nokona Baseball Gloves provided gloves and mitts to servicemen, whether they were stationed in Fort Hood, Texas, or Iwo Jima, Japan.[21] Veterans wrote to Bob Storey, telling him what it meant to have an American-made glove delivered from Texas to them while they were so far from home. Troops played the American game of baseball wherever they were stationed. To survive the cold in the trenches, some soldiers in Europe ended up burning their gloves for heat.[22]

In 1988, another military contract came Nokona's way. The contract was to manufacture headgear straps and carry bags for night vision apparatus worn by helicopter pilots used in the Gulf War.[23]

Nokona does not do a big-money business with player endorsements, but back when the Fort Worth Cats were a AA team of the Brooklyn Dodgers (1946–56), the team had an agreement where a player would give his signature to Nokona and in exchange receive two free

Most Nokona gloves sport an embroidered geometric logo, but the red "retro" logo of a Native American is available as a custom option.

gloves. Dick Williams, Chico Carrasquel, and Carl Erskine were some of those players who signed on with Nokona. These signatures would be stamped in the pocket. Today, MLB players such as Michael Kopech and Ryan Pressly lend their names and images to Nokona products including gloves and belts.[24]

Carroll Beringer was a pitcher on those Fort Worth teams. Later, he was a bullpen coach for over 10 years with the Los Angeles Dodgers and Philadelphia Phillies. "I put one of their catcher's gloves on in the bullpen, where they really take a beating," said Beringer. "We just couldn't wear 'em out."[25]

That may have been true in Beringer's day. But times have changed. The leather used now is not as durable as it was in past years. It would be a joke to say they don't make cows like they used to, but that's exactly the case. "Nowadays a steer comes out of a feedlot by the time it's a year-and-a-half old. Which means we're using 1½-year-old leather in our gloves instead of material that's seven years old," said Jim Storey, one of Bob's sons.[26]

As a result, one glove today may make it through one season, maybe two. One alternative is to choose kangaroo leather, which is lighter and four times stronger than cow, but it's also more expensive. But people buying Nokona ball gloves are not looking for a bargain price. "Our niche in the market is sentiment," said Rob Storey, Bob's grandson. "People want the best and they want American."[27] The other American glove companies like Wilson and Rawlings began offshoring their operations in 1960, leaving Nokona now the last manufacturer of gloves still in the United States.[28]

Hollywood has also made calls to Nokona. In the 1951 biopic movie *Jim Thorpe—All-American*, the production company (Warner Bros.) ordered 10 snub-nosed footballs from Nokona to be used in the movie.[29] In *Field of Dreams* (1989) and *A League of Their Own* (1992), replica vintage Nokona baseball gloves were used in the production of each movie.[30]

Nokona Gloves is a family-run business that treats their employees like kin. Bob Storey's sons, Jim and

Bob, also led the company, before passing the reins on to Rob. On July 18, 2006, a fire broke out, engulfing Nokona's 75,000 square foot factory in flames that blazed for two days. The fire was believed to have begun in the shipping department and spread quickly. About 80 firefighters from eight fire departments battled to extinguish the fire, nearly depleting the city of its water supply. The cost of the damage was an estimated $5 million (around $8 million in today's dollars).

Rob Storey vowed to rebuild the plant. "The building wasn't the company," said Storey. "The employees were the company."[31] Although their work hours were irregular during rebuilding, not one employee missed a paycheck and the entire staff of over 40 people were paid for all 51 days they were out of work.[32] The factory had to move into the old Nocona Boot Co. building. It was a makeshift setup, but it was the only building large enough to accommodate the space Nokona needed. (Eventually, in 2017, the old boot factory became the permanent home for Nokona gloves.) The fire was a major setback, and in 2010 Nokona was forced into bankruptcy. Another sporting goods company, Cutters, bought a majority stake in Nokona, and aided them in modernizing their marketing and focusing the business on direct sales of ball gloves, revitalizing the company.[33]

In 2018, Nokona launched its online custom glove store, which allows a customer to custom-build a glove by dictating every aspect, including the color, type of leather, and stamping on each element of the glove's style, lining, webbing and more. At the same time, they launched a line of accessories called ShowBelts, referencing "the Show" as a nickname for Major League Baseball, custom designing belts to MLB player preferences. Nowadays when you see players wearing anything other than the standard-issue uniform belt—for example, Arizona Diamondbacks pitcher Zac Gallen wearing snakeskin or Bryce Harper's belt sporting his player number on his belt's keeper loop—you can be sure that custom belt was manufactured by Nokona. The belts are also fully customizable, just like the gloves. In 2024, Nokona announced that All-Star shortstop Bobby Witt Jr. of the Kansas City Royals would be the brand ambassador for ShowBelts, and in 2025 they added Pittsburgh pitching phenom Paul Skenes.[35]

In 2020, because of the COVID-19 pandemic, Nokona Gloves started manufacturing face masks. They came in three different styles: form-fitted, draw string, and woven.[36]

Today, Nokona produces gloves that come in all varieties and colors. Baseball, softball (fast pitch or slow pitch), Little League, and of course left-handed gloves and mitts. A quick check in a Dallas-area sporting goods store reveals that Nokona gloves retail between $300-$400, while Rawlings and Wilson models can be purchased for as low as $150.

The evolution of baseball gloves has generated many additions from the flat mitt with no fingers to the high-tech variations available today. One thing that has not changed, though, is the thrill of picking out that first glove.

"That was my first glove, and I still have it today," said Nolan Ryan of his Nokona. "The reason it was so meaningful to me is that… I was the last of six kids. We didn't have a lot of disposable income, so it was very big when I got to go down and pick out my own glove."[37]

Nokona brings these memories, like the one expressed by Nolan Ryan, to thousands across the country and beyond. The smell of the leather, the rubbing in of the glove oil, the pounding of the pocket, are personal acts that connect us to the game of baseball. We're fortunate that this element of our National Pastime still has a home in America. ∎

Notes

1. Kirk Bohls, "An Old Glove Story," *Austin American-Statesman*, July 16, 2006: C9.
2. City of Nocona Texas website, https://cityofnocona.com/home, accessed January 22, 2025.
3. Nocona Chamber of Commerce website, https://www.nocona.org/heritage/leather-goods.html, accessed January 22, 2025.
4. Helen Fenoglio, "Miss Enid Justin's Story: From Catalog Sacker to Boot Factory," *Wichita Falls Times*, December 15, 1968: 15C.
5. 1930 United States Census, Ancestry.com.
6. Barbara Green, "Nokona building fits new purpose like a glove," *Wichita Times Record*, February 25, 2018: 21.
7. Nokona Chamber of Commerce website.
8. "Exotic," online catalog page features ostrich, alligator, giraffe, elephant, and shark skin. https://nokona.com/product-category/ballgloves/exotic/, accessed April 2, 2025.
9. Jim Fuquay, "Nokona runs hand-on-game," *Fort Worth Star-Telegram*, September 9, 1990: 4-2.
10. Mark McDonald, "Family Takes Pride in Making Ball Gloves," *Sunday Oklahoman*, March 7, 1993: B9
11. Brian Schildhorn, "How a Nokona Baseball Glove is Made," Bloomberg News, September 13, 2018, https://www.bloomberg.com/news/videos/2018-09-13/how-a-nokona-baseball-glove-is-made-video, accessed April 7, 2025.
12. McDonald, "Family Takes Pride."
13. "Ballgloves," https://nokona.com/ballgloves/baseball/, accessed April 2, 2025.
14. McDonald, "Family Takes Pride."
15. Ann DeFrange, "Labor of Glove: Factory Makes Baseball Memories," *The Oklahoman*, May 15, 1994: 22.
16. Bohls, "An Old Glove Story."
17. Schildhorn, "How a Nokona Baseball Glove is Made."
18. "Our Story: A New Look for a New Generation," Nokona Ball Gloves website, https://nokona.com/our-story/, accessed April 7, 2014.
19. John Austin, "Leather and Laces," *Fort Worth Star-Telegram*, October 25, 2003: 10C.

20. DeFrange, "Labor of Glove."

21. In 2023, Fort Hood, named after a Confederate general, was renamed after General Richard Edward Cavazos, the first American Mexican four-star general; Mark McDonald, "Family Takes Pride in Making Ball Gloves,": B9.

22. DeFrange, "Labor of Glove."

23. Jim Fuquay, "Nokona runs hand-on-game," *Fort Worth Star-Telegram*, September 9, 1990: 4-1.

24. "Pros," Nokona company website, https://nokona.com/pros/, accessed April 7, 2025.

25. Austin, "Leather and Laces."

26. Carroll Copelin, "The Business of Baseball," *Wichita Falls Record News*, May 8, 1986: C1.

27. DeFrange, "Labor of Glove."

28. Jeff Miller, "Inside America's Last Domestic Manufacturer of Baseball Gloves," Texas Monthly, June 3, 2024, https://www.texasmonthly.com/arts-entertainment/nokona-last-domestic-baseball-glove-manufacturer/, accessed April 7, 2024.

29. Dick Collins, "Nokona Leather Firm Colors Baseball Gloves," *Wichita Falls Times*, November 16, 1952: 4B.

30. "Our Story."

31. Kevin Robbins, "With Bare Hands and Heavy Hearts, Nokona Will Rise Again," *Austin American-Statesman*, July 23, 2006: C1.

32. Kat de Naoum, "Nokona: The Last American Manufacturer of Baseball Gloves is Here for the Long Haul," Thomas Business Insights, June 25, 2024, https://www.thomasnet.com/insights/nokona-the-last-american-manufacturer-of-baseball-gloves/, accessed April 7, 2025.

33. Kat de Naoum, "Nokona: The Last American Manufacturer of Baseball Gloves is Here for the Long Haul."

34. Paul Lukas, "The Company that's Revolutionizing MLB Belts," Inconspicuous Consumption, August 30, 2023, https://www.inconspicuous.info/p/the-company-thats-revolutionizing, accessed April 7, 2024.

35. "Nokona Announces ShowBelts™ Partnership with All-Star Shortstop Bobby Witt Jr." PR Newswire, https://www.prnewswire.com/news-releases/nokona-announces-showbelts-partnership-with-all-star-shortstop-bobby-witt-jr-302260619.html, September 27, 2024;"Nokona Adds to the Star-Studded ShowBelts® Roster," PR Newswire, February 14, 2025, https://www.prnewswire.com/news-releases/nokona-adds-to-the-star-studded-showbelts-roster-302377376.html, accessed April 7, 204.

36. Lauren Roberts, "Nokona Ball Gloves Starts Making Masks," *Wichita Falls Times Record News*, April 30, 2020: 1A.

37. *Tim Madigan, "Leather and Laces," Fort Worth Star-Telegram*, August 7, 2008: L3.

From Athens, Texas, to the Cincinnati Reds

The Saga of Pete Donohue

Steve Krevisky

Reds pitcher Pete Donohue pitched 100 years ago and his career is worth exploring, as he was one of the mainstays of the Reds pitching staff in the 1920s. His accomplishments are notable, even in a short career. He was born in Athens, Texas, in the eastern part of the state. He became a North Side High School pitching star in Fort Worth, where he pitched in 31 games, and won 24 of them.[1] He also excelled at the semipro level. Pete led the Athens Hornets, a semipro level baseball team, to district titles, going 25–5, with a 1.75 ERA and 175 Ks, winning All-District and All-State honors.[2] He then pitched for Texas Christian University (TCU), going 29–4 and hurling four no-hitters, before he signed with Cincinnati. His TCU coach, Kid Nance, taught Pete the change-up, which he used with great success.[3]

According to the *Fort Worth Star-Telegram*, Pete's record over five years in school and semipro pitching was 107–17.[4] The Reds gave Pete a $5,000 signing bonus as an amateur free agent in 1920. Pete told the *Dallas Morning News* that he was swayed to sign with them because they seemed to care about him: "[T]hey took a real interest in me. The other club representatives seemed to be only interested in my alleged pitching powers. It seemed to me that they only wanted me as a chattel to win games for them. They only wanted me as a bolt or a rod or a can to go into the old machinery. But the Cincinnati folks showed an interest in Pete Donohue."[5] By 1921, at the ripe age of 20 years old, he was hurling for Cincy. From then until 1926, he was a key member of the Reds rotation, which also featured Dolf Luque and Eppa Rixey, whom "the Cincinnati Reds Hall of Fame dubbed the 'most successful and durable staff in Reds history…the Big Three.'"[6]

The following table shows his pitching stats from 1921 through 1926.

Table 1 demonstrates Donohue's significant accomplishments over this six-year time period. He was a 20-game winner three times in four years, with 1925 being his best season, featuring his best ERA, best ERA+, best WAR, and he led the league in games

started and complete games. He was good in 1926, too, as he led in wins, games started, and shut-outs (5). In 1925 and 1926 he bore the heaviest workload of any pitcher, leading the league both seasons with 301 and 285⅔ innings respectively. The 1925 season is worth special emphasis, not only because 2025 is 100 years since his best season, but also because various sources listed Pete as one of the top moundsmen in the NL that year. For example, the 1926 *Sporting News Record Book* lists Donohue as the fourth best NL pitcher for 1925, with only three hurlers having better ERAs than him.[8] *The Hidden Game of Baseball* rates him as the second best NL hurler, behind only Dolf Luque.[9] And the 2006 *ESPN Baseball Encyclopedia* ranks Pete second only to Luque in pitcher wins.[10]

Table 1. Pete Donohue Pitching Stats from 1921 through 1926[7]

Year	W	L	Era	Era+	Gs	Cg	War
1921	7	6	3.35	107	11	7	2.0
1922	18	9	3.12	127	30	19	3.0
1923	21	15	3.38	115	36	19	2.3
1924	16	9	3.60	104	31	16	2.4
1925	21	14	3.08	133	38*	27*	6.1
1926	20*	14	3.37	109	36*	17	2.0

*Asterisks indicate where the statistic led the league.

A top Texas high school, semipro, and college pitcher, Pete Donohue excelled with the Cincinnati Reds for several years before his effectiveness fell off, possibly due to overuse.

Donohue enjoyed some fine performances in 1925. Highlights include:

1. April 18 at Redland Field: A 4-hitter against the Pirates where Pete went 2-for-4, with a double, triple and 3 RBIs, in a 12–2 win.

2. April 25 at Sportsman's Park: A 3 hitter against the Cardinals, resulting in a tight 3–1 triumph.

3. July 3 at Forbes Field: An 8–0, 4-hit white-wash of the Pirates, with Pete going 2-for-3.

4. September 13 at Cubs Park A 5-hitter against the Cubs, a 5–2 victory.

Pete was a fairly good hitter, especially for a pitcher, as exemplified on May 22, 1925, when he went 5-for-5, with a homer and three RBIs. He batted .294 for that season, and even garnered a vote or two for NL MVP (with 4 total points, good for 15th on the list, one slot below Dolph Luque, who had 5 points). Interestingly, of the 21 players receiving at least one vote for MVP that year, Donohue had the second highest WAR (7.0), topped only by the MVP winner, Rogers Hornsby, who led the league with 10.2 WAR.

Donohue was dubbed one of "The Big Three" in the Reds rotation, along with Eppa Rixey and Dolf Luque.

The 1925 Reds scored 690 runs, the fewest in the NL, but also only gave up 643 runs, also the fewest in the NL. Both Pete and the Reds were better at home than on the road. Table 2 shows how good the Big Three were.

Table 2. Pitching Stats for the Reds Big 3 in 1925[11]

Pitcher	W	L	Era	Era+	Cg	War
Donohue	21	14	3.08	133	27*	6.1
Luque	16	18	2.63*	156*	22	6.3
Rixey	21	11	2.88	142	22	6.5*

*Asterisks indicate where the statistic led the league.

Table 3 shows how the team performed during Donohue's six strong seasons. Hall of Famer Edd Roush was the main offensive threat in 1925. He batted .339, with 28 doubles, 16 triples, 8 homers and 83 RBIs. Curt Walker was solid, batting .318, with 22 doubles, 16 triples and 71 RBIs. Rube Bressler weighed in with a .348 BA and 61 RBIs. This team's strength is underscored by their achievements in the standings from 1922 to 1926. They finished 2nd in 1922, 2nd in 1923, 4th in 1924, 3rd in 1925, and a close 2nd in 1926, two games behind the Cardinals. Cincinnati had a big improvement over 1921, as the Reds jumped from 70 wins and 6th place to 86 wins and 2nd place in 1922. Some of that was due to a stronger offense, but Donohue's emergence as a strong pitcher also played a part. After this season, Pete and some other Reds went on a Midwest barnstorming trip, where he pitched in a 6–1 victory, and many of Edd Roush's fans were present.[13]

Table 3. Cinncinnati Reds 1921–25[12]

Year	Rs	Ra	Rs–Ra	Standings
1921	618	649	–31	6th
1922	766	677	+89	2nd
1923	708	629	+79	2nd
1924	649	579	+70	4th
1925	690	643	+47	3rd
1926	747	651	+96	2nd

In 1922, Donohue finished 2nd in pitching runs, behind Pirates ace Wilbur Cooper, meaning Cooper prevented the most runs compared to an average pitcher. Although the Reds played in a park that favored pitching, even by normalized ERA, adjusted for league conditions and park factor, Donohue finished third.[14]

The 1925 season saw Luque, Rixey, and Donohue finish 1–2–3 in pitching runs, park adjusted pitching runs, and normalized ERA. Rixey and Donohue were tied for 2nd in percent of team wins, and Pete was ranked 2nd in the NL in pitchers overall.[15] Also,

Luque, Donohue, and Rixey were in the top four in Opponents OBP, ERA and adjusted ERA. The Big Three were also 1–2–3 in Pitcher Wins, according to the 2006 *ESPN Baseball Encyclopedia*.

In 1926, the Cincy boys finished a mere two games behind the pennant winning Cardinals.[16] Donohue pitched well down the stretch, hurling three shutouts in September, even though they fell short.[17]

After Donohue's 588 ⅔ innings pitched 1925–26, whether due to injury or illness, his performance dropped substantially and he was never the same again. Pete's nephew, Jim Pemberton, reported "[Pete] told me he'd been spiked and nearly died of blood poisoning. They'd actually given him up, but he came back. But after that, he favored the injured leg and ruined his pitching motion.'"[18] Donohue also claimed that he was overworked, but a 1927 article in the *Cincinnati Enquirer* reported he had also been hit by a batted ball in the ankle during batting practice, causing him to miss three weeks of the season.[19] After a few subpar years, he was traded to the Giants. He then went to Cleveland, and ended up in Boston. He also made minor league appearances, finally retiring in 1933.

He remains one of the few Reds pitchers to have three or more 20-win seasons. Noodles Hahn had four such seasons, and Paul Derringer did as well. Pete Donohue deserves to be better remembered for his accomplishments. ■

Additional References

Carter, Craig. *Daguerreotypes 8th Edition*. New York: Sporting News, 1990.

"Pete Donohue." Retrosheet. Accessed April 22, 2025. https://www.retrosheet.org/boxesetc/D/Pdonop102.htm

Sugar, Bert Randolph and Ken Samelson. *The Baseball Maniac's Almanac*. New York: Sports Publishing, 2023.

Notes

1. Bill Nowlin, "Pete Donohue," Society for American Baseball Research, https://sabr.org/bioproj/person/pete-donohue/, accessed April 22, 2025.
2. Nowlin, "Pete Donohue."
3. Nowlin, "Pete Donohue."
4. *Fort Worth Star-Telegram*, June 12, 1921: 11.
5. Nowlin, "Pete Donohue."
6. Nowlin, "Pete Donohue."
7. "Pete Donohue," Baseball Reference, https://www.baseball-reference.com/players/d/donohpe01.shtml, accessed April 22, 2025.
8. Paul Rickart, *The Sporting News Record Book for 1926* (St. Louis: CC Spink, 1926), 8.
9. John Thorn and Pete Palmer, *The Hidden Game of Baseball* (New York: Doubleday, 1985), 344.
10. Gary Gillete and Pete Palmer, *The 2006 ESPN Baseball Encyclopedia* (New York: Sterling Publishing, 2006), 1544.
11. "Giants Return Home: All Will Be Seen in Games with Yale at Polo Grounds To-day," *The New York Times*, April 9, 1913: 10.
12. Thorn and Palmer, *The Hidden Game of Baseball*, 340–345.
13. Thomas Barthel, *Baseball Barnstorming and Exhibition Games, 1901–1962* (Jefferson: McFarland Publishing, 2007).
14. John Thorn and Pete Palmer, *The Hidden Game of Baseball*, 341.
15. Thorn and Palmer, *The Hidden Game of Baseball*, 342.
16. Thorn and Palmer, *The Hidden Game of Baseball*, 345.
17. Nowlin, "Pete Donohue."
18. Nowlin, "Pete Donohue."
19. Jack Ryder, "Winning Streak Narrowly Escapes Ruin ad Reds Win, 11–10," *Cincinnati Enquirer*, July 27, 1927, 9; Nowlin, "Pete Donohue."

Semipro and Collegiate Baseball in Enid, Oklahoma

Thomas E. Van Hyning

The town of Enid, Oklahoma, had minor-league baseball in the early twentieth century, with such teams as the 1922 Enid Harvesters in the Class C Western Association.[1] They did well at first—a 104–27 record— but after going 80-65 in 1923, they folded in 1924 due to poor attendance. Enid's baseball glory would instead come in the realms of semipro and college baseball. Enid was a hotbed of semipro excellence from 1935 through 1945—with 1935 to 1941 considered the "Golden Age"—thanks to sponsorship by oil companies such as Eason and the Champlin Refining Company, located in Enid. Four Enid semipro teams won National Baseball Congress (NBC) tournaments in Wichita, Kansas, including the 1937 Enid Eason Oilers, the 1940 and 1941 Enid Champlin Refiners, and the 1945 Enidairs, a World War II Army Air Field ballclub. Located 120 miles south of Wichita, Enid was runner-up in the 1938, 1943, and 1944 events.[2] More recently, Enid has become the host for some of the twenty-first century's top collegiate baseball. Since 2009, Enid has been home to the National Junior College Athletic Association (NJCAA) Division II World Series at David Allen Memorial Ballpark, with its open seating capacity of 3,000.[3]

This article's dual purpose recognizes Enid's semipro teams of a bygone era and its relevance in hosting a collegiate World Series through—at least—2028.

ENID EASON OILERS AND DUNCAN HALLIBURTON CEMENTERS: 1935–39 POWERHOUSES

The Enid-Duncan rivalry was akin to Boston Red Sox-New York Yankees. Duncan, Oklahoma, captured the 1936 and 1939 NBC semipro crowns while Enid won the 1937 laurels. The first NBC tournament in Wichita—which has hosted the event continuously from 1935 through 2025—featured the Bismarck (North Dakota) Churchills, headlined by Satchel Paige, as one of 32 teams from 24 states. Enid lost two of three games in the double-elimination series while second-place Duncan finished 6–2, losing to the Churchills (3–1 and 5–2), paced by Paige's four wins and 66 strikeouts in 39 innings.[4] Quincy Trouppe, Paige's teammate, noted

it was a "fun tournament, players took it seriously, and promoter Ray Dumont did a fine job."[5]

In the 1936 NBC, Enid topped Bismarck (8–2)—sans Paige and other Negro Leaguers who had other obligations—but was eliminated by Duncan, 15–4. Then Enid won seven straight Wichita contests to take home the 1937 NBC trophy. In the semifinals, Buford, Georgia eliminated Duncan, before Enid's Bus Talley—ex-House of David hurler—bested Buford, 7–4.[6]

In August 1938, Enid lost the title game, 5–4, to the Buford Bona Allens. The All-Tournament Team included Silverton, Oregon, shortstop Johnny Pesky, and Eddie Waitkus, first baseman for Lisbon Falls, Maine.[7] A bad omen for the 1939 Enid Champlin Refiners—the same team but now sponsored by oil baron H.H. Champlin—was three straight pre-Wichita tournament losses to Buford on the Refiners' home turf. Enid was eliminated by eventual NBC champion Duncan, 5–3, after losing their opener to Mount Pleasant, Texas.[8] Duncan traveled to Puerto Rico for the September 1939 Semipro World Series and was defeated, four games to two, by the Guayama Brujos, 1938–39 Puerto Rico semipro league champions.

TWO NBC CROWNS AND 1940 SEMIPRO WORLD SERIES TITLE FOR ENID CHAMPLIN REFINERS

Enid claimed back-to-back NBC titles in 1940 and 1941 plus a September 21–October 1, 1940, Semipro World Series win—four games-to-three—versus 1939–40 Guayama. The Refiners qualified for Wichita in 1940 by edging the Stillwater (Oklahoma) Boomers, 7–6.[9] They won the NBC under skipper Nick Urban, and star hurler Vince Cauble, whose four wins in Wichita—including a 5–1 finale versus the Mount Pleasant Cubs—tied Satchel Paige's 1935 win total. Enid lost two tune-up games to Duncan, on September 7–8, 1940, before traveling to Puerto Rico in mid-September by ship. The Refiners copped Game Seven, 7–5, with a four-run rally in the ninth. Guayama's Juan Esteban "Tetelo" Vargas got a Gold Medal for going 16-for-24.[10] Guayama player Luis Olmo and Enid shortstop Red Barkley were later teammates on the 1943 Brooklyn Dodgers.[11]

On October 10, 1940, 300 baseball fans honored the Refiners in Enid's Oxford Hotel. The Global Semipro Championship trophy was presented to H.H. Champlin.

Ray Dumont instituted the Designated Hitter (DH) rule for the 1941 NBC, 32 years before the 1973 American League, and established a 20-second time limit between pitches, seven-plus decades ahead of Major League Baseball.[12] Red Barkley, a Childress, Texas, native and MVP of the 1941 NBC, played for the 1937 St. Louis Browns and 1939 Boston Bees, pre-Brooklyn. Enid's 7–0 record included topping the Waco, Texas, Dons, 9–3, for the title. Monty Basgall, Enid's second baseman, played 200 combined games with the 1948, 1949, and 1951 Pittsburgh Pirates. Enid declined a trip to Puerto Rico in 1941 to defend their Global title versus the Caguas Criollos since four of their key players worked in defense industry jobs.[13]

ELLIS "COT" DEAL, TWO-TIME NBC MVP AND THREE-TIME ALL-AMERICAN

Cot Deal, born in Arapaho, Oklahoma, 100 miles southwest of Enid, was stationed at Enid Army Flying Field as a physical instructor. The Enid Army Flying School Enidairs were three-time NBC finalists, second in 1943 and 1944, and 1945 champs. On August 29, 1943, Deal lost the title game, 5–3, to Cecil Travis and the Camp Wheeler Spokes from Macon, Georgia. An NBC record 12,000 fans saw Deal allow seven hits. He was named to the semipro All American team.[14] In 1944, the Enidairs were upended, 5–4, by the Sherman Field Flyers for the Gold. Deal's grand slam versus Sioux Falls Army Air Field propelled the Enidairs to the finals. He was 10–1 on the mound for the 54–18 Enidairs, with a .371 batting average, pre-NBC tournament, before being voted 1944 MVP in Wichita.[15] The 1945 Enidairs went 7–0 as Deal played the outfield in all seven games and pitched stellar relief twice. He became a two-time Wichita MVP and three-time All-American. "I was glad to serve my country and polish my baseball skills," said Deal. "Enid's Vance Air Force Base trains world-class pilots for our Air Force, Navy, Marine Corps, and allies."[16]

ENID'S TWENTY-FIRST CENTURY COLLEGIATE BASEBALL COMEBACK

Semipro baseball in Enid waned from the end of World War II until 1999. A catalyst for jump-starting Enid's amateur baseball story, which went decades without a first-class baseball stadium, was the building of David Allen Memorial Ballpark. The downtown ballpark opened on September 14, 1999. The stadium is a successful public-private partnership involving the non-profit ballpark association, Enid, its public schools,

and Northern Oklahoma College (NOC). The outfield fence is classic brick, and measures 328 feet down the left-field line, 390 feet to center, and 300 feet down the right-field line.[17] In addition to high school and semipro games, the ballpark has hosted the Connie Mack League, NJCAA Division II World Series, and Division II NJCAA Regional baseball events. The May 24–31, 2025, World Series was its 16th Classic.

Enid is heavily invested in its World Series, 2009 to 2025, hosting players and coaches for meals, assigning Little League "cheerleaders and buddies" to participating teams, and educating participants about Enid's baseball history. All Junior College (JUCO) team coaches, players, and fans are a boon to the local economy in terms of week-long hotel stays, purchases of meals, fuel, souvenirs, and other incidentals. Players are transported to David Allen via motorcoach. Tommy Graham, a 2024 East Central (Mississippi) Warriors bus driver, noted: "Enid's hospitality is great—they support the World Series and visiting teams. I drove the Warriors from Memphis, Tennessee, to Enid. They got to Memphis from Decatur, Mississippi."[18]

Enid's 12-team World Series is a double-elimination format. The LSU-Eunice Bengals won their sixth title since 2009, and eighth overall, including 2006 and 2008. They eliminated St. John's River (Florida) in the semifinals, 6–5, before defeating Brunswick (North Carolina), 9–3, in the finals. Brunswick edged East Central, 2–1, in the other semifinal.[19] LSU-Eunice is 48–12 in 11 NJCAA Division II World Series. Table 1 lists the 2009-2024 JUCO winners.

Table 1. NJCAA Division II World Series Champions, 2009–24

JUCO	Location	Year (s)
Parkland	Champaign, IL	2009
LSU	Eunice, LA	2010, 2012, 2015, 2018, 2021, 2024
Western Oklahoma	Altus, OK	2011
Murray State	Tishomingo, OK	2013
Mesa	Mesa, AZ	2014
Jones	Ellisville, MS	2016
Kankakee	Kankakee, IL	2017
Northern Oklahoma	Enid, OK	2019
Pearl River	Poplarville, MS	2022
Heartland	Bloomington, IL	2023

The 2020 World Series was canceled due to COVID-19.
SOURCE: 2024 World Series Program.

INTERNATIONAL FLAVOR: 2024 ENID REGIONALS

The eight-team 2024 Enid Regionals, held May 9–13, preceded the May 25-June 1 World Series. South Arkansas Community College from El Dorado won it.

Luis Olmo played for Guayama against Enid in 1940. By 1943, he and Enid shortstop Red Barkley were teammates on the Brooklyn Dodgers.

Player rosters were set at 30, the same as for Enid's World Series. The event had an international flavor since 18 of Western Oklahoma State's 30-player roster were Latino—from the Dominican Republic (7), Puerto Rico (3), Colombia (2), Aruba, Curacao, and Panamá with three others via the Bronx, Miami, and Texas.[20] This tournament attracted visitors like Jhamil Rivera Sr., from Canóvanas, Puerto Rico, who came to Enid to watch his son, Jhamil Jr., play for Western Oklahoma. He flew from Puerto Rico to Dallas, then to Oklahoma City, then rented a car to drive to Enid.[21] The other seven teams mainly had players from Arkansas, Florida, Oklahoma, and Texas. ■

Acknowledgments

Thanks to Jorge Colón Delgado, Cot Deal, Tommy Graham, Luis Olmo, Jhamil Rivera Sr., and Quincy Trouppe.

Sources

Player data from Baseball Reference.

Notes

1. Lloyd Johnson and Miles Wolff, *The Encyclopedia of Minor League Baseball*, Third Edition (Durham, NC: Baseball America, 2007), 286.
2. The Free Library. S.v. "Semipro baseball's golden era (1935-1941): a tale of two cities." Located at: https://www.thefreelibrary.com/ Semipro+baseball%27s+golden+era+(1935-1941)%3a+a+tale+of+ two+cities.-a0157255634, acccessed January 7, 2025.
3. "Welcome to David Allen Memorial Ballpark," *NJCAA Division II Baseball World Series Program* (Enid, OK: David Allen Memorial Ballpark, 2024), 3.
4. Dean A. Sullivan, *Middle Innings: A Documentary History of Baseball, 1900–1948* (Lincoln, NE: University of Nebraska Press, 1998), 157–60.
5. Quincy Trouppe, in-person interview, New York, June 1991. Trouppe was fluent in Spanish, having played in Cuba, Mexico, Puerto Rico, and Venezuela.
6. *Official Guide National semipro Baseball for 1938* (Wichita, Kansas: National Semipro Baseball Congress, 1938), 14.
7. *Official Guide National semipro Baseball for 1939* (Wichita, Kansas: National Semipro Baseball Congress, 1939), 14. Pesky later starred for the Boston Red Sox and became famous for Fenway Park's "Pesky Pole." Waitkus may have loosely inspired Bernard Malamud's 1952 book *The Natural*, later made into a 1984 film starring Robert Redford.
8. Bob Burke, Kenny Franks, and Royse Parr, *Glory Days of Summer: The History of Baseball in Oklahoma* (Oklahoma City, OK: Oklahoma Heritage Association, 1999), 40–41.
9. *Official Guide National semipro Baseball for 1941* (Wichita, Kansas: National Semipro Baseball Congress, 1941), 120.
10. Thomas E. Van Hyning, "Enid, Oklahoma's Baseball Links: Late Nineteenth Century to the 21st Century (Part II)," beisbol101.com, May 19, 2024, https://beisbol101.com/enid-oklahomas-baseball-links-late-nineteenth-century-to-the-21st-century-part-ii/, accessed January 7, 2025. This was a five-part series.
11. Luis R. Olmo, in-person interview, Santurce, PR, December 1991.
12. Travis M. Larsen, "Ahead of the Curve: A History of the National Baseball Congress Tournament in Wichita, Kansas, 1935–2005," (Hays, KS: Fort Hays State University, 2006), 31. Master's Theses 2208, https://scholars.fhsu.edu/cgi/viewcontent.cgi?article=3207&context= theses, accessed January 8, 2025.
13. Burke, Franks, and Parr, 49.
14. Gary Bedingfield, "Cot Deal," *Baseball in Wartime*, March 6, 2008, https://www.baseballinwartime.com/player_biographies/deal_cot.htm, acccessed January 8, 2025.
15. Bedingfield, March 6, 2008.
16. Cot Deal, telephone interview, January 25, 1992. Deal had a storied 1950–54 Puerto Rico Winter League and minor-league playing career before becoming the Houston Colt 45s' first pitching coach (1962–64); managing the 1968 and 1969 Oklahoma City 89ers; returning as 89ers coach/interim manager, 1979–82; serving as the Houston Astros 1983–85 outfield coach and defensive coordinator.
17. "Welcome to David Allen Memorial Ballpark," 3.
18. Tommy Graham, in-person interview, Enid, OK, May 29, 2024.
19. Author's scorecards, May 31 and June 1, 2024. The author resided in an Enid RV Park, from mid-April to mid-June 2024, and attended the eight-team Regional Tournament and 12-team World Series.
20. NJCAA Baseball 2024 Region II, Division II Tournament Program, 7.
21. Jhamil Rivera Sr., in-person conversation, Enid, OK, May 10, 2024.

The 1943 Camp Hood Baseball Season

Andrew Jett

When searching "Camp Hood Baseball," three words come up often: Jackie, Robinson, and court-martial. Numerous articles have been written about Robinson's time at Camp Hood—many about his August 1944 court-martial after refusing to move to the back of a non-segregated bus[1]—but far, far less attention has been paid to the baseball actually played at the camp. This article intends to rectify that oversight. Camp Hood featured a full baseball league, with a skillful mix of pro, semipro, and amateur players, as well as multiple segregated Black teams which formed their own ecosystem in the camp and surrounding areas.

Initial construction for Camp Hood was completed in September 1942, and the camp was quickly used to begin training Tank Destroyer (TD) Battalions.[2] These Battalions were formed, unsurprisingly, with the goal of destroying Axis tanks and other armored vehicles during World War II. As Army members and their families moved in, they increasingly needed facilities for recreation and non-military uses. Sports at Camp Hood exploded in popularity; by September 1943, an estimated $75,000 had been spent on 140 softball fields, 15 baseball diamonds, a dozen tennis courts, two swimming pools, and more smaller recreation areas than the camp newspaper could be asked to count.[3]

The baseball diamonds played host to a camp-wide baseball league that ran throughout the summer, featuring 15 teams and weekly standings reports in the *Hood Panther*, the camp newspaper. Many games were reported on, and I have reconstructed as much of each roster as possible. Teams were divided by military units and split into "A" and "B" Leagues, reminiscent of the AL and NL. The victors of each league, based on win percentage, faced off in a three-game series to decide the year's champion. The A League consisted of the Student Regiment, the Academic Regiment, the 605th, 635th, 651st, 652nd, and 825th Tank Destroyer Battalions, and the 520th Ordnance Company. The B League consisted of the 113th Cavalry Regiment, the Officer Candidate School, the 744th Tank Battalion, and the 603rd, 650th, 653rd, 656th, 657th, and 801st Tank Destroyer Battalions.

By May 27, the season was underway. The first games were reported in the May 27 edition of the *Hood Panther*, which ran every two weeks until becoming weekly in early July 1943.[4] The *Panther* was an invaluable resource for my research, and almost all my data on rosters and games come from it. To open their season, the Officer Candidate School (OCS) played against the 520th Ordnance Company, winning, 6–5, on five hits.[5]

The exact status of this game in the standings is questionable; the 520th only begins appearing in standings at the end of July, with a 0–0 record.[6] The early season was marked by a feeling-out process, in which teams were formed and disbanded as games were played and reported on inconsistently, and with indeterminate effects on standings. It was only in July, when the paper began running weekly, that games were more well-reported and overall standings were published semi-regularly.

Several teams disbanded early in the season, or joined the season late and did not substantially affect the standings. These teams include the previously-mentioned 520th Ordnance Company, the 744th Tank Battalion, and the 603rd and 656th Tank Destroyer Battalions. The 744th team withdrew prior to June 8, replaced with the 657th Tank Destroyer Battalion. Their final record was 2–1; their one loss came at the hands of the 801st TD Battalion, 11–9.[7] The 520th Ordnance Company officially joined the standings at the end of July, but (excluding the previously mentioned game) only played their first games in mid-August; the final reported record was 0–4.[8] The 656th TD Battalion also only played games in late August, with a final published record of 0–3, with no further information.[9] The 656th was eventually deployed to Europe, serving in the Rhineland and Central European campaigns.[10]

The 603rd Tank Destroyer Battalion fared much better than its other late-joining compatriots. By August 26, the team had accumulated 4 wins and 1 loss, including a win over the high-performing 113th Cavalry Regiment.[11] The team unfortunately fell at the end, losing out to the OCS in a three-game series to determine the

B League champion.[12] They went on to play another game against the 635th TD Battalion after the season had concluded.[13] The baseball roster included Pvt. Bud Giannini (RF), Pvt. Bill Christopher (P), and "Babe" Goforth (P).[14] The Battalion landed in France in July 1944 before fighting in the Battle of the Bulge in the winter of 1944–45. The Battalion would also help to liberate Buchenwald concentration camp on April 11, 1945.[15]

The 650th, 651st, 652nd, and 653rd TD Battalions all had middling, but full, seasons; their games were largely unreported except where they played the top teams, and their roster info is near non-existent. The two notable games are a 651st win over the 652nd, 7–3, early in the season, and a 17–0 trouncing of the 651st by the Camp Training Brigade.[16] The only players noted are from the 651st: Cpl. Jack Jiacomini (P) and Pvt. Savage (C).[17] The 650th, 651st, and 653rd were all reorganized into other units; The 652nd served only in the US, guarding and escorting German POWs.[18]

The Academic Regiment also had little luck during their season, albeit with a few interesting games. The first came in the week before July 29, when they suffered a hefty 22–2 loss to the 635th Tank Destroyer Battalion.[19] The second was a victory over the McCloskey Hospital team, played in Temple.[20] This game (among others) indicates that off-camp games were not unheard of, even outside of specific events.

The 605th TD Battalion began the season strong, winning three out of their first four games to sit second in the A League.[21] However, the wheels quickly fell off; their first loss, to the 635th TD Battalion, came off four home runs.[22] The 605th failed to win a single game over the next month, falling to 3–4 and out of contention.[23] The unit later served in the Rhineland and Central European campaigns. Regrettably, no information on the baseball roster is provided in any sources, however the 605th Tank Destroyer Battalion website—created and maintained by families of those in the unit—has a wealth of information, including a step-by-step look at the entire unit history.[24]

The 801st Tank Destroyer Battalion had a season middling in results, but with a number of standout games. Their final reported record was 6–7, but the newspaper tells some further stories.[25] They held close contests with some of the high performing teams, including a victory over the 657th TD Battalion, and a tight 3–2 loss to the 113th Cavalry Regiment.[26] Towards the end of August, however, the team was falling short; an early August loss to the OCS left the team needing a spark.[27] They tried to fan the flames of competition before a game with the 603rd, with the 801st Drum and Bugle Corps playing the team into the game.

Unfortunately, the grand entrance seemed to have the opposite effect—the 801st lost, 19–0.[28]

As the season came to a close, the needs of the Army clashed with the 113th Cavalry Regiment's baseball schedule. While the unit departed Camp Hood the week after August 26, the baseball team stayed behind to make a last gasp at the Camp Championship.[29] The 113th had a very strong season, with a 14–3 record just before playing a final game against the OCS team, also 14–3, to determine who would play the 603rd for the B League title.[30] The 113th had beaten the OCS recently: a 7–0 win the week before August 5 and an 8–2 victory off 10 OCS errors a week later.[31] T-5 Walter Wlazlek started for the 113th and went three scoreless innings before leaking two runs in the fourth. In the fifth, however, the dam burst, with four additional runs coming off Wlazlek and his replacement, Cpl. John Hubiak, the game ending, 6–2, along with the 113th's season.[32] The unit eventually served in the European Theater, seeing action in Normandy, Northern France, the Rhineland, and Central Europe.

THE SEMIPRO TOURNAMENT TEAMS

From July 15 through August 8, the Texas State Semi-Pro Tournament was played.[33] The tournament was also open to military teams, and this drew three participants from Camp Hood: the 657th and 635th Tank Destroyer Battalions, and the Student Regiment Team.

The tournament also welcomed a number of teams and players from other military bases, including some bona-fide professional players.[34] In all, the estimated value of the contracts of players in the tournament was greater than $1,000,000 (approximately $18,250,000 inflation-adjusted).[35] This included The Fort Worth Army-Air Field, featuring Dutch Meyer and Clyde "Rabbit" McDowell; Camp Wallace, featuring Bruce Divers; San Marcos, featuring McLee Baker.[36] The tournament winner would be Waco Army-Air Field, featuring Buster Mills, Hoot Evers, Ernest Nelson, Birdie Tebbetts, and Sid Hudson.[37]

The Camp Hood Teams interrupted their normal seasons to participate in the tournament. The 657th TD Battalion had a middling performance in both their season and the tournament. They ended 5th in the B League, as well as suffering a difficult 8–1 no-hit defeat at the hands of Jack Smiley and the Camp Wallace team in the semipro tournament.[38] The 657th's colleagues performed much better in the tournament. The 635th would eventually fall in the A League to the Student Regiment at the end of the season but would finish with an impressive 13–2 record.[39] The team also made quite a bit of noise in the semipro tournament.

Pvt. Bob Shepard pitched the first no-hitter in the tournament's history (about a week before the above-mentioned Smiley performance), leading the team to an 18–0 win over the Bryan Navigators.[40] They would eventually bow out of the tournament at 1–2 but would be awarded the tournament's Sportsmanship Award due to their cheering section.[41] The 635th landed at Omaha Beach on D-Day before participating in campaigns in Northern France, the Rhineland, Ardennes-Alsace, and Central Europe.[42] The Student Regiment also managed to pull out a victory, defeating the San Marcos Flying School, 1–0, off the pitching and batting of Herb Karpel, before falling, 8–3, to the Houston Shipbuilders.[43]

THE "WORLD SERIES"

At the end of the season, the winners of the A and B Leagues faced each other. Emerging from the A League was the Student Regiment, a collection of students now in the military and including an impressive lineup with genuine professional-level talent. From the B League came the Officer Candidate School, a collection of prospective officers and those who trained them. Both teams had dominated their respective leagues but were set on a three-game series to decide the champion of the 1943 season.

The highlights of the Student Regiment lineup come from two players in particular: T-5 Herb Karpel (P) and Pvt. Henry Stram. Karpel, the team's ace, was in the Yankees farm system before beginning his military service. He would make several solid performances during the 1943 season and eventually be called up to the Yankees in 1946. There, he would pitch 1.2 innings across two games, giving up two runs. Perhaps more time in the league could have steadied him out, but he never received the opportunity; he languished in AAA until his retirement. Hank Stram has a far more interesting and fruitful story. He never made it to the majors, but after playing football and baseball for Purdue he became a professional football coach, going on to coach the 1960–62 Dallas Texans of the AFL, just before the team became the Kansas City Chiefs. The team won three AFL Championships and a Super Bowl in Stram's 15 years with them. He went on to be inducted into both the Chiefs and Pro Football Halls of Fame.[44]

The OCS won an overwhelming majority of their games. The roster consisted of no major-league talent, but some players had amateur and semi-pro experience: David Madison (P) had played previously at LSU, James Newberry played at Texas A&M, and Al Scanland had played football at Oklahoma St. and was selected

in the 1943 NFL Draft.[45] The graduates of the school would become Second Lieutenants before being distributed across the Army.[46] Of players on the team, 2nd Lt. James Newberry, 2nd Lt. Al Scanland, and Cpl. John Scroggins would be killed in action in Europe.[47]

Game One saw Karpel, the Studes' ace, hold the OCS to a measly two hits to preserve a 7–0 victory for the Student Regiment.[48] Game Two saw the series draw even when the OCS's David Madison held the Students scoreless in a 5–0 rout, forcing a winner-take-all Game Three.[49] Before a crowd of 7,500, Karpel once again took the mound for the Student Regiment, facing off against 2nd Lt. Therone Botoher for the OCS.[50] The OCS got off to a strong start, with a pair of singles forcing one man across the plate in the top of the third.[51] Karpel quickly regained his composure to shut down the Candidates for the inning.[52] Help arrived in the bottom of the fourth, with two runs scoring for the Studes and knocking Botoher out, with the OCS bringing in Madison to attempt to clean up the game.[53] Madison stemmed the bleeding in the fourth, but gave up one in the fifth, the game ending in a 3–1 Student Regiment victory off only six hits allowed by Karpel.[54]

THE "NEGRO LEAGUE" TEAMS

Segregated Black units also formed their own baseball teams at Camp Hood. While they did not play in the A or B Leagues or the semi-pro tournament, they did play fairly consistently against each other and competition outside of Camp Hood. Two teams were particularly represented in the Panther articles: the 827th and 829th Tank Destroyer Battalions.

The 829th "Black Panthers" were reported to have won two games, one against the Trucking Battalion and one against the 827th.[55] They also lost two against competition outside of camp, but those were the team's only two losses by August 12.[56] No 829th players are named in the articles. The unit only served in the continental US before being disbanded in March 1944.[57]

Before serving in the European Theater, the 827th Battalion more regularly caught the eyes of the authors of the *Panther*, with 10 games explicitly mentioned.[58] These include victories throughout the year against the Trucking Battalion and the 614th Tank Destroyer Battalion, as well as draws to the 614th (11–11[59]) and the 758th Tank Destroyer Battalions (6–6[60]). All units mentioned thus far were explicitly Black Battalions, though some were headed by White officers. Outside of the camp, the 827th played the Temple All-Stars and Marlin All-Stars, semipro teams from those towns.[61] I could find no evidence of the racial makeup of those teams, including in the *Marlin Democrat*.

One Camp Hood team, most likely the 827th, also played and defeated the Dallas Green Monarchs, a Black semipro team.[62] The last game we know the 827th played, however, is exceptional. Reported in the *Panther*, the 827th played Camp Hood's Student Regiment.[63] This is the only game I could find evidence for where a White unit played a Black one. It is, to an extent, the "exception that proves the rule": racism's longstanding hold on American life and baseball were still firmly in place. But it also illustrated the start of a wider sea-change across American culture. In 1945, the OISE All-Stars, an integrated team, would win the GI World Series in a defeated Germany.[64] The next year, Bob Feller and Satchel Paige would lead a "Major League vs. Negro League" barnstorming tour, before finally Camp Hood's own—or perhaps disowned—Jackie Robinson would break the segregation barrier in 1947. ■

Rosters and other details regarding Camp Hood baseball can be found in the online appendix at SABR.org.

Acknowledgments

I would like to thank Aaron Jett, Anne Hanisch, and the Eisenhower Presidential Library for their assistance in my research.

Notes

1. Erin Clancey, "United States v. 2LT Jack R. Robinson," National World War II Museum, accessed February 17, 2025, https://www.nationalww2museum.org/war/articles/united-states-v-jack-r-robinson.
2. Frederick L. Briuer, "Fort Cavazos: History, Significance, and Community Impact." Handbook of Texas Online, accessed February 17, 2025, https://www.tshaonline.org/handbook/entries/fort-hood. Published by the Texas State Historical Association.
3. PFC Keith Quick, "On The Ball," *Hood Panther*, September 16, 1943, 8, https://tankdestroyer.net/images/stories/ArticlePDFs2/CHP_Issue_26_Vol._1_9-16-43.pdf.
4. "OCS Baseball Nine Defeats Ordnance," *Hood Panther*, May 27, 1943, 8, https://tankdestroyer.net/images/stories/ArticlePDFs2/CHP_Issue_13_Vol._1_5-27-43.pdf; "Panther Now Published On Weekly Basis," *Hood Panther*, July 8, 1943, 1, https://tankdestroyer.net/images/stories/ArticlePDFs2/CHP_Issue_16_Vol._1_7-8-43.pdf.
5. "OCS Baseball Nine Defeats Ordnance," *Hood Panther*, May 27, 1943, 8, https://tankdestroyer.net/images/stories/ArticlePDFs2/CHP_Issue_13_Vol._1_5-27-43.pdf.
6. "Baseball Standings," *Hood Panther*, July 29, 1943, 8, https://tankdestroyer.net/images/stories/ArticlePDFs2/CHP_Issue_19_Vol._1_7-29-43.pdf.
7. "Baseball Standings," *Hood Panther*, July 8, 1943, 8, https://tankdestroyer.net/images/stories/ArticlePDFs2/CHP_Issue_16_Vol._1_7-8-43.pdf.
8. "Baseball Standings," *Hood Panther*, August 26, 1943, 8, https://tankdestroyer.net/images/stories/ArticlePDFs2/CHP_Issue_23_Vol._1_8-26-43.pdf.
9. "Baseball Standings," *Hood Panther*, August 26, 1943, 8, https://tankdestroyer.net/images/stories/ArticlePDFs2/CHP_Issue_23_Vol._1_8-26-43.pdf.
10. "656th Tank Destroyer Battalion," tankdestroyer.net, accessed February 12, 2025. https://tankdestroyer.net/units/battalions600s/292-656th-tank-destroyer-battalion/.
11. "Baseball Standings," *Hood Panther*, August 26, 1943, 8, https://tankdestroyer.net/images/stories/ArticlePDFs2/CHP_Issue_23_Vol._1_8-26-43.pdf; "Undefeated in Eight Games," *Hood Panther*, August 19, 1943, 8, https://tankdestroyer.net/images/stories/ArticlePDFs2/CHP_Issue_22_Vol._1_8-19-43.pdf.
12. "OCS Nine Wins 3 To 1 From 603rd in Seventh," *Hood Panther*, September 2, 1943, 8, https://tankdestroyer.net/images/stories/ArticlePDFs2/CHP_Issue_24_Vol._1_9-2-43.pdf; "OCS Nine Wins 'B' League Title; Post Series Starts Friday Night," *Hood Panther*, September 9, 1943, 8, https://tankdestroyer.net/images/stories/ArticlePDFs2/CHP_Issue_25_Vol._1_9-9-43.pdf.
13. "635th Wins From 603rd," *Hood Panther*, September 30, 1943, 8, https://tankdestroyer.net/images/stories/ArticlePDFs2/CHP_Issue_28_Vol._1_9-30-43.pdf.
14. "OCS Wins 3 To 1 From 603rd," *Hood Panther*, September 2, 1943, 1, https://tankdestroyer.net/images/stories/ArticlePDFs2/CHP_Issue_24_Vol._1_9-2-43.pdf; "OCS Nine Wins 3 To 1 From 603rd in Seventh," *Hood Panther*, September 2, 1943, 8, https://tankdestroyer.net/images/stories/ArticlePDFs2/CHP_Issue_24_Vol._1_9-2-43.pdf; PFC Walter H. Glaser, "OCS Nine Wins 'B' League Title; Post Series Starts Friday Night," *Hood Panther*, September 9, 1943, 8, https://tankdestroyer.net/images/stories/ArticlePDFs2/CHP_Issue_25_Vol._1_9-9-43.pdf.
15. "603rd Tank Destroyer Battalion," tankdestroyer.net, accessed February 12, 2025. https://tankdestroyer.net/units/battalions600s/198-603rd-tank-destroyer-battalion/.
16. "651st Bn. Ball Club Victors," *Hood Panther*, July 22, 1943, 5, https://tankdestroyer.net/images/stories/ArticlePDFs2/CHP_Issue_18_Vol._1_7-22-43.pdf; "Training Brig. Wins 17 to 0 Game From 651st Battalion," *Hood Panther*, September 9, 1943, 8, https://tankdestroyer.net/images/stories/ArticlePDFs2/CHP_Issue_25_Vol._1_9-9-43.pdf.
17. "651st Bn. Ball Club Victors."
18. "652nd Tank Destroyer Battalion," tankdestroyer.net, accessed February 12, 2025. https://tankdestroyer.net/units/battalions600s/240-652nd-tank-destroyer-battalion/.
19. "635th Team Back In Race," *Hood Panther*, July 29, 1943, 7, https://tankdestroyer.net/images/stories/ArticlePDFs2/CHP_Issue_19_Vol._1_7-29-43.pdf.
20. "Academic Team Wins 6 To 2 From Hospital," *Hood Panther*, July 29, 1943, 8, https://tankdestroyer.net/images/stories/ArticlePDFs2/CHP_Issue_19_Vol._1_7-29-43.pdf.
21. "Baseball Standings," July 8, 1943.
22. PFC Keith Quick, "On the Ball," *Hood Panther*, July 8, 1943 8, https://tankdestroyer.net/images/stories/ArticlePDFs2/CHP_Issue_16_Vol._1_7-8-43.pdf.
23. "Baseball Standings," August 5, 1943.
24. See https://www.605tdb.com/.
25. "Baseball Standings," *Hood Panther*, August 26, 1943, 8, https://tankdestroyer.net/images/stories/ArticlePDFs2/CHP_Issue_23_Vol._1_8-26-43.pdf.
26. "801st Baseball Team Wins From 657th 7 to 6," *Hood Panther*, July 29, 1943, 8, https://tankdestroyer.net/images/stories/ArticlePDFs2/CHP_Issue_19_Vol._1_7-29-43.pdf; "113th Wins Again," *Hood Panther*, July 29, 1943, 7, https://tankdestroyer.net/images/stories/ArticlePDFs2/CHP_Issue_19_Vol._1_7-29-43.pdf.
27. "OCS Team Wins 7–0 From 801st," *Hood Panther*, August 5, 1943, 8, https://tankdestroyer.net/images/stories/ArticlePDFs2/CHP_Issue_20_Vol._1_8-5-43.pdf.
28. "Undefeated in Eight Games," *Hood Panther*, August 19, 1943, 8, https://tankdestroyer.net/images/stories/ArticlePDFs2/CHP_Issue_22_Vol._1_8-19-43.pdf.

29. "113th Team Stays Here But Loses," *Hood Panther*, September 2, 1943, 8, https://tankdestroyer.net/images/stories/ArticlePDFs2/CHP_Issue_24_Vol._1_9-2-43.pdf.

30. "Baseball Standings,"August 26, 1943. "113th Team Stays Here But Loses."

31. "113th Cavalry Adds Another Win To List," *Hood Panther*, August 5, 1943, 7, https://tankdestroyer.net/images/stories/ArticlePDFs2/CHP_Issue_20_Vol._1_8-5-43.pdf; "113th Cavalry Defeats OCS Regiment Players," *Hood Panther*, August 12, 1943, 7, https://tankdestroyer.net/images/stories/ArticlePDFs2/CHP_Issue_21_Vol._1_8-12-43.pdf.

32. "113th Team Stays Here But Loses."

33. "Semi-Pro Tourney Opens at Waco," *The West News*, July 16, 1943, 9, https://texashistory.unt.edu/ark:/67531/metapth589773/m1/9/.

34. "Semi-Pro Tourney Opens at Waco."

35. "Semi-Pro Tourney Opens at Waco."

36. "Texas Semi-Pro Opener Tonight," *Abilene Reporter-News*, July 22, 1943, 9, https://texashistory.unt.edu/ark:/67531/metapth1757685/m1/9/; "Camp Hood Teams Set New Records in Semi-Pro," *Hood Panther*, August 5, 1943, 8, https://tankdestroyer.net/images/stories/ArticlePDFs2/CHP_Issue_20_Vol._1_8-5-43.pdf; "No Hitter Features Semi-Pro Tourney," *Abilene Reporter-News*, July 29, 1943, 11, https://texashistory.unt.edu/ark:/67531/metapth1635806/m1/11/.

37. "Waco Fliers Win," *Abilene Reporter-News*, July 24, 1943, 2, https://texashistory.unt.edu/ark:/67531/metapth1635801/m1/2/; PFC Keith Quick, "On the Ball," *Hood Panther*, July 29, 1943, 8, https://tankdestroyer.net/images/stories/ArticlePDFs2/CHP_Issue_19_Vol._1_7-29-43.pdf; "Waco Nabs Texas Semi-Pro Title," *Abilene Reporter-News*, August 9, 1943, 7, https://texashistory.unt.edu/ark:/67531/metapth1635817/m1/7/.

38. "Baseball Standings," August 26, 1943. "Camp Hood Teams Set New Records in Semi-Pro," *Hood Panther*, August 5, 1943, 8, https://tankde-stroyer.net/images/stories/ArticlePDFs2/CHP_Issue_20_Vol._1_8-5 43.pdf.

39. "Baseball Standings," August 26, 1943. "Studes Win 'A' League," *Hood Panther*, August 26, 1943, 7, https://tankdestroyer.net/images/stories/ArticlePDFs2/CHP_Issue_23_Vol._1_8-26-43.pdf.

40. "No Hitter Features Semi-Pro Tourney."

41. Quick, "On The Ball."

42. "635th Tank Destroyer Battalion," tankdestroyer.net, accessed February 17, 2025. https://tankdestroyer.net/units/battalions600s/222-635th-tank-destroyer-battalion/; Gene Smith, "Kansans retrace their steps from Omaha Beach to Austria," *Topeka Capital-Journal*, June 3, 1984. https://tankdestroyer.net/images/stories/ArticlePDFs2/635th-Top-Cap_Jnl_Article.pdf.

43. "Student Nine Wins Opener In Semi-Pro," *Hood Panther*, July 29, 1943, 8, https://tankdestroyer.net/images/stories/ArticlePDFs2/CHP_Issue_19_Vol._1_7-29-43.pdf; Quick, "On the Ball."

44. "Hank Stram," Sports Reference, accessed February 17, 2025. https://www.pro-football-reference.com/coaches/StraHa0.htm; "1987 I Hank Stram I Coach," Chiefs Hall of Honor, accessed February 17, 2025. https://www.chiefs.com/hallofhonor/players/hankstram.

45. "OCS Team Wins 7–0 From 801st," *Hood Panther*, August 5, 1943, 8, https://tankdestroyer.net/images/stories/ArticlePDFs2/CHP_Issue_20_Vol._1_8-5-43.pdf; "James Newberry," Baseball's Greatest Sacrifice, accessed February 17, 2025, https://www.baseballsgreatestsacrifice.com/biographies/newberry_james.html; "1943 NFL Draft," Sports Reference, accessed February 17, 2025, https://www.pro-football-reference.com/years/1943/draft.htm.

46. "Sport Stars to Get Bars," *Hood Panther*, November 4, 1943, 8, https://tankdestroyer.net/images/stories/ArticlePDFs2/CHP_Issue_33_Vol._1_11-4-43.pdf.

47. "James Newberry," Baseball's Greatest Sacrifice, accessed February 17, 2025. https://www.baseballsgreatestsacrifice.com/biographies/newberry_james.html; "38th Armored Infantry Battalion Deaths in Europe," 7thArmdDiv.org, accessed February 17, 2025. https://www.7tharmddiv.org/38deapho.htm; "Cpl. John Paul Scroggins," findagrave.com, accessed February 17, 2025. https://www.findagrave.com/memorial/62987595/john-paul-scroggins.

48. "Student Regt. Camp Champs Defeats OCS Nine, 3 To 1, In Last Tilt," *Hood Panther*, September 16, 1943, 8, https://tankdestroyer.net/images/stories/ArticlePDFs2/CHP_Issue_26_Vol._1_9-16-43.pdf

49. PFC Keith Quick, "Two Baseball Squads Finish Unusual Season," *Hood Panther*, September 23, 1943, 8, https://tankdestroyer.net/images/stories/ArticlePDFs2/CHP_Issue_27_Vol._1_9-23-43.pdf.

50. "Student Regt. Camp Champs Defeats OCS Nine, 3 To 1, In Last Tilt," *Hood Panther*, September 16, 1943, 8, https://tankdestroyer.net/images/stories/ArticlePDFs2/CHP_Issue_26_Vol._1_9-16-43.pdf.

51. "Student Regt. Camp Champs Defeats OCS Nine, 3 To 1, In Last Tilt."

52. "Student Regt. Camp Champs Defeats OCS Nine, 3 To 1, In Last Tilt."

53. "Student Regt. Camp Champs Defeats OCS Nine, 3 To 1, In Last Tilt."

54. "Student Regt. Camp Champs Defeats OCS Nine, 3 To 1, In Last Tilt."

55. "The 'Black Panthers' Win Baseball Game From Trucking Bn.," *Hood Panther*, August 12, 1943, 7, https://tankdestroyer.net/images/stories/ArticlePDFs2/CHP_Issue_21_Vol._1_8-12-43.pdf; "829th Bn. Ball Club Victors," *Hood Panther*, July 15, 1943, 8,. https://tankdestroyer.net/images/stories/ArticlePDFs2/CHP_Issue_17_Vol._1_7-15-43.pdf.

56. "The 'Black Panthers' Win Baseball Game From Trucking Bn."

57. "829th Tank Destroyer Battalion (AA)," tankdestroyer.net, accessed February 14, 2025. https://tankdestroyer.net/units/battalions800s/287-829th-tank-destroyer-battalion/.

58. "827th Tank Destroyer Battalion (AA)," tankdestroyer.net, accessed February 17, 2025. https://tankdestroyer.net/units/battalions800s/285-827th-tank-destroyer-battalion-aa/.

59. "827th and 614th Teams Battle Io Tie," *Hood Panther*, September 2, 1943, 8, https://tankdestroyer.net/images/stories/ArticlePDFs2/CHP_Issue_24_Vol._1_9-2-43.pdf.

60. "827th Ties With 758th," *Hood Panther*, September 23, 1943, 8, https://tankdestroyer.net/images/stories/ArticlePDFs2/CHP_Issue_27_Vol._1_9-23-43.pdf.

61. "827 Bn. Club Beats Temple Team, Truck. Bn.," *Hood Panther*, July 15, 1943, 8, https://tankdestroyer.net/images/stories/ArticlePDFs2/CHP_Issue_17_Vol._1_7-15-43.pdf; "827th Loses Two Games," *Hood Panther*, August 19, 1943, 8, https://tankdestroyer.net/images/stories/ArticlePDFs2/CHP_Issue_22_Vol._1_8-19-43.pdf.

62. Elgin Hychew, "Monarch Face Army in Three Gamer at Rebel," *Dallas Express*, June 19, 1943, 10, https://texashistory.unt.edu/ark:/67531/metapth1760037/m1/10/.

63. "827th Loses Two Games," *Hood Panther*, August 19, 1943, 8, https://tankdestroyer.net/images/stories/ArticlePDFs2/CHP_Issue_22_Vol._1_8-19-43.pdf.

64. John Rosengren, "GI World Series of 1945 Featured Diverse Heroes of the Diamond," National Baseball Hall of Fame, accessed February 17, 2025. https://baseballhall.org/discover/gi-world-series-of-1945-featured-diverse-heroes-of-the-diamond.

Baseball in the Middle of Nowhere

The Unique Story of Herbert Kokernot and the Alpine Cowboys

C. Paul Rogers III

Thanks to a successful, quiet, unassuming, and very generous rancher named Herbert Kokernot, the most remote part of the great state of Texas, sometimes referred to as Far West Texas, has a rich baseball history. Alpine, Texas sits about 25 miles southeast of the Davis Mountains and about 80 miles north of Big Bend National Park. It's the land of cactus, desert willows, mule deer and javelinas, and, surprisingly enough, baseball.

Alpine has about 6,000 residents with the nearest commercial airport about three hours away, whether one chooses the Midland-Odessa Airport or El Paso. It is the seat of Brewster County, the largest by far of Texas's 254 counties with almost half as many square miles (6,169) as people (about 9,500). Marfa, better known because of the mysterious Marfa Lights and as an art haven, 25 miles to the west, has all of 1,600 people and is the county seat of neighboring Presidio County. Fort Davis, population 855 and the county seat of Jeff Davis County, lies 25 miles to the northwest.

Baseball had been played in Alpine and the Big Bend area since the late nineteenth century with the soldiers at Fort Davis squaring off against cowboys from local ranches, especially on the Fourth of July. By the turn of the century, Alpine had a town team which played against teams from Fort Stockton, Marfa, Marathon, Fort Davis, Pecos, and Sanderson. With the arrival of the Orient Railroad in Brewster County around 1910, the local club became known as the Orient Team for a few years. Later they were called the Alpine Blues, and then the Vaqueros.[1]

Around 1945 a man named C. West, reputed to be a former big-league pitcher, moved to Alpine, opened the Texas Café and organized a local baseball team called the Alpine Cats. Fitted with new uniforms, the Cats won 11 of 12 games and attracted the attention of Herbert J. Kokernot Jr. Generally known as "Mr. Herbert," he was the wealthy scion of the sprawling Kokernot O6 (pronounced "oh six") Ranch, which covered some 320,000 acres in Brewster, Jeff Davis, and Pecos Counties. Kokernot had played baseball in high school at the San Marcos Baptist Academy and later

as a .300 hitting infielder for the Alpine Independents town team.[2] To say he had a passion for the game would be an understatement. Before the 1946 season began, Kokernot had donated land for a ballpark for the Cats and he oversaw the construction of a some-what makeshift ballpark with wooden planks, chicken wire, a corrugated tin roof, and the O6 brand on the wooden fences.[3]

Kokernot was soon all in and bought the Cats that summer, renaming the team the Cowboys and outfitting them with new uniforms. Herbert Kokernot Sr. had long ago turned over the running of the O6 Ranch to his son and lived in the more civilized San Antonio. On the father's annual visit to Alpine that summer, Herbert Jr. told his dad—who cared little for baseball—about his purchase of the ballclub and drove him by the ballpark. Days later, when Herbert Sr. was about to board a train back to San Antonio, he turned and looked his boy in the eye and said, "Son, if you're going to put the O6 brand on something, do that thing right." He then climbed on the train and left.[4]

That was all the encouragement Herbert Jr. needed. He decided to start over with a new ballpark and picked a spot just west of the Sul Ross State College campus. Herbert Jr. spared no expense, spending an estimated $1.25 million on Kokernot Field, which opened in May 1947. The ballpark had a completely roofed, concrete, 1,200-seat grandstand, with wooden seats with individual arm and was rests, faced with local reddish-brown stone. On a visit to Georgia, Kokernot had admired the state's rich, red clay, and so ordered enough for the infield and had it shipped to Alpine by boxcar. Real Bermuda grass covered the playing field. The stone outfield wall was adorned with the O6 brand, with center field a daunting 430 feet from the plate.

Mr. Herbert also paid attention to detail, commissioning decorative iron baseballs from a San Antonio metalworks and having red stitches painted on them. They were hung in clusters over the stone entrance gates.[5] A rose garden led to the concession stand which sported a red Spanish tile roof and was framed by pewter bats.[6] Gardeners planted flowers and ivy outside the park and the outfield walls were painted bright blue, making Kokernot Field appear to be a baseball oasis in the middle of its arid surroundings.[7] One writer describe the décor as "Early Cooperstown."[8]

Kokernot outfitted the team with new uniforms with the O6 brand on the sleeve and soon sought to bring in talented semiprofessional players from throughout the state, rather than rely on those available locally. Soon the team became mostly college players, including a number from Sul Ross. His goal was to qualify for the National Baseball Congress Tournament in Wichita, Kansas, which annually attracted the best semiprofessional teams in the country. In 1947, the Cowboys won 20 of 26 games and also won the Sixth Annual Southwestern Semiprofessional Baseball Tournament in El Paso, thus qualifying for Wichita. Mr. Herbert chartered a Pullman for the team to travel in style. After four wins in the Wichita tournament, they lost to the Florida Railroaders in their first bid for a national championship.[9]

Tom Chandler of Baylor was a stalwart on the first Cowboys teams. He developed a close relationship with Kokernot and in 1952 began a very successful run as coach of the team.[10] Together they recruited college stars including Adrian Burk and Larry Isbell of Baylor, and Yale Lary of Texas A&M, later an all-pro defensive back with the Detroit Lions. Later in the decade, future major leaguers Carl Warwick of TCU and Rick Herrscher of SMU played for the Cowboys, as well as other Southwest Conference stars like SMU's Tommy Bowers and Larry Click and Jerry Mallett of Baylor.

Sul Ross had a strong NAIA baseball program, winning the national championship in 1957, held at Kokernot Field, and many of their top players suited up for the Cowboys in the summer, including Norm Cash, who went on to a stellar major league career with the Detroit Tigers.[11]

Kokernot and Chandler developed nationwide baseball contacts and in 1957 were called by Milwaukee Braves scout Gil English about a high school farm boy from North Carolina's Tobacco Road area who threw very hard but was a raw talent. The Cowboys had never had a high schooler, but were convinced to give this one, whose name was Gaylord Perry, a shot. Perry, however, had flunked his English class that spring, and had to somehow make it up to be eligible for his senior year. The team arranged for Perry to take a correspondence course from Texas Tech to make up the course.[12]

Manager Chandler initially told Perry not to throw too hard in response to Perry's concern that he might hit someone because he was so wild.[13] In a game against the Sinton Oilers, Perry was getting knocked around until he asked Chandler, "Can I just throw harder?" Chandler said yes, and Perry was pretty much untouchable for the rest of the summer.[14]

Perry's off-the-field problem, passing English, persisted. Willowdean Chandler, Tom's wife, was Perry's correspondence course tutor, but the lack of a workbook hindered his progress in the course. Mrs. Chandler took to filling in the answers to his assignments—careful not to answer them all correctly—and then sending them in. The final exam posed a problem, however, because it had to be taken in front of a high school principal. It turned out that Chuck Ellis, the principal of Marathon High School, 25 miles east of Alpine, loved the Cowboys baseball team, so he and his wife and Chandler and Willowdean took the exam for Perry while in the car driving to a road game.[15]

Under NCAA rules, college athletes were not allowed to be paid for playing their sport in the summer, so Kokernot hired the players for $400 a month to work on his ranch, while they played baseball for the Cowboys ostensibly for free. One of the typical jobs was killing jackrabbits, which were a plague on the ranch. The players used old Jeeps and drove through the prairie armed with .22s and even pistols, chasing the rabbits down until the critters tired and stopped.[16]

In 1955, the big local event was the filming of the movie *Giant* in Marfa, 25 miles away. The movie starred Elizabeth Taylor, Rock Hudson, and James Dean, and included a 19-year-old Dennis Hopper. During the shooting, it was arranged for the Alpine team to visit the famous house set and meet the actors. Doyle Stout, one of pitchers for the Cowboys, had a conversation with James Dean in which Dean asked. "What do you guys do here for excitement?" Stout replied that hunting jackrabbits from the hood of his car, armed with 35-inch baseball bats, was one of his favorite pastimes. Dean thought that sounded great, and a couple of days later joined some of the ballplayers, "yelling, cursing, and swinging and having a great time, although he didn't hit a lot of rabbits."[17]

Mr. Herbert was nothing if not generous with his players and annually donated bushels of scholarships to enable students to attend Sul Ross. He often rewarded players for home runs or well-pitched games with a $50 or $100 bill and hosted frequent barbecues at his ranch for the entire team. In the early years of the Cowboys, the players stayed at the Holland Hotel in downtown Alpine and just signed for their meals; Mr. Herbert took care of all their food and lodging. However, after Larry Isbell, a high-profile player from Baylor, abused the practice by buying a new set of tires for his car and a trolling boat on Kokernot's credit, the players were relegated to the dorms at Sul Ross.[18]

Kokernot, ever the baseball enthusiast, also sometimes enlisted major league teams to play spring training exhibition games in Alpine, beginning with a Cubs-Browns tilt in 1949, played before a sellout crowd.[19] In 1951, Satchel Paige and the St. Louis Browns took on the Chicago White Sox as a reported 6,000 fans from all over the area crammed into Kokernot Field. Mr. Herbert announced that he would pay $100 to the player on each team who got the most hits, plus other cash prizes for most total bases, strikeouts, and assists.[20] Paige, who pitched one inning of the game, remarked to Kokernot before the game how much he liked his white Stetson. By the time of the postgame barbeque at the O6 ranch, Kokernot had arranged to pass out white cowboy hats to the entire Browns team.[21]

In 1953 the Browns and Cubs again played at Kokernot Field as Mr. Herbert handed out $1,900 in "bonuses" for top performances, including $500 to the Browns for the winning the game.[22] In early April 1956, another jammed house saw Ernie Banks blast two home runs over the left-field fence during a Cubs-Orioles exhibition game that the Cubs won 16–4.[23] In the third inning, an Air Force fighter jet, probably stationed in Del Rio, zoomed over the field at about 500 feet, causing some, like Cubs pitcher Russ Meyer and umpire Stan Landes, to dive for cover.[24]

Also in 1953, Kokernot arranged for the Brooke Army Medical Center team to play a series in Alpine, since the Brooke team featured major leaguers Don Newcombe and Bob Turley, who were both in the service. Mr. Hebert promised to pay Newcombe $1,000 an inning pitched and Newcombe remembered, "I don't care if my arm was sore, I pitched five innings."

Newcombe never forgot Mr. Herbert's generosity and left tickets for him for Game Seven of the 1955 World Series.[25] Of course, Johnny Podres, who had just turned 22, famously pitched the Brooklyn Dodgers to their first World Championship in that game with a 2–0 shutout over the New York Yankees. Afterwards, Kokernot managed to push his way up to Podres in the Dodgers clubhouse. Mr. Herbert told Podres he wanted him to come to Alpine to pitch sometime, and when he whispered a figure in Podres' ear, he got the lefty's attention.[26]

The opportunity probably came sooner than expected. In 1956, the Cowboys fielded a very strong team behind such stalwarts (and future big leaguers) as Rick Herrscher of SMU and Jacke Davis of Baylor and qualified for the National Baseball Congress Tournament in Wichita. Teams often used ringers in Wichita and the Cowboys made a real splash by adding Podres—who was then in the Navy—and future National League Rookie of the Year Jack Sanford, who was also in the service. Podres flew to Wichita and struck out seven in four innings in an eventual 23–2 Cowboys victory, while also going 4-for-5 at the plate.[27] Podres later recalled that Mr. Herbert paid him $1,000 to pitch, plus $100 a strikeout.[28]

Sponsor Herbert L. Kokernot Jr. and manager Tom Chandler view the Cowboys practice at Kokernot Field in 1956.

Jack Sanford also pitched and won a game for the Cowboys in Wichita, but protests ensued, and the military leaves of both players were canceled. The Cowboys ended up finishing third in the tournament.[29]

For years Kokernot planned to add lights to the field, so people with weekday jobs could attend games, and he visited ballparks around the country to find the best lighting available. He was ready to have them installed before the 1958 season, telling his contractor, "I want lights better than Yankee Stadium." When

Kokernot Field

the lights were switched on before the Cowboys' first game of 1958, a tilt against the Dyess Air Force Base Sonics, the crowd gasped and cheered as 435,000 watts bathed the field.[30]

Before the game, Mr. Herbert visited the Cowboys' dugout and offered a $100 bill to the first player to hit a home run under the lights. The result was that everyone swung from the heels, with few making good contact and no one hitting a homer. In fact, it took several games before Gene Leek of the University of Arizona finally sent one out of the park.[31]

Those '58 Cowboys were a juggernaut, led by future major league pitcher Joe Horlen and his shortstop brother, Bill, from San Antonio. They finished the summer with a 45–5 record—with Horlen going 12–1—and again qualifying for the National Baseball Congress tournament in Wichita. There the team advanced to the championship game, but fell to the Drain, Oregon, Black Sox in a nail-biting final, 8–7, to finish second.[32]

In 1959, with it becoming more difficult for the Cowboys to find semipro and military teams in the region to play, Kokernot, perhaps against his better instincts, entered into a working agreement with the Boston Red Sox to field a team in the Class D Sophomore League. Mr. Herbert insisted that the team be called the Cowboys and refused to permit the typical outfield fence advertising signs favored by minor league teams.[33] Alpine was the smallest city in affiliated baseball and literally half the town, 2.500 people, turned out for the opener, an 18–1 shellacking of San Angelo.[34] It was a precursor of the season to come as the team won 88 games against just 34 losses. Led by Don Schwall, who won 23 games, and Chuck Schilling, who batted .340, the Cowboys at one juncture won 15 games in a row and topped their four-team division by a whopping 34 games. Just two years later with the Boston Red Sox, Schwall would be named American League Rookie of the Year while Schilling would place fourth in the balloting.[35]

The 1960 club, led by future American League All-Star Jim Fregosi—who later called Kokernot Field the best ballpark he ever played in[36]—won the regular season by six games with a 76–52 record before losing the playoffs to Hobbs, two games to one. Mel Parnell, the former Red Sox ace, was sent to manage the '61 club, but before the season was out, Boston announced it would not renew its working agreement. That was fine with Mr. Herbert, who lamented how the Red Sox treated the players, buying and selling them like cattle.[37]

Kokernot Field then became the home park to Sul Ross, and when Sul Ross dropped baseball in 1968, to

Aerial view of Kokernot Field in the early 1950s.

the Alpine High School Fighting Bucks. But the field gradually fell into disrepair until Sul Ross restarted its baseball program in 1984. The school leased the park and put $150,000 into its refurbishment.[38] Mr. Herbert consented to throw out the first pitch for the Lobos' first game in 16 years. Kokernot passed away in 1987, at age 87, leaving behind a beautiful ballpark, plus a legacy of generosity, kindness, and love for the game of baseball.

In 2009, professional baseball returned to Alpine and Kokernot Field for the first time in 48 years with the debut of the Big Bend Cowboys of the independent Continental League. Two years later the team reorganized as a non-profit and as the Alpine Cowboys became charter members of the far-flung independent Pecos League.[39] There they have thrived through 2024, winning their division championship eight times and the league championship three times. In 2024, the Cowboys had a truly incredible season, winning 45 games and losing only four before sweeping through the league playoffs with six more wins against a single loss.[40]

Mr. Herbert's paean to the great game in Far West Texas thus lives on. ∎

Notes

1. Betty L. Dillard and Karen L. Green, "Beeves and Baseball: The Story of the Alpine Cowboys," *The Journal of Big Bend Studies* (Vol. 11, 1999): 172.
2. Dillard and Green, 173–75.
3. Nicolas Dawidoff, "The Best Little Ballpark in Texas (Or Anywhere Else)," *Sports Illustrated* (July 31, 1989).
4. Dick Sheffield, "A Field of West Texas Dreams," *Boston Sunday Globe*, March 21, 1999: A12; Dawidoff.
5. Dillard and Green, 177.
6. William M. Adler, "Just Imagine: the Kokernot Yankees," *New York Daily News*, February 20, 2000: 1245.
7. Dillard and Green, 177.
8. Ray Buck, "Love Field," *Fort Worth Star-Telegram*, June 29, 2003: 48.

9. In 1948 the Cowboys made it back to Wichita, only to exit the tournament early. When Mr. Herbert learned that the team from Glen Ridge, New Jersey was out of funds and stranded, he charitably offered them the hotel rooms being vacated by Alpine and paid their expenses for the balance of the tournament. Glen Ridge, dubbed the New Jersey Cowboys, finished the tournament in fourth place. Dillard and Green, 178; Buck, 48.

10. Tom Chandler went on the become the highly successful baseball coach at Texas A&M University, where in 26 years, he won five Southwest Conference championships and was named Coach of the Year seven times. He was elected to the Texas A&M Athletic Hall of Fame in 1991.

11. Dawidoff.

12. David Vaught, *Spitter—Baseball's Notorious Gaylord Perry* (College Station, TX: Texas A&M University Press, 2023): 69.

13. DJ Stout, *The Amazing Tale of Mr. Herbert and His Fabulous Alpine Cowboys Baseball Club* (Austin: University of Texas Press, 2010): 147.

14. Sheffield, A12.

15. Stout, 147; Vaught, 70–71.

16. Robert L. McCartha, *Texas Heat, Chicago Fire: The Remarkable Life of Joe Horlen* (North Charleston, SC, 2017): 57–58.

17. Stout, 159.

18. Interview with Rick Herrscher, January 21, 2025; Sheffield, A12.

19. The Cubs won 7–6 as Roy Smalley hit a home run for the Cubs and Al Zarilla and Gerry Priddy hit for the circuit for the Browns. L.A. McMaster, "Browns Find Baseball In Alpine, Tex., Costs Plenty to Kokernots," *St. Louis Post-Dispatch*, April 1, 1949: 36.

20. The White Sox won 3–1 with two runs in the bottom of the eighth to break a 1–1 tie. "3,000 See Chisox Victory At Alpine," *San Angelo Standard-Times*, March 31, 1951: 4.

21. Dawidoff; Dillard and Green, 185.

22. The final score was 9–4 behind 16 hits by the Browns. L.A. McMaster, "Browns Collect 16 Hits, A 9–4 Victory and $1330 In Big Payoff With Cubs," *St. Louis Post-Dispatch*, April 3, 1953: 33.

23. Chuck Whitlock, "Chicago Cubs Slaughter Baltimore Orioles, 16–4," *El Paso Times*, April 6,1956: 34.

24. "Cubs Rout Orioles, 16–4, At Alpine's Kokernot Field," *San Angelo Standard-Times*, April 6, 1956: 19; Stout, 175.

25. Sheffield, A12.

26. Dawidoff.

27. Stout, 179.

28. Dawidoff.

29. Stout, 179.

30. Stout, 202.

31. Stout, 213.

32. McCartha, 59–60.

33. "Kokernot To Skip Fence Signs," *El Paso Times*, January 25, 1959: 34.

34. Dawidoff.

35. In other words, both would jump from Class D to starring roles in the Major Leagues in just two years.

36. Dawidoff.

37. Stout, 235. Seventeen year-old Dalton Jones, who played nine years in the big leagues, was on the '61 Cowboys, who finished 62–63, good for fourth place in the six team Sophomore League.

38. Mark Rogers, "Field of Dreams," *Odessa American*, October 16, 1989: 9; Buck, 48.

39. Bill Rogan, *Life Ain't the Same in the Pecos League* (Self-published, 2020).

40. http://pecosleague.com/pecosleague.asp?page=2.

Four Hundred Hitters, Home Run Barrages, and Jim Crow

The Post-War Bush Leagues in Texas, (1946–61)

C. Paul Rogers III

Texas has always been a baseball bastion, with more of its towns represented in the history of so-called "Organized Baseball"—at least 102—than any other state.[1] The post-war baseball boom not only revitalized the Texas League, lower classification circuits also sprang up around the state. The result was some amazing performances, both good and bad. Home runs flew out of ballparks, especially in West Texas, and earned run averages soared. Many of the stats from the era read more like one would expect from slow pitch softball.

For example, the Class C West Texas-New Mexico league began a ten-year run in 1946 with Joe Bauman of the Amarillo Gold Sox slugging 48 home runs and driving in 159 runs in a 140-game season.[2] With teammate Bob Crues, Bauman would form one of the greatest power hitting tandems in minor league history in 1946–47, hitting a combined total of 167 home runs in those two years with Amarillo.[3] Quanah, Texas' Bill Evans—who would later have cups of coffee with the White Sox and Red Sox—went 26–7 in 1946 for the Gold Sox while future big leaguer Warren Hacker recorded a 20–4 line for the Pampa Oilers, who edged out the Gold Sox for second place.[4] At the other end of the standings, the Lamesa Lobos won only 36 of 140 games and finished 62½ games behind the pennant-winning Abilene Blue Sox. On June 8, the Lobos set a record for futility by losing to Amarillo 32–0.[5]

The East Texas League made a one-year appearance in 1946, also at the Class C level. The highlight was undoubtedly the comeback of former major league hurler Monty Stratton who won 18 games against 8 losses for the Sherman Twins. Stratton, raised on a farm near Greenville, pitched with an artificial leg—the result of a hunting accident eight years before—which had ended a promising big-league career.[6] Hollywood took note and Stratton was paid a reported $100,000 for the rights to his story, which resulted in a 1949 movie called *The Stratton Story* starring Jimmy Stewart and June Allyson.[7]

The post-war rise in lower-level minor league baseball in Texas was due in part to the passion, energy, and creativity of men like Howard Green. A native of Swenson in West Texas, Green served as a gunner on a B-24 during the war and returned with the goal of owning and operating a franchise in the West Texas-New Mexico League. Before the 1946 season, he put together a small investment group and founded the Abilene Blue Sox, even though professional baseball had failed three times in Abilene. He secured an affiliation with the Brooklyn Dodgers, which provided the Blue Sox with prospects like first baseman (and future big-league manager) Danny Ozark (31 homers, 142 RBIs, .325 batting average), Leo Thomas (.363 batting average) and player-manager William Greer (.358 BA with 131 RBIs). Pitchers John Hall (20–9), William Werbowski (20–7), Ken Olsen (19–7), Richard Tross (16–3), and Joe Tysko (13–2) were stellar on the mound as the Blue Sox compiled a 97-40 record and finished with the second highest winning percentage in baseball.[8]

Green wasn't content with the success of the Blue Sox and organized an entirely new league for 1947, the Class D Longhorn League with franchises in Odessa, Midland, Big Spring, Ballinger, Sweetwater, and Vernon to become, at age 25, the youngest league president in history. Although there were many naysayers, the Longhorn League lasted until 1955. Pat Stasey, a native of Stephenville, batted a cool .416 for Big Spring in the league's first year, driving in 153 runs in 123 games. Stasey didn't even win the batting title as James Prince of the Midland Indians batted an incredible .429 for the season. Stasey would play in the league for nine years, only once batting below .341.

The 30-year-old Stasey was Big Spring's manager and part-owner and, funding the team with his own money, hit upon a plan to recruit light-skinned Cuban players to stock his roster. Cubans were happy to play for lower salaries and were not subject to the US military draft, which ramped up with the Korean Conflict. From 1947 through 1952 the Broncs were made up largely of Cuban players, who made Big Spring a lower minor league powerhouse. Stacey's Big Spring teams won three pennants, finished second twice, and third once in six years.[9] In 1949 the Broncs won the regular season pennant by 20½ games and then swept the playoffs by winning eight games without a loss. Future big league pitchers Camilo Pascual, Mike Fornieles, and Raul Sanchez all got their start with Big Spring, as did Camilo's older brother, Carlos "Potato" Pascual, who was such an exciting two-way player for the Broncs that he jumped from Class D directly to the major league Washington Nationals at age 19.[10]

The first Longhorn League season in 1947 was marred by the death of Ballinger Cats outfielder James "Stormy" Davis, who was struck in the head by a pitched ball in Sweetwater on July 3. He died seven days later of a brain hemorrhage. The twenty-year-old Davis, whose roommate was Bonham native and future big-league shortstop Roy McMillan, was considered a bona fide prospect and was batting .333, with 19 homers, and 59 RBIs in just 48 games at the time of his fatal injury.[11]

The West Texas-New Mexico League cemented its reputation as the top hitters' league in baseball in 1947 as Lubbock swept to the pennant by 14 games over Amarillo, averaging almost nine runs a game.[12] The Hubbers were led by 5'9", 175-pound future Chicago Cub Bill Serena, who played shortstop, clubbed 57 home runs, and drove in 190 while batting .374. In 14 September playoff games, Serena hit 13 more taters, for a total of 70 for the year.[13] Borger's Leon Cato batted a lusty .410 to lead the league. The league had some quality pitching, however, as William "Lefty" Jones went 24–4 for Lamesa while Paul Hinrichs, who would later have a cup of coffee with the Red Sox, was 18–5 for the Hubbers with a league-leading 3.34 earned run average.[14]

The Class C Lone Star League began a two-year run in 1947 with franchises in East Texas cities such as Kilgore, Longview, Tyler, Marshall, Jacksonville, and Lufkin. John Stone of the Henderson Oilers won the Triple Crown with a .396 batting average, 32 homers, and 185 runs batted in. Perhaps the low point came in July when a game in Bryan was interrupted in the fifth inning when a snake slithered into right field.[15]

The Class B Big State League also began an eleven-year run in 1947 with teams like the Paris Red Peppers, the Greenville Majors, the Gainesville Owls, and Texarkana Bears, among others. Vern Washington of the Bears batted .404 to lead the league, while Chicota's Buck Frierson of the Sherman-Denison Twins smashed 58 homers and drove in 197 runs to complete an eye-popping campaign. D.C. "Pud" Miller of Wichita Falls was right behind with 57 homers and 196 runs batted in. On August 17 Frierson peaked with three home runs and eight runs driven in, all against Monty Stratton of the Waco Dons, who went the distance in absorbing the 16–14 loss.[16]

The following year, 1948, saw more gargantuan performances in the West Texas-New Mexico League as six of the eight teams batted over .300 for the season.[17] Bob Crues of Celina, Texas, tied a record in affiliated baseball by clouting 69 home runs, up from 52 the previous year.[18] He also drove in an unbelievable 254 runs in 140 games and batted .404, which was only the third highest average in the league.[19] Crues had lost his right index finger in a childhood accident and had broken in as a pitcher, winning 20 games in 1940 for the Lamesa Lobos before learning to hit at Camp Hood while serving in the military. After the war, he switched to the outfield and was rediscovered by Gold Sox owner/manager Bob Seeds.[20]

The league's sluggers augmented their monthly paychecks by "fence" money that fans stuck into the chicken-wire screens after home runs. Crues hit 41 of his 69 home runs at home and on the night he hit number 69 he was said to have gone home with about $400 in bills stuck through the screen and another $300 in change dropped into two-gallon buckets that were passed around the stands. It was about double his monthly $375 salary.[21]

In 1947 and 1948 the league also had Len Glica, a popular teenage second baseman for the Abilene Blue Sox. Glica moved up to Class B in 1949 and 1950 before he was drafted due to the Korean Conflict. Sadly, he was killed in action on May 26, 1951, only four days after arriving in the war zone. He was just 22 years old and the second professional baseball player to die in Korea.[22]

The Lone Star League was beset with bad luck in 1948 when, within the space of nine days in August, ballparks in Tyler and Henderson were destroyed by fire. Kilgore's Joe Kracher batted .433 to lead the minors (and majors). In the far-flung Longhorn League, a June 20 game in Vernon between the Vernon Dusters and Del Rio Cowboys was called off because of travel fatigue.[23]

By 1949 the Lone Star League had faded into history, but Frank Saucier of the Wichita Falls Spudders in the Big State League gained national attention by hitting .446 to win the Hillerich & Bradsby Silver Slugger Award as the top hitter in the minor leagues.[24] It was the highest season batting average up until that point in the history of affiliated baseball. In the hitters paradise that was the West Texas-New Mexico League, Lamesa's Pud Miller broke the 50-homer barrier for the second time by slamming 52 four-baggers—all the more remarkable because he missed the first 31 games of the league season while he suited up for the Glade-water Bears in the East Texas League.[25] Miller also batted .404, trailing only Roberto Fernandez of Abilene, whose .408 average led the league.

Miller was a 6'2", right-handed slugger who tried to launch one on every trip to the plate, mostly to reap the financial rewards from fans sticking cash in the fence after a round-tripper. Soon after T-bone—as he was known locally—joined Lamesa, he slugged four straight home runs but was unhappy because he reaped only $149 for the evening. The next day he threatened to leave the team unless team president Horace Duke gave him $100, so Duke went to the bank and got a $100 bill and handed it over. Surprisingly, when Miller returned to his hometown, Hickory, North Carolina, he praised the generosity of the Lamesa fans, saying he got as much as $150 for a homer and never less than $35.[26]

The Rio Grande Valley League began a two-year run in 1949, first as a Class D circuit and then advancing to Class C in 1950. The latter year Jess McClain had a gargantuan season for Harlingen with 53 home runs, 173 runs batted in, and a .356 batting average to lead the Capitols to the pennant by a single game over the Laredo Apaches. Lloyd Pearson of the Corpus Christi Aces hit .383 to win the batting title while driving in 154 runs, second to McClain. Gonzales' Dick Midkiff, who had appeared briefly for the Boston Red Sox in 1938, won 22 games for the Del Rio Cowboys. When several teams, led by Corpus Christi and including Harlingen, Brownsville, and Laredo, jumped to the Class B Gulf Coast League for 1951, the league was forced to discontinue operations.[27]

Mansfield, Texas, native Roy Parker had a dual threat season to remember in 1950 for Pampa in the West Texas-New Mexico League, leading the Oilers to the regular season pennant by posting 27 wins on the mound. When not pitching, Parker played left field, batting .346 for the year with 21 home runs. Joe Fortin, however, led the team in batting average with a .401 batting average and led the league with 236 hits and 171 RBIs in 145 games.[28] Oilers' catcher Jim Martin narrowly escaped tragedy on April 28 when knocked unconscious by lightning in a game in Abilene. The bolt launched his catcher's mask 20 feet past

the pitcher's mound, but Martin was back behind the plate the next evening. In August the Abilene Blue Sox tried wearing new style shorts for two games to try to beat the heat, but quickly abandoned the experiment because of mosquitoes.[29]

In the Class B Big State League, the Texarkana Bears swept to the pennant by 11½ games over the second place Gainesville Owls thanks in large part to Rice University alum Frank Carswell who batted an even .400, improving over his .386 batting average for the Bears in 1949. Milan Vucelich helped mightily with 144 runs batted in to lead the league. Down in Class D, the Odessa Oilers won their first Longhorn League pennant by seven and a half games, led by player-manager Alex Monchak, the all-league second baseman.

In 1951 in the Class C Longhorn League, Dean Franks chalked up 30 wins for the Roswell Rockets, who still finished third behind the San Angelo Colts. Nineteen-year-old Mike Fornieles led the second-place Big Spring Broncs with a 17–6 record and a league leading 2.85 earned run average. He made his big-league debut with the Washington Nationals the following year at age 20 to begin a 12-year major league career. Pat Stacey, then 34 years old, again led the league in batting with a lofty .384 average.

Kyle Rote, All-American halfback from SMU and first overall choice in the draft by the New York Football

AUTHOR'S COLLECTION

The East All-Stars for the 1953 Longhorn League All-Star game played July 25 in Midland, Texas. Front row (L to R): John Malgarini of San Angelo, Roger Dalla Betta of Midland, Scooter Hughes of Midland, John Tayoan of San Angelo, and Barney Batson of Odessa. Second row (L to R): Joe Riney of Big Spring, Art Bowland of Midland, Glenn Groomes of Big Spring, Glenn Burns of San Angelo, Julio De la Torre of Midland. Back row (L to R): Mario Saldana of San Angelo, Ben Bonine of San Angelo, Jim Carson of Odessa, Bobby Gregg of San Angelo, and Rudy Briner of San Angelo.

Giants made his professional baseball debut on April 24, 1951, with the Corpus Christi Aces of the Class B Gulf Coast League. Two nights later he clobbered three home runs in a game against Galveston. In 22 games for the Aces, Rote batted .349 with seven home runs. Then on May 23 he turned in his uniform to report to training camp for the Giants, never to return to the diamond.[30]

In the same circuit, 46-year-old rubber-armed Texan Earl Caldwell, a veteran of eight major league seasons, won 19 games (against only six losses) for the Harlingen Capitols and led the league with a 2.22 earned run average. Caldwell followed in 1952 with a 20–11 record and a 2.74 ERA and won 11 and 12 games the next two seasons, both with sparkling earned run averages to cap off a minor league career that spanned 24 seasons and included 302 wins.[31]

Outfielder Glenn Burns of the Lamesa Lobos in the West Texas-New Mexico League had a mammoth year in 1951, batting .392 with 197 RBIs in 141 games. Lamesa, however, made much bigger waves when manager Jay Haney signed two African American players, John Wingate of Beaumont and Connie Heard of Texas City, in spite of considerable local opposition. Although Heard did not make the team, Wingate did as a shortstop. He began the year by hitting safely in his first six games and the so-called Negro (segregated) stands were full in what was still very much the Jim Crow south. Overall attendance declined, however, as many Whites stopped attending and after just 27 games in which Wingate batted .250, he was released.[32]

As the decade wore on, the lower classifications struggled financially, but were home to some incredible performances and unusual events. For example, in 1952 Patricio Lorenzo batted .415 to lead the West Texas-New Mexico League and was traded mid-season from the Lamesa Lobos to the Borger Gassers. Joe Bauman, playing for Artesia, New Mexico, terrorized pitchers in the Longhorn League with 50 home runs and 157 runs batted in. The Big Spring Broncs, still relying on Cuban players like Gilberto Guerra who went 26–11, finished in second place, a single game behind the Odessa Oilers. In the Class B Big State League, the Waco Pirates suffered through one of the most futile seasons in minor league history, finishing 56 games out of first place with a 29–118 record, good for a .197 winning average.

Unfortunately, Waco's luck was even worse in 1953. On May 11 a devastating tornado swept through the city, destroying the business district and Katy Park where the Pirates played. The twister had actually first touched down in San Angelo and then swiftly traveled

190 miles before striking Waco, where it killed 114 people and injured another 597.[33] Without a ballpark, the Pirates moved to Longview for the rest of the season. The team improved greatly from the previous year and finished in fourth place with a 77–68 record.

The 1953 season was the swan song for the Gulf Coast League, with Harlingen and Corpus Christi migrating to the Big State League after the league shut down. That final season was a memorable one, however, at least for on-field shenanigans. On June 4 Brownsville Charros manager Stubby Greer threw a flurry of punches at umpire Dick Valencourt and earned a 45-day suspension. Without Greer, on July 13 the Charros scored 17 runs in the second inning of a 25–5 victory over the Corpus Christi Aces. In August the so-called "leaded bat controversy" erupted, with first Port Arthur and then Laredo complaining that the Galveston White Caps, who ran away with the regular season title, were using leaded and "studded" bats with nails driven in.[34] Bill Bagwell of Texas City won 26 games, but his Texans still finished eight games behind the suspect White Caps.

The thin air of West Texas and the Panhandle continued to benefit hitters in 1953 as the Plainview Ponies' Don Stokes batted an amazing .426 with 174 RBIs in 141 games to lead the West Texas-New Mexico League. No one-year wonder, Stokes had batted .384 and .363 the previous two years with Lamesa before the franchise moved to Plainview. In 1954, Stokes again topped the four hundred mark, batting .405 to once more lead the league.[35]

Also in 1953, Amarillo's Jim Matthews polled 50 homers while batting a cool .393. Longhorn League hurlers "held" Artesia's Joe Bauman to 53 home runs. Unseasonably cold weather affected the start of the season for many teams. For example, in the Big State League on April 18, only 30 fans in Tyler braved temperatures in the 40s to witness the Tyler East Texans defeat the Austin Pioneers 5–2.[36] Wichita Falls would go on to claim the Big State League pennant and the postseason championship over Tyler. The Spudders were led by outfielder Al Neil, who led the league in five hitting categories, including the triple crown (.356 batting average, 39 home runs, and 137 RBIs).

Joe Bauman brought national attention to the Longhorn League in 1954 when he smashed 72 homers for the Roswell Rockets in 138 games. He went into the last day of the season with 69 circuit clouts and launched three more that day to become the first player in organized baseball to top 70.[37] Bauman also batted an even .400 for the year and drove in an astounding 224 runs.[38] Making less of a lasting impression but still contributing to the second place Rockets was hometown hero Tom Brookshier, who won seven of eight decisions before leaving for the NFL's Philadelphia Eagles, where he would twice make All-Pro.[39]

In the Big State League, the Waco Pirates were back home in a rebuilt Katy Park. Led by outfielders Jack Falls (.349) and future major leaguer Roman Mejias (.354), the club had a memorable resurgence, winning 105 games against only 42 losses to claim the regular season pennant by 13 games over the Tyler Tigers. The Pirates then won the league playoffs, defeating the Corpus Christi Clippers in seven games in the final round.

The dangers of bus travel in the bush leagues were apparent on May 17 when five members of the Abilene Blue Sox of the West Texas-New Mexico League were hospitalized for carbon monoxide poisoning from gas fumes coming from the team bus.[40] On April 23 the following year, dust storms played havoc in the Longhorn League, causing postponements of games in Midland, Big Spring, and Hobbs, New Mexico.[41]

Plainview Ponies player-manager Jodie Beeler enjoyed the arid weather on August 21, 1955. In a West Texas-New Mexico League doubleheader against the Amarillo Gold Sox in Amarillo, Beeler smoked two home runs in the first game in an 8–6 defeat and four more in the second game in an 18-13 victory. Both games were seven inning affairs, so Beeler smacked his six home runs for the day in only 14 innings of play. Sonny Tims of the Pampa Oilers and the Gold Sox's Paul Mohr both also hit four homers in a single nine-inning game which for Mohr included 11 runs batted in.[42] Plainview's Isaac Palmer led the league in batting with a .406 average.

In 1956, the Class B Southwestern League replaced the lower classification Longhorn League and the West Texas-New Mexico League with teams in El Paso, Pampa, San Angelo, Plainview, Ballinger, Midland and four New Mexico cities.[43] Len Tucker of Pampa batted .404 to lead the league while Plainview's Forrest "Frosty" Kennedy smashed 60 home runs (with 184 RBIs) to become one of 9 minor leaguers to reach the 60 homer mark. He hit number 60 on the last day of the season against San Angelo. No flash in the pan, Kennedy had batted .410 with 38 homers and 169 RBIs for Plainview in 1953. According to Kennedy, it was tougher to hit 60 homers in the minor leagues than in the majors:

A shorter season, rotten lights at rotten little ballparks, rotten pitchers who couldn't or wouldn't throw me a pitch to hit, freezing weather in the spring, hot as hell in the summer. Don't let anyone ever tell you there was anything cheap about my getting 60 home runs. I was there.[44]

In the Big State League, Wichita Falls player-manager (and future Philadelphia Phillies manager) Danny Ozark had a memorable day by slugging four home runs in a 7–3 triumph over the Beaumont Exporters. Confusion ensued in a game between Lubbock and Beaumont when a combined five players named Smith were in the box score, including three *George* Smiths. Paris was the lone Texas team competing in the Class D Sooner State League and the Orioles featured Johnny Wartelle, the top fire-baller in the league. Wartelle struck out a loop record 22 batters on May 5 against Seminole and 16 in his next start against Ardmore.[45] For the season he struck out 268 batters in 217 innings.

Also in 1956, Amarillo jumped from the defunct West Texas-New Mexico League up to the fast Class A Western League as the only Texas franchise in the league. The Gold Sox promptly won the pennant behind Art Cuitti's league-leading .364 batting average to go with 46 homers and 139 runs batted in. Thirty-seven-year-old player-manager Chuck Stevens, a former Pacific Coast League star, chipped in with a .334 batting average in 98 games. The Gold Sox finished second the next two years in close pennant races. They were led by Al Pinkston who batted .372 and .337 with 133 and 126 runs batted in 1957 and 1958. Pinkston was a 40-year-old African American who, despite rarely batting below .300 in 16 years in the minor leagues and the Mexican League, never got a real shot with a major league team. According to Gold Sox teammate Clay Dalrymple, who played 12 years in the big leagues, "He could really pop the line drives to all fields—right-center on over to left field. It was just amazing."[46]

Year after year the bush leagues continued to dwindle in Texas and throughout the US. Forty-three leagues began the season in 1952 and by 1959 the number was down to only 21.[47] The advent and spread of television had a great impact: the Game of the Week with Dizzy Dean and Buddy Blattner, later replaced by Pee Wee Reese, provided a major league baseball game in living rooms in the hinterlands every Saturday.[48]

The Big State League hung in there until 1957, and the Longhorn and West Texas-New Mexico Leagues until 1955, while the Gulf Coast League shut down after the 1953 season. The El Paso Texans played in the Arizona-Texas League until the league folded in 1954 and Gainesville, Paris, Greenville, and Sherman/Denison fielded teams sporadically in the Class D Sooner State League, which also lasted until 1957.[49] The Paris Orioles won the last Sooner State League regular season pennant by a half game and featured 19-year-old flame-throwing southpaw Steve Barber, who would soon go on to a 15-year big league career. But even the Class A Western League was gone after 1958.

Surprisingly in the face of this downturn, the Class D Sophomore League began a four-year run in 1958 with franchises in San Angelo, Plainview, and Midland to go with three eastern New Mexico outfits. It, too, was a hitters league, as evidenced by Midland's 15-run second inning in a 19–9 win over Plainview on May 6. Alpine and Odessa joined the league for the 1959 season.

The Alpine Cowboys had been a top-notch semipro team for 13 years under the ownership of rancher and baseball mavin Herbert Kokernot, Jr. He had built a beautiful $1.25 million ballpark in Alpine which opened in 1947 and attracted many of the top collegiate players in the country for a summer of high caliber baseball in far West Texas. In 1959, Kokernot decided to try professional baseball and entered into a working agreement with the Boston Red Sox. With a population of 5,261 people, Alpine became the smallest town in the nation with a professional baseball team.[50]

Officially known as the Big Bend-Davis Mountains Cowboys, the club won their home opener 18–1 over San Angelo and didn't look back. By mid-season they were 30–6 at home and were clearly the class of the league.[51] During one stretch, the Cowboys won 15 games in a row. They raced to the South Division title by an astounding 34 games with an 88–34 record and then swept Hobbs and Carlsbad in the league playoffs. The Cowboys were led by Don Schwall, who posted a 23–6 mound record, and second baseman Chuck Schilling, who batted .340. Just two years later Schwall and Schilling would be starting for the Boston Red Sox and Schwall would be named American League Rookie of the Year after going 15–7.

Jim Crow still reigned in West Texas and eastern New Mexico in the late 1950s and future Hall of Famer Wilver "Willie" Stargell's experience in the Sophomore League was not atypical. The Pittsburgh Pirates signed the 19-year-old out of the Bay Area for a $1,500 bonus in 1959 and sent him to San Angelo, their Class D affiliate. The team went bankrupt six weeks into the season and abruptly moved to Roswell, where Stargell had difficulty finding a place to live. The team finally located a bed for him in a house rented by a black Air Force Sergeant who was stationed at Walker Air Force Base.

Accommodations on the road for young Wilver were even worse, and were often fold-up beds on the back porches of homes of African American families. For meals, White teammates would bring him sandwiches on the bus, since most restaurants would not serve him. He remembered that in general "people treated me like a dog."[52] A defining moment occurred in Plainview early one evening when Stargell decided to walk to the ballpark alone from his place of lodging. On Stargell's way through town, a White man jumped out from an alley, pointed a shotgun at Willie at point blank range, called him a racial epithet, and threatened to shoot him if he played in the game that night. Stargell overcame his fear and played, but never forgot the incident.[53]

Outfielder Gilbert Carter, another African American, led the league in home runs in 1959 with 34. Playing for the Carlsbad Potashers, he made an indelible impact on August 11 in a contest against the Odessa Oilers. Heading into the bottom of the seventh, the Oilers' pitcher Wayne Schaper had a 6–0 lead and a no-hitter. Carter ended the shutout and the no-hitter with a run-scoring double. The score was still 6–1 when Carter batted again in the ninth. This time he laid into a fastball and hit one of the longest—if not *the* longest—home runs in baseball history. The ball cleared the 50-foot light poles behind the fence in left-center field and landed in a yard thought to be about 650 feet from home plate.[54] Some estimates had the ball traveling over 700 feet.[55] The mammoth blast forged a bond between Carter and Schaper and they kept in touch until Carter passed away in 2015.[56]

The Sophomore League continued in 1960 and 1961 as the only Texas minor league other than the Texas League. In 1960, however, only Alpine and Odessa were teams from Texas. Alpine, led by 18-year-old shortstop Jim Fregosi, repeated as regular season champions before losing to Hobbs in the playoff final. Fregosi would quickly advance in 1961 to the Triple A Dallas-Fort Worth Rangers and would be the starting shortstop for the major league Los Angeles Angels by the time he was 21.

In 1961 Odessa dropped out of the Sophomore League while the El Paso Sun Kings joined the circuit and finished second to Hobbs. El Paso was led by a seventeen-year-old Cuban named Jose Cardenal, who batted .355 while leading the league in home runs with 35 and driving in 108 runs to finish second in that category. Two years later, a nineteen-year-old Cardenal batted .312 with 36 homers for the Sun Kings after El Paso had joined the Double A Texas League and soon would be on to an 18-year major league career.

The Sophomore League called it quits after 1961, ending the bush league era in Texas.[57] The hiatus lasted until the rise of independent, unaffiliated leagues in the 1990s. But it was a time marked by incredible performances on the diamond and segregation off it when baseball was indeed the National Pastime in spite of itself. ■

Notes

1. Robert Obojski, *Bush League: A History of Minor League Baseball* (New York: Macmillan Publishing Co., 1975):179. "Organized Baseball" as a historical term refers to the American and National Leagues and all other teams and leagues participating in contractual agreements with those leagues, including minor leagues, team-affiliated "farm teams," affiliated independent teams, and instructional leagues.
2. Bauman's RBI total was surpassed by the Borger Gassers' Gordon Nell who drove in 175 runs.
3. Toby Smith, *Bush League Boys—The Postwar Legends of Baseball in the American Southwest* (Albuquerque: University of New Mexico Press, 2014): 1–24.
4. The Abilene Blue Sox won the pennant by 5½ games with a 97–40 record.
5. Smith, 7.
6. Stratton had won 15 games for the White Sox in both 1937 and 1938 against 5 and 9 losses respectively.
7. Gary Sarnoff, "Monty Stratton," SABR BioProject at https://sabr.org/bioproj/person/monty-stratton/.
8. David Pietrusza, *Minor Miracles—the Legend & Lure of Minor League Baseball* (South Bend, IN: Diamond Communications, 1995): 49–51.
9. Gaylon H. White, *Left on Base in the Bush Leagues: Legends, Near Greats, and Unknowns in the Minors* (Lanham, MD: Rowman & Littlefield Publishing Group, 2019): 111–34.
10. Carlos Pascual pitched two games for the Nationals late in 1950, winning one and losing one but sporting a 2.12 earned run average on 17 innings. After he reported to the Nationals' spring training in 1951, he became quite homesick and returned to Cuba where he pitched for several years for the Class B Havana Cubans before injuring his arm. He then continued to play as a position player and eventually returned to play for Pat Stasey with Hobbs in the Longhorn League in 1955 and then with Hobbs and Midland/Lamesa in the Southwestern League in 1956 and 1957. He never returned to the big leagues and played in the minor leagues through 1962. White, 119–20.
11. Pietrusza, 52–53.
12. Clay Coppedge, *Texas Baseball: A Lone Star History from Town Teams to the Big Leagues* (Charleston, SC: The History Press, 2012): 63–64.
13. Lloyd Johnson and Miles Wolff, *The Encyclopedia of Minor League Baseball*, 2nd ed. (Durham, NC: Baseball America, Inc., 1997): 366.
14. Smith, 39–41.
15. Johnson and Wolff, 366.
16. Johnson and Wolff, 366.
17. White, 39.
18. Many believed that Crues had actually hit 70 homers. Future big league umpire Frank Secory ruled that a blast Crues hit in Abilene had hit high off the wall and bounced back onto the playing field, but many, including Crues, insisted that the ball had hit the scoreboard above the fence. White, 38–39.
19. Former major leaguers Hershel Martin of Albuquerque and Eddie Carnett of Borger batted .425 and .409 respectively.
20. White, 45.
21. White, 40–41.
22. Smith, 106.
23. Johnson and Wolff, 377.
24. Jim Ball, *Frank Saucier*, SABR Bio Project at https://sabr.org/bioproj/person/frank-saucier/.
25. White, 19–20.
26. White, 20–22.
27. Noe Torres, *Ghost Leagues: A History of Minor League Baseball in South Texas* (Coral Springs, FL: Llumina Press, 2005): 102–3.
28. Future big leaguer Harry Bright of the Clovis Pioneers, however, led the league in hitting with a .413 average.
29. Johnson and Wolff, 399.
30. Torres, 105–11. Rote would play 11 seasons with the football Giants and would retire as the team's all-time leader in passes caught, receiving yards, and receiving touchdowns. He captained the team for eight of those years.
31. Caldwell compiled a 33–43 record in his eight major league seasons, pitching for the Phillies, Browns, White Sox and Red Sox. His best year was 1946 when he went 13–4 with a 2.08 earned run average for the White Sox.
32. White, 24–28. After serving two years in Korea, Wingate played for two years in the Longhorn and Big State Leagues with limited success before returning to his native Beaumont. Smith, 123–25.
33. Smith, 48–50.
34. A.C. Becker, Jr., "Charges of 'Leaded Bats,' Forfeit Stir Up Gulf Coast," *The Sporting News*, August 26, 1953: 34.
35. Stokes had earlier played for four years for the Sherman-Denison Twins in the Class B Big State League, batting over .300 in each year.
36. Johnson and Wolff, 427.
37. White, 57–85.
38. The seemingly ubiquitous Pat Stasey was player-manager of Roswell from 1953 through 1955. He finished his 14-year minor league playing career in 1955 with a cumulative .343 batting average, almost all of it in the bush leagues of West Texas and eastern New Mexico.
39. Post-football, Brookshier had a long career as a NFL broadcaster.
40. A similar incident occurred just a week before, on May 10 when seven members of the Decatur Commodores of the Mississippi-Ohio Valley League narrowly escaped death from carbon monoxide poisoning on t he team bus. Johnson and Wolff, 434.
41. Johnson and Wolff, 441.
42. Pietrusza, 109.
43. The New Mexico franchises were the Hobbs Sports, the Carlsbad Potashers, the Roswell Rockets, and the Clovis Pioneers.
44. White, 4–5.
45. Johnson and Wolff, 447.
46. White, 166.
47. Johnson and Wolff, 411.
48. Gene Kirby with Bo Carter and Mark S. McDonald, *Dizzy Dean of Baseball and My Podnah* (San Antonio: Cool Cat Publications, 2016).
49. Peter G. Pierce, *Baseball in the Cross Timbers: The Story of the Sooner State League* (Oklahoma Heritage Association Publishing, 2009); Peter G. Pierce, *Red Dirt Baseball: The Post-War Years, Small Team Professional Baseball in Oklahoma 1946–1961* (Oklahoma Heritage Association Publishing, 2015).
50. DJ Stout, *The Amazing Tale of Mr. Herbert and His Fabulous Alpine Cowboys Baseball Club* (Austin: University of Texas Press, 2010): 215.
51. Stout, 225.
52. James Forr, Willie Stargell, SABR Bio Project at https://sabr.org/bioproj/person/willie-stargell/.
53. Smith, 117–21. Forr.
54. Smith, 25–36.
55. White, xx.
56. Smith, 35–36.
57. The Texas League would carry on, but as one of the premier minor leagues; it could hardly be considered a "bush" league.

When the Babe Came to Dallas, 1947

Bob LeMoine

Babe Ruth's plane landed at Love Field in Dallas on the afternoon of Tuesday, July 8, 1947. There to greet baseball's greatest celebrity was Dallas mayor Jimmie Temple, Harry Rubin of the American Legion, and officials of the Ford Motor Company which sponsored the Bambino's appearance. Before Ruth was even halfway down the ramp, Temple handed him a ten-gallon Stetson hat. Ruth tossed his familiar flat, tan hat aside in favor of the Stetson, hearing the roar of the 200 fans who turned out for a glimpse of the once mighty, but now declining, Sultan of Swat. They watched him ride off in a lemon-colored Ford convertible, headed for the Baker Hotel, located at Commerce and Akard Streets in downtown Dallas.

This visit to Dallas was one of several stops Babe Ruth made around the country as a "consultant" for Ford, which promoted the American Legion Youth Baseball Program. The title didn't mean that much, but it gave Ruth a purpose and rekindled a passion. "They call me a 'consultant,' but I want to tell you that I plan to work hard at this job—just as hard as my health permits," Ruth said. "I owe everything I am to the kids. They didn't get up there and hit for me, but they were my inspiration all the time. Now, I want to pay them back."[1]

"I've always been for the youth of America," Ruth promised, "and I will be till the day I die."[2]

Ruth had dreamed of managing a major league club before his final season flop in 1935. But after retiring from playing, he found himself an outsider to the game he loved and helped establish as big business. He filled time golfing, making personal appearances, playing some exhibition games, and even suiting up as a wrestling referee to fill the void. "My old game does not appear to want me anymore," Ruth lamented.[3] Ford gave Ruth a new lease on life to "help the kids of America by spending the rest of my life teaching them baseball," Ruth said.[4] He knew time was not on his side. This new adventure would be his last, as it coincided with his battle with cancer which he would lose in 1948 at the age of 53.

Ruth made the most of his opportunities, talking to youth while his own body shuddered in pain. Before Dallas, Ruth made Legion stops in Syracuse and Detroit, then spent the remainder of the month at Mount Sinai Hospital. The suffering could be seen on Ruth's face. "The eyes that once picked out home run pitches are deep pools," observed Felix R. McKnight of the *Dallas Morning News*. "The bull shoulders that rocketed 714 home runs out of major league parks are bent and sloped. The massive frame is slender and stooped and the hair is grey. The voice is raspy and the slight coughs frequent. But the heart? Bigger than ever!"[5]

Ruth slumped into a chair at the Baker Hotel and gave an 8:30PM press conference. He gave the predictable rant of kids having it easy compared to his day, "when we sewed two pieces of cloth together for a glove and made balls out of yarn raveled from our socks." Ruth also complained that night baseball negatively affected young players who have to "develop a different set of eyes."[6]

Ruth had a full itinerary on July 9. The City of Dallas threw a downtown morning parade in his honor and presented Ruth with a belt and silver spur to match his ten-gallon hat. Later, Ruth was the guest at an American Legion luncheon where he spoke of legacy. "When we get too old to help ourselves," he said, "we can help others." To the youth he advised, "The men out there are trying to do something for you. When you think you know enough to do something, too, pitch in and help the boys that come on behind you."[7] The toastmaster, Colonel Alvin Owsley, said to Ruth while posing for a picture, "It must be wonderful to be a champion, but it must be greater to be a champion of America's youth."[8]

One attendee finally received the Ruth autograph he had waited 20 years for. Father M.W. Ross, athletic director at nearby Jesuit High School, played on a youth team in New Orleans in 1927. The Bambino paid a visit. Ross sought an autograph but couldn't find a pencil. Someone found Ross a fountain pen, but when Ruth attempted to sign, it was out of ink. Ross made sure he brought his own pen this time, and Ruth gladly signed it.[9]

DALLAS HISTORY & ARCHIVES DIVISION, DALLAS PUBLIC LIBRARY

Babe Ruth is handed a 10-gallon Stetson hat by Dallas Mayor Jimmie Stetson (right) upon his arrival at Love Field on July 8, 1947. A joyous Claire Ruth (left) looks on.

That evening, Ruth arrived at Rebel Stadium to see American Legion youth play a tournament double-header. Ruth missed the opener, the Forest Lions defeating the Crozier Tech Wolves in a nail-biter, 1–0. Ruth arrived between games in his convertible, wearing his ten-gallon hat and puffing on a black cigar. He thanked the crowd of 2,500 (two-thirds teenagers) who roared in approval. Ruth watched the nightcap, a 9–3 win by W.H. Adamson over North Dallas, from the private box of George Schepps, the owner of the Dallas Rebels, a Detroit Tigers' affiliate in the Texas League.[10]

In 1938, Schepps had purchased the Dallas Steers, a Chicago White Sox affiliate at the time. He changed the name of the team to Rebels and renamed Steer Stadium, at 1500 E. Jefferson Boulevard, to Rebel Field, and later Rebel Stadium. The park would later serve as a whistle-stop for Harry S. Truman's re-election campaign and in 1960 provided a practice field for the expansion Dallas Cowboys of the NFL. Later known as Burnett Field, the facility was razed in 1964. Schepps later founded the Texas Baseball Hall of Fame.[11]

Babe Ruth Day wouldn't be complete without him being accosted by a group of boys. It happened at the hotel and made for a front-page photo in the *Dallas Morning News*. The boys were Kenneth Fowler, Perry Tarver, John Nance Garner, Tommy Crittenden and his little five-year-old brother, Carlton Crittenden. Ruth inspected the muscles on young Carlton's arm.

"Gee, fellow," Ruth bellowed, "that muscle is just the size of the handle on my old bat!"

Carlton's eyes bulged, wrote McNight.

"I'll betcha' play baseball too—don't you?" Ruth asked.

Second base, Carlton told him.

"Good boy, good boy."[12]

Almost 60 years later, Kevin Sherrington of the *Dallas Morning News* caught up with Carlton. He didn't have many memories of that day other than the family stories told to him. His mom read about Ruth being at the Baker Hotel and drove Carlton and Tommy from their home in Detroit, Texas, 120-something miles to Dallas. They saw the Bambino passing in the hallway and a reporter asked if they would like to meet Ruth. Carlton didn't know what was going on, but looking at the picture 60 years later acknowledged the moment.

"That's my one claim to fame," he told Sherrington.[13]

Crittenden was one of the last boys to chat with Babe Ruth. Ruth wasn't a slugging, robust athlete anymore, but a declining, cancer-ridden man from Baltimore. The great sportswriter Grantland Rice reflected on Ruth's last years and thought they were his greatest. "It is the story of a man who is much greater nearing the trail's end of glory," Rice eloquently wrote, "than he ever was when hitting his 714 home runs and giving a vast nation the greatest thrills that sport has ever known." Rice added that Ruth was "broken but not beaten, a relic of the king that he was, he is an even greater man today." Nothing could stop Ruth from visiting a sick kid or "a broken or blind human being. He seems to feel they belong to him—and he belongs to them." Rice saw Ruth as a "better man" who did not fear the grave but whose "only thought has been that he will travel the few remaining miles for the betterment of the kids…those who might need help and inspiration as he once needed such help so badly."[14]

The City of Dallas, and particularly a few young lucky ballplayers, were the beneficiaries of that inspiration for one day in July of 1947. As McKnight summarized, "Yes, a pretty important piece of America was in town Wednesday."[15] ∎

Author's Note

For more on Babe Ruth's final season of 1935 and his life's final journey, see the author's book: *When the Babe Went Back to Boston: Babe Ruth, Judge Fuchs and the Hapless Braves of 1935* (McFarland, 2023).

References

Cohen, Alan, "Babe Ruth's Final Legacy to the Kids." Society for American Baseball Research. Retrieved January 11, 2025. https://sabr.org/journal/article/babe-ruths-final-legacy-to-the-kids/.

Wilonsky, Robert, "For Sale: A Rare Photo Taken on 'Babe Ruth Day in Dallas' at Rebel Stadium on July 10, 1947. *Dallas Observer*, May 23, 2011. Retrieved January 9, 2025. https://www.dallasobserver.com/news/for-sale-a-rare-photo-taken-on-babe-ruth-day-in-dallas-at-rebel-stadium-on-july-10-1947-7135649.

Notes

1. Joseph M. Sheehan, "Ford Co. Signs Ruth to Life Post As Consultant in Legion Baseball," *The New York Times*, April 8, 1947: 37.
2. Hy Turkin, "Ruth Signed by Legion to Aid Young Players," *New York Daily News*, April 8, 1947: 49.
3. Associated Press, "Babe Ruth Says Mat Jobs Taken Since Baseball 'Does Not Want Me,'" *Hartford Courant*, April 3, 1945: 14.
4. Turkin.
5. Felix R. McKnight, "Babe Ruth Greets Texas Boys," *Dallas Morning News*, July 10, 1947: 1.
6. Bill McClanahan, "Start Young, Play Often, Babe Says," *Dallas Morning News*, July 9, 1947: 14.
7. Associated Press, "Ruth Urges Youths to Help Others," *Abilene Reporter-News*, July 10, 1947: 4.
8. McKnight.
9. Associated Press, "After 20 Years Fan Gets Ruth's Autograph," *Wichita Daily Times*, July 10, 1947: 11.
10. Mike Haikin, "Babe Ruth's Appearance Thrills Fans," *Dallas Morning News*, July 10, 1947: 5.
11. Frank Jackson, "The History of Burnett Field: Dallas' Minor League Baseball Home," Texas State Historical Association. March 24, 2021. Retrieved January 11, 2025. https://www.tshaonline.org/handbook/entries/burnett-field.
12. McKnight.
13. Kevin Sherrington, "'My Claim to Fame'—Nearly 60 Years Ago, Ruth Made a Boy's Day," *Dallas Morning News*, March 11, 2007: 2c.
14. Grantland Rice, "Rice Calls Ruth Greater Than Ever, Forgetting Own Pain to Cheer Others," *Boston Globe*, March 24, 1948: 18.
15. McKnight.

Bobby Layne, 28–0

Hall of Fame Caliber Pitcher for the Texas Longhorns (1944, 1946–48)

Herm Krabbenhoft

During the 1944 and 1946-48 baseball seasons, while playing for the University of Texas Longhorns, Bobby Layne compiled an amazing 28–0 won-lost ledger vs. Southwest Conference teams. In doing so, Layne helped the team win the SWC championship in each of the latter three years.[1]

OBJECTIVES

The focus of this research is Bobby Layne's phenomenal 28 consecutive victories versus the other five teams constituting the Southwest Conference: the Baylor University Bears, Rice University Owls, Southern Methodist University (SMU) Mustangs, Texas A&M Aggies, and Texas Christian University (TCU) Horned Frogs. The principal objectives are 1) to examine key details for selected games in the victory streak, and 2) assess how Layne's achievement ranks now, some 75 years later.

RESEARCH PROCEDURE

Using Newspapers.com and GenealogyBank, I searched newspapers for "Layne" in "Texas" from early March through mid-June (the time period covering the collegiate baseball seasons) for the years 1944 and 1946–48. In addition, I also examined the information presented in two biographies about Bobby Layne.[2,3]

RESULTS

Brief summaries of every Longhorns baseball game Bobby Layne participated in are provided in Appendix A (available on the SABR website). Summaries for twelve of his games involving SWC teams are given here.

1944

April 21: Bobby Layne had his first SWC game versus Rice University. Layne tossed five innings of shutout ball, giving up but three hits, walking none and striking out eight. He took over in right field for the last four innings. Texas won the game, 5–0, with Layne being credited with the victory.[4]

May 19: Layne recorded another victory against Rice, even though he hurled only two innings (one hit, one walk, two strikeouts). Thanks to robust hitting, Texas built up an 11–0 lead going into the bottom of the third. Following the "Large Lead" custom, Layne was awarded the W as Texas defeated Rice by a final score of 16–12.[5,6]

May 20: Thanks to his arm-saving short outing in the May 19 game, Layne was able to take the hill the very next day and hurl a complete game against the Rice Owls, emerging with a 7–1 triumph. Permitting only seven hits, Layne walked four batters and fanned 13.[7,8]

For the 1944 season overall, Layne finished with a 7–5 W-L ledger. Excluding his 1–4 W-L record against non-collegiate opponents, such as teams composed of United States military personnel (such as servicemen stationed at the San Marcos Army Air Field), Bobby compiled a 6–1 ledger against collegiate foes. See Table 1.

Table 1. Bobby Layne's Pitching Stats vs. Collegiate Opponents (1944).

Game	OPP	IP (S/R)	R/ER	H	W	K	W/L
3–25	SWU	9.0 (S*)	1/0	3	4	15	W
4–21	*RIC*	*5.0 (S)*	*0/0*	*3*	*0*	*8*	*W*
4–22	*RIC*	*5.1 (R)*	*0/0*	*1*	*0*	*8*	*W*
4–28	SWU*	8 0 (S*)	5/?	8	?	?	L
5–11	*TAM*	*9.0 (S*)*	*1/0*	*3*	*6*	*8*	*W*
5–19	*RIC**	*2.0 (S)*	*0/0*	*1*	*1*	*2*	*W*
5–20	*RIC**	*9.0 (S*)*	*1/1*	*7*	*4*	*13*	*W*

NOTES: (1) The "OPP" column gives the opposing team. SWU (Southwestern University), RIC (Rice University), TAM (Texas A&M University). SWC teams in bold italics. An asterisk indicates the game was played at the opponent's ballpark.
(2) For the "IP (S/R)" column, "IP" gives the Innings Pitched; "S" indicates Starting pitcher and "R" indicates Relief pitcher. An asterisk indicates a complete game.

1946

After having spent much of 1945 in the Merchant Marine, Bobby Layne returned to the University of Texas in the fall and resumed pitching the next spring.

April 13: In his second outing of the season, versus Rice in Houston, Layne twirled a three-hitter and shut out the Owls, 16–0. Layne struck out 16 batters, the most in a single game during his college career.[9]

May 4: On May 1 the AP reported that "Bobby Layne, the Longhorns' star pitcher, might not be able to start against the Texas A&M nine at College Station Saturday [May 4] because of an ankle injury."[10] Layne had suffered a badly bruised ankle in an automobile accident. But Layne did start the game and threw a no-hitter. Bobby struck out 14 Aggies and walked two as the Steers won a tight game, 2–1. The lone run came on a couple of fielding errors—batter Earl Beasley hit a grounder to third baseman Ransom Jackson and went all the way to second on the error. Beasley then "stole third and came home on a squeeze play when Layne threw wide to [catcher] Jack O'Reagan at the plate." Bobby also did pretty well from the batter's box, getting three singles in four trips to the plate.[11]

May 13: By twirling a four-hit 4–0 shutout against the Rice Owls, Layne and the Longhorns clinched the Southwest Conference championship. Layne struck out 11 and walked just two batters in the decisive victory.[12]

Overall, for 1946 Layne finished with a 12–1 W-L ledger. Excluding his three games against non-collegiate opponents (in which he went 1–0), Bobby produced an 11–1 ledger against collegiate foes. See Table 2.

Table 2. Bobby Layne's Pitching Stats vs. Collegiate Opponents (1946).

Game	OPP	IP (S/R)	R/ER	H	W	K	W/L
3–22	OKL	6.0 (S)	7/?	8	1	9	L
3–26	SWU	9.0 (S*)	0/0	0	4	16	W
3–30	MMC	9.0 (S*)	0/0	1	7	13	W
4–04	BAY*	9.0 (S*)	6/5	8	6 + 1 HBP	9	W
4–08	SWU*	0.0 (S)	4/3	1	3	0	—
4–13	RIC*	9.0 (S*)	0/0	3	2	16	W
4–19	TCU	9.0 (S*)	1/1	5	4	9	W
4–24	SMU	4.0 (R)	0/0	1	3 + 1 HBP	7	W
5–04	TAM*	9.0 (S*)	1/0	0	2	14	W
5–08	BAY*	6.0 (R)	3/2	7	6	5	W
5–13	RIC	9.0 (S*)	0/0	4	2	11	W
5–17	TAM	9.0 (S*)	4/1	7	1	5	W
5–25	SMU*	9.0 (S*)	2/0	4	6	8	W

NOTES: (1) See Table 1. (2) The "OPP" column gives the opposing team: OKL (Oklahoma University), MMC (McMurray College), BAY (Baylor University), TCU (Texas Christian University), SMU (Southern Methodist University).

1947

April 22: In front of the largest Clark Field crowd in history (estimated at 7,000), Layne outdueled Baylor's Rickey Rowe in a minimum-run game, Layne himself tallying the only run. In tossing a 1–0 shutout, Layne surrendered only four hits and issued four walks; he struck out

six. The Steers victory put them a half game ahead of the Bears in the race for the SWC championship.[13]

April 28: Layne turned in another solid mound performance, defeating the SMU Mustangs, 4–1. The only run he permitted was scored by his former high school teammate and future pro football teammate, Doak Walker, who received one of Layne's four walks, which was followed by Layne's fielding error on a grounder, and a timely single.[14,15]

May 1: As reported in the *Austin American*, "The junior right-hander [Bobby Layne], who has never dropped a conference contest in three seasons of play, literally backed into this [win]. Ineffective and in trouble most of the time, Layne was replaced by Pinch Hitter George Schwoebel in the last of the sixth. The Steers had gone into the last half of that frame on the short end of a 5–2 score, but rallied to score five runs before a second Rice relief pitcher quelled the disturbance." Charles Tankersley relieved Layne and the Longhorns' 7–5 lead en route to an 8–6 win. Layne received credit for the win despite being smacked for nine hits and five runs, walking four and striking out seven.[16]

Overall, for the 1947 collegiate season, Layne finished with an 11–1 W-L ledger. Excluding his record against non-collegiate opponents (1–0), Bobby produced a 10–1 W-L ledger against collegiate foes. See Table 3.

Table 3. Bobby Layne's Pitching Stats vs. Collegiate Opponents (1947).

Game	OPP	IP (S/R)	R/ER	H	W	K	W/L
3–24	MMC	9.0 (S*)	5/?	7	4	11	W
3–27	SMU	9.0 (S*)	7/6	8	7	3	W
4–02	RIC*	9.0 (S*)	2/2	4	7	7	W
4–05	OKL	7.0 (S)	4/?	4	5	3	W
4–11	TAM	8.0 (S)	4/0	5	2	7	—
4–17	BAY*	8.1 (S)	6/3	9	3	8	W
4–22	BAY	9.0 (S*)	0/0	4	4	6	W
4–25	TCU*	9.0 (S*)	3/?	9	7	8	W
4–28	SMU*	9.0 (S*)	1/0	4	4	11	W
5–01	RIC	6.0 (S)	5/?	9	4	7	W
5–06	TCU	6.0 (S)	4/1	7	0	7	W
5–14	TAM*	7.2 (S)	5/4	8	3	6	—
6–20	OKL#	0.1 (R)	3/?	2	2	0	—
6–22	CAL#	5.0 (R)	2/2	5	3	5	L

NOTES: (1) See Notes in Tables 1 and 2. (2) The "OPP" column gives the opposing team—CAL (University of California, Berkeley). A hashtag indicates that the game was played in Denver, Colorado (NCAA Western Regional Playoffs).

Table 3 shows that Layne produced an 8–0 W-L ledger versus SWC teams and a 2–1 W-L record versus non-SWC teams. His only setback was in a relief role in the final game of the NCAA Western Regional Playoffs, five and a half weeks after his last SWC game. Appendix B (available on the SABR website) provides pertinent information on Layne's non-collegiate diamond activity during that interval and his performance in the Western Regional Playoffs.[17]

1948

April 9: After TCU had raked Layne in the top of the first for three runs on four hits, the Longhorns responded with a six-run outburst, capped off by Layne himself. "Joe Randerson doubled and Al Hunt brought him home with a single. Shortstop Chick Zomlefer, who was sensational in the field, then hit a double and [after Tom Hamilton was retired] Hobbs Williams reached first when he was hit by a pitched ball. Hunt and Zomlefer scored on a single by Charlie Munson. [The next batter, Don Russell, was retired.] With two out and two men [Williams and Munson] on base and two men out [and three runs already in], the TCU board of strategy elected to issue Dan Watson an international [sic] base on balls in order to get to Layne. The Blond Bomber responded in typical Layne fashion, slapping out a single—his first hit of the season—to score Williams, [Munson], and Watson [giving the Longhorns a 6–3 lead]."[18] However, with the Steers ahead, 6–4, after four frames, Layne could not survive the fifth inning: "Layne was relieved early in the fifth after Rick Kramer walked and Jim Busby hit his circuit clout."[19] Layne was rocked for six earned runs on eight hits before being relieved by Murray Wall, who earned the win, 7–6.

April 23: Bobby Layne earned his second consecutive shutout by hurling a 3–0 complete game over the Rice Owls. Layne tossed a three-hitter while fanning fifteen.[20,21]

May 14: Going into the final two-game series of the season between the first-place Longhorns (with an SWC record of 11–1) and the second-place Aggies (11–2), Texas needed to win just one of the games to claim at least a tie for the SWC championship.[22] Not surprisingly, Bobby Layne was chosen by Steers' manager Bibb Falk to start the first game. Layne did the job as Texas won the game, 16–4. Layne allowed nine hits and walked four while striking out six, and carving out his 28th SWC victory without a defeat.[23] Texas then claimed the SWC championship outright for the fourth straight season by winning the second game, 3–2.[24]

Overall, for the regular 1948 collegiate season, Layne finished with a 9–0 W-L ledger. Excluding his record

Bobby Layne is the only Longhorns pitcher to throw two nine-inning no-hitters, both in 1946—versus the Southwestern University Pirates (March 26) and the Texas A&M Aggies (May 4).

against non-collegiate opponents (1–0), Bobby produced an 8–0 W-L ledger against collegiate foes. See Table 4. Thus, Layne extended his streak of consecutive regular-season wins versus collegiate teams to 29.

Table 4. Bobby Layne's Pitching Stats vs. Collegiate Opponents (1948).

Game	OPP	IP (S/R)	R/ER	H	W	K	W/L
3–25	OSU	9.0 (S*)	6–3	6	6	7	W
3–26	OSU	0.2 (R)	0/0	0	0	1	SV
3–29	OKL	8.0 (S)	5/5	5	7	8	W
4-02	*TAM**	*9.0 (S*)*	*4/4*	*8*	*2*	*9*	*W*
4-09	*TCU*	*4.0 (S)*	*6/6*	*8*	*4*	*1*	*—*
4-13	*SMU*	*9.0 (S*)*	*0/0*	*4*	*3*	*6*	*W*
4-23	*RIC**	*9.0 (S*)*	*0/0*	*3*	*4*	*15*	*W*
5-01	*BAY*	*9.0 (S*)*	*1/1*	*9*	*2*	*5*	*W*
5-07	*SMU**	*9.0 (S*)*	*2/2*	*7*	*1*	*7*	*W*
5-14	*TAM*	*9.0 (S*)*	*4/4*	*9*	*4*	*6*	*W*

NOTES: The "OPP" column gives the opposing team—OSU (Ohio State University). See also the Notes in Tables 1 and 2.

Layne takes a swing in this photo from the 1948 University of Texas Yearbook.

SUMMARY

As shown in Table 5, during the 1944 and 1946–48 diamond campaigns the Texas Longhorns fashioned an overall regular-season W-L ledger of 68–20 (.773). Versus collegiate teams, the Steers compiled a 63–8 (.887) W-L record. The 17 Longhorns' games versus non-collegiate teams included military service clubs (10), an industrial team (1), and minor league clubs (6). Against SWC foes the Steers assembled a 47–3 (.940) W-L record. Layne's corresponding W-L stats [39–6 (.867), 35–2 (.946), and 28–0 (1.000)] clearly show that he was the top of the hill.

Layne pitched in 31 (62%) of the Longhorns 50 SWC games. Layne was the game-starting hurler 28 times, and won 25 of them, 20 as complete games. The Longhorns also won each of the three games in which he had a no-decision. Layne came in from the bullpen in three games and earned the win each time. Pertinent information for the seven Texas pitchers who started the other 22 SWC regular-season games is given in Appendix C (available on the SABR website).

Also of significance, based on my research, Bobby Layne concluded his collegiate career with a streak of 29 consecutive *regular-season* victories. According to the baseball records information provided on the NCAA website, the longest streak for consecutive victories by a Division 1 pitcher is 26, shared by Kyle Sleeth (Wake Forest, 2001–03) and Scott Nielse (Brigham Young University, 1978, 1982–83).[25] The following introductory/explanatory note was also provided: "Official NCAA Division I baseball records began with the 1957 season and are based on information submitted to the NCAA statistics service by institutions participating in the statistics rankings. Career records of players include only those years in which they competed in Division I." Thus, Bobby Layne's record of 29 consecutive regular-season triumphs versus collegiate teams—achieved from March 26, 1946, through May 14, 1948—is three games longer than the post-1956 record of 26 given in the NCAA record book. In Table 6 we will examine how Layne compares to six members of the College Baseball Hall of Fame.

NON-PITCHING, NON-COLLEGE AND NON-BASEBALL CAREER

Bobby Layne was also a star quarterback on the gridiron, both in college and in the National Football League. He led the football Longhorns to New Year's Day triumphs in 1946 (Cotton Bowl) and 1948 (Sugar Bowl), and sparked the Detroit Lions to four Division titles and three NFL Championships (1952, 1953, and 1957). With regard to Bobby Layne's performance as a batter and as a fielder during his college years, Appendix D (available on the SABR website) provides the pertinent information on a game-by-game basis for his SWC games. His fielding average was .950. Overall for his SWC games, Layne manufactured a triple-slash line of .224/.333/.255, demonstrating that he hit neither for average nor power. Layne hit only one home run while hurling for the Longhorns. In a March 24, 1947, game versus the McMurray College Indians, Layne tossed a complete-game seven-hitter as the Steers won, 9–5. "Blond Bobby contributed a home run over the right field fence [at Clark Field] in the seventh inning for the Longhorns' final run."[26]

Prior to beginning his professional football career with the Chicago Bears in the fall of 1948, Layne also played professional baseball. While Layne's collegiate pitching career was stellar, his brief time as a professional baseball player—a dozen games for the Lubbock Hubbers (Class C West Texas New Mexico League) between June 11 and July 25, 1948—yielded mediocre performance stats. As given in the 1949 edition of *Official Baseball Guide* (published by *The Sporting News*), Layne fashioned a 6–5 W-L pitching ledger with an ERA of 7.29. He struck out 74 and walked 55. Appendix E (available on the SABR website) provides game-by-game information for Layne's professional baseball career.

CONCLUDING REMARKS

Not surprisingly, Bobby Layne's name is best remembered for his football accomplishments. Layne is enshrined in both the College Football Hall of Fame (1968) and the Pro Football Hall of Fame (1967). However, it seems curious, if not incredible, that Layne is not in the College Baseball Hall of Fame. The Texas

Table 5. Regular-Season W-L Records for Texas and Bobby Layne (1944, 1946-1948).

Year	All Opponents		Collegiate Opponents		SWC Opponents	
	Texas	Layne	Texas	Layne	Texas	Layne
1944	8–10 (.444)	7–5 (.583)	7–3 (.700)	6–1 (.857)	6–1 (.857)	5–0 (1.000)
1946	20–4 (.833)	12–1 (.923)	19–2 (.905)	11–1 (.917)	14–0 (1.000)	9–0 (1.000)
1947	20–4 (.833)	11–0 (1.000)	19–2 (.905)	10–0 (1.000)	14–1 (.933)	8–0 (1.000)
1948	20–2 (.909)	9–0 (1.000)	18–1 (.947)	8–0 (1.000)	13–1 (.929)	6–0 (1.000)
1944, 46–48	**68–20 (.773)**	**39–6 (.867)**	**63–8 (.887)**	**35–2 (.946)**	**47–3 (.940)**	**28–0 (1.000)**

NOTE: Including Texas's 1–1 W-L record for the 1947 post-season (NCAA Western Regional Playoffs) gives Texas an overall record of 69–21 (.767) and a collegiate record of 64–9 (.876); Layne had an 0–1 W-L record which gives him an overall record of 39–7 (.848) and a collegiate record of 35–3 (.921).

Table 6. Annual Regular-Season Collegiate Pitching Stats for Bobby Layne and Six College Baseball Hall of Famers (from the University of Texas).[27]

Pitcher	Seasons	Collegiate W–L (average)	SWC W–L (average)
Bobby Layne	1944 (1)	6–1 (.857)	5–0 (1.000)
	1946*	11–1 (.917)	9–0 (1.000)
	1947*	10–0 (1.000)	8–0 (1.000)
	1948*	8–0 (1.000)	6–0 (1.000)
Total	*1944, 1946–48*	*35–2 (.946)*	*28–0 (1.000)*
Burt Hooton	1969*	9–0 (1.000)	5–0 (1.000)
	1970*	8–1 (.889)	5–0 (1.000)
	1971*	11–1 (.917)	5–1 (.833)
Total	*1969–71*	*28–2 (.933)*	*15–1 (.938)*
Richard Wortham	1973*	10–0 (1.000)	4–0 (1.000)
	1974*	10–2 (.833)	3–2 (.600)
	1975*	13–0 (1.000)	7–0 (1.000)
	1976*	12–1 (.923)	6–1 (.857)
Total	*1973–76*	*45–3 (.938)*	*20–3 (.870)*
Jim Gideon	1973*	4–3 (.571)	1–1 (.500)
	1974*	17–1 (.944)	11–0 (1.000)
	1975*	14–0 (1.000)	7–0 (1.000)
Total	*1973–75*	*35–4 (.897)*	*19–1 (.950)*
Greg Swindell	1984*	11–1 (.917)	6–1 (.857)
	1985*	15–1 (.938)	8–0 (1.000)
	1986*	10–3 (.769)	6–3 (.667)
Total	*1984–86*	*36–5 (.878)*	*20–4 (.833)*
Kirk Dressendorfer	1988*	14–2 (.875)	7–1 (.875)
	1989	14–2 (.875)	8–1 (.889)
	1990	12–3 (.800)	6–1 (.857)
Total	*1988–90*	*40–7 (.851)*	*21–3 (.875)*
Brooks Kieschnick	1991*	6–1 (.857)	3–1 (.750)
	1992*	9–1 (.900)	5–1 (.833)
	1993	14–3 (.824)	6–2 (.750)
Total	*1991–93*	*29–5 (.853)*	*14–4 (.778)*

NOTES: (1) The Southwest Conference was not operative in 1944 as a consequence of World War Two. (2) The W-L records do not include W-L records for the District Playoffs and the College Baseball World Series. The W-L records do include the W-L records for the end-of-the-regular-season Southwest Conference Tournaments played since 1979. (3) In the "Seasons" column, an asterisk indicates the Longhorns had the best W-L record in the Southwest Conference.

Longhorns have had six pitchers elected—Brooks Kieschnick (2006), Burt Hooton (2008), Greg Swindell (2008), Kirk Dressendorfer (2009), Richard Wortham (2010), and Jim Gideon (2020). Table 6 provides pertinent performance stats for each of these pitchers.[27]

Inspection of Table 6 reveals that Bobby Layne's still-standing 28-0 SWC W-L record dwarfs those achieved by these collegiate Hall of Fame pitchers. His college mound performance is absolutely worthy of consideration. ■

Acknowledgments

Special thanks to Kevin Rodriguez (University of Texas Athletics, Associate Director, Communications), David Lentz (NCAA, Assistant Director of Media Coordination and Statistics), and Sean Straziscar (NCAA). For permission to use pictures of Bobby Layne, grateful thanks are extended to Emily Cohen (Director for Marketing and Advertising, University of Texas at Austin) and Richard Tijerina (Sports Editor) and Briana Sanchez (Director of Photography) with the Austin (Texas) *American Statesman*. Thanks also to Karl Green, Jeff Robbins, Gary Stone, Patrick Todgham, and Dixie Tourangeau for valuable inputs/discussions.

Notes

1. *Texas Longhorns, 2023 Baseball Fact Book*, 87, https://s3.us-east-2. amazonaws.com/sidearm.nextgen.sites/texassports_com/documents/ 2023/2/15/23-fact-book-FULL-web.pdf, accessed October 1, 2024. The Southwest Conference was not operative in 1944 as a consequence of World War II.

2. Bobby Layne with Bob Drum, *Always On Sunday* (Prentice Hall, 1962).

3. Bob St. John, *Heart of a Lion—The Wild and Wooly Life of Bobby Layne* (Taylor Publishing Co, 1991).

4. Morris Williams, "Longhorns Take First of 2 Games With Rice, 5–0," *Austin American*, April 22, 1944, 7.

5. "Layne Builds Up 11-Run Lead And Retires," *Austin American*, May 20, 1944, 7.

6. The "Large Lead" custom: Pete Palmer, email to the author, November 2, 2023: "If you leave the game with a large lead, you can get the win because the manager is saving you for the next game. I don't know when that practice was in effect. There were no [official] rules for 'winning' and 'losing' pitchers until 1950." For an example, see Herm Krabbenhoft, "The Pitcher's Cycle," *Baseball Research Journal* (Volume 53, Number 2, Fall 2024) page 34—Christy Mathewson was relieved after the first inning with the New York Giants leading the St. Louis Cardinals 13–0. "Having the game in hand, [manager John] McGraw took Mathewson out of the box, so as to save him for another game and he put [Rube] Marquard in the box." ["Did Anyone See Bresnahan's Goat?," *The* (New York) *World, Evening Edition*, May 13, 1911, 11]. The Retrosheet box score shows Mathewson having been credited as the winning pitcher and Marquard having earned a save. See also: Frank Vaccaro, "Origin of the Modern Pitching Win," *Baseball Research Journal* (Volume 42, Number 1, Spring 2013) 50; Frank J. Williams, "All the Record Books Are Wrong," *The National Pastime*, 2013, 50; Joe Wayman, "The Matty-Alex Tie," *Baseball Research Journal* (Number 24, 2013) 25.

7. "Longhorn Nine Takes Second Game From Rice," *Austin American*, May 21, 1944, 12.

8. Johnny Lyons, "Texas Wins, 7–1, on Six Unearned Runs," *Houston Post*, May 21, 1944, Section 2, 3.

9. "Layne Pitches Three-Hitter, Fans 16 Owls," *Austin American*, April 14, 1946, 18.

10. "Bobby Layne May Not Start Against Aggies Saturday," [AP] *Amarillo* (Texas) *Daily News*, May 2, 1946, 10.

11. Wilbur Evans, "Layne Pitches No-Hitter as Texas Tops A&M, 2–1," *Austin American*, May 5, 1946, 17.

12. Wilbur Evans, "Steer Nine Takes Title…Layne Scores Seventh Win in Blanking Rice," *Austin American*, May 14, 1946, 7.

13. Morris Williams, "Bears Fall to Longhorns, 1–0," *Austin American*, April 23, 1947, 11.

14. Harry Gage, "Steers Down SMU Nine by 4–1 Margin," *Dallas Morning News*, April 29, 1947, 10; "Layne Stops SMU with 4 Hits, 4–1," *Austin American*, April 29, 1947, 9.

15. Bobby Layne and Doak Walker were classmates at Highland Park High School in University Park, Texas (just north of Dallas) and teammates on the Detroit Lions (1950–55) during which they led the Lions to three Division Titles and two NFL Championships. In their college years at Texas and SMU they squared off mano-a-mano in four baseball games: (1) March 27, 1947: playing left field and batting leadoff, Walker went 0-for-4 with a walk against Layne. (2) April 28, 1947: playing left field and batting leadoff, Walker went 1-for-4 with a single and a walk. (3) April 13, 1948: playing center field and batting leadoff, Walker went 1-for-4 with a single. (4) May 7, 1948: playing center field and batting second, Walker went 0-for-3 with a sacrifice hit.

16. Wilbur Evans, "Steers Nip Rice, 8–6," *Austin American*, May 2, 1947, 17.

17. Layne's postseason loss to California snapped a streak of 21 consecutive victories vs collegiate teams. However, adhering to the official rules of Major League Baseball for "Cumulative Performance Records" (Rule 9.23), his streak of 21 straight *regular-season* triumphs remained intact: "Guidelines for Cumulative Performance Records (Rule 9.23)," *Official Baseball Rules*, 2024 Edition, 144. See, for example: Matt Kelly, "Pitchers with the longest win streaks," https://www.mlb.com/news/the-longest-pitcher-win-streaks-in-mlb-history#, August 25, 2020 (accessed October 17, 2024—"(1) Carl Hubbell, 24 straight wins (July 17, 1936, to May 27, 1937); (2) Roy Face, 22 straight wins (June 7, 1958, to August 30, 1959); (3-Tied) Gerrit Cole 20 straight wins, (May 27, 2019, to August 14, 2020); (3-Tied) Jake Arrieta (August 4, 2015 to May 25, 2016); (3-Tied) Roger Clemens (June 3, 1998 to June 1, 1999); (3-Tied) Rube Marquard October 1, 1911 to July 3, 1912)." Kelly also provided this: "NOTE: These streaks do not include postseason appearances, which means that Cole's loss to the Nats in Game 1 of last year's World Series [i.e., 2019] did not preclude him from [possibly tying] Hubbell's record."

18. Jimmy Banks, "Longhorns Edge TCU," *Austin American*, April 10, 1948, 8. It is noted that the box score in the *Austin American* shows Layne with three RBIs, suggesting that Layne's single knocked in the three runners on base (Williams, Munson, and Watson). However, an AP article describing the first inning suggested that an error was involved in the scoring of the six runs: Associated Press, "3 Tilts Today in SWC Loop," *San Antonio Evening News*, April 10, 1948, 5: "Texas erased a three-run Frog lead in the bottom half of the first with a six-run splurge on five hits and an error." Thus, considering both the *Austin American* account and the AP story, it seems that the five of the six runs were scored on five hits—Randerson (who had doubled) scored on Hunt's single; Hunt and Zomlefer (who had doubled) scored on Munson's single; Willams and Munson scored on Layne's single—and that Watson scored on an error in the fielding of Layne's single, the *Austin American* box score generously giving Layne RBI credit for the run scored by Watson. According to the *Austin American* box score, TCU committed three errors and five of Texas's seven runs were earned runs. Texas's seventh run in the bottom of the fifth inning, scored by Russell, was also unearned, although no details were provided in the game story.

19. "Frogs Chase Layne But Lose," *Houston Post*, April 10, 1948, 8.

20. Morris Frank, "Layne Says Farewell to Rice, 3–0," *Houston Post*, April 24, 1948, 13.

21. "Steers Defeat Rice, 3–0…Layne Pitches Three-Hitter for 25th Win," *Austin American*, April 24, 1948, 6.

22. The various scenarios resulting from the two-game Steers-Aggies series were as follows: (a) If Texas wins both games, Texas is the SWC champion outright. (b) If Texas A&M wins both games, Texas A&M is the champion outright. (c) If the Longhorns and the Aggies each win one game, then Texas will have to go back to Fort Worth and play the TCU game that was rained out May 10. If Texas wins that game, it is the SWC champion outright; if TCU wins that game, then the Longhorns and Aggies would tie for the SWC title (although Texas could claim bragging rights since it would have won two of the three games between the two clubs).

23. Weldon Hart, "16–4 Triumph Clinches Title Tie for Steers," *Austin American*, May 15, 1948, 7.

24. Despite winning the SWC championship, the University of Texas decided to remove itself from consideration to be the sixth district representative in the NCAA tournament for the 1948 College Baseball World Series. Longhorns' manager Bibb Falk said, "Graduation of four first-stringers, including pitcher Bobby Layne and shortstop Chick Zomlefer, would require a makeshift lineup if we went to the tournament. Summer school, one or two boys' professional plans, and the length of time between the end of our season and the tournament all add up." From "Longhorn Nine Out…Steers Shun NCAA Bid," *Austin American*, May 15, 1948, 19.

25. NCAA Division 1 Baseball Records, Individual Records: Pitching: Victories, Consecutive, page 3, http://fs.ncaa.org.s3.amazonaws.com/Docs/stats/ baseball_RB/D1.pdf, accessed October 22, 2024.

26. Morris Williams, "Layne Stingy as McMurray Falls to Longhorns, 9–5," *Austin American*, Marc 24, 1947, 11.

27. The performance stats for the pitchers included in Table 6 were ascertained from the box scores and game accounts in relevant newspapers for each of Texas's regular-season games in the seasons the pitchers played for Texas. The identities of the Texas pitchers elected to the College Baseball Hall of Fame were obtained from the list of "Hall of Fame Honors" section (page 161) in the *Texas Longhorns, 2023 Baseball Fact Book*. The dates and opponents of Texas's pertinent regular-season games were obtained from the "Year-By-Year Results" section (pages 81–104) and the "Year-By-Year Conference Standings" section (pages 109–15) in the *Texas Longhorns, 2023 Baseball Fact Book*.

The "Savior" Does Not Answer Letters

Dave Hoskins and the Uneven, Unheralded, and Unfinished Integration of the Texas League

Jason A. Schwartz

"I received three letters that morning, one at a time. First one said I'd be shot if I sat in the dugout. Second one said I'd be shot if I went on the field and the third one said I'd be shot if I took the mound."

—Dave Hoskins[1]

On March 19, 1951, a group of 20 young Black ballplayers gathered on a cold day in West Texas for what was then billed as an "All-Negro Tryout Camp." By day's end, two players—outfielder Connie Heard and shortstop J.W. Wingate—impressed manager Jay Haney sufficiently as to earn invitations to camp.

Neither the tryout nor its results were remarkable in any way, even in the South, except for one detail. The team hosting the tryout, the Lamesa Lobos of the Class C West Texas-New Mexico League, was entirely White.[2] Four years after Jackie, the seeds of integration had reached the Lone Star State. Or had they?

Though Haney had hoped to land players of Cuban ancestry, perhaps to limit backlash, he seemed otherwise genuine in his openness, if not enthusiasm, to integrate the squad, stating, "Negroes can play ball and the time is not far off when Negroes will be playing on White teams in Texas." His time in the military helped shape this view. "I lost my opposition to [Black players] when I played with and against them in service ball."[3]

Haney backed up his words with action, playing both Heard and Wingate in the Lobos' spring training opener.[4] However, less than two weeks later, Haney sent both players packing. Though he found them to be "excellent types," he concluded that neither had the skills to compete at the Class C level.

As much as the Black players' dismissal, right down to the rationale, echoed any number of previous perfunctory "attempts" at integration, a plot twist followed. Not only was Wingate back with the team by the season opener, but he was one of *three* Black players on the

Lobos Opening Day roster.[5] (The others were pitcher Roberto Leyva and catcher Douglas McBean, both Black Cubans.) Both Wingate and McBean saw action in the opener.[6] The date was April 21, 1951: Organized Baseball in Texas had officially integrated, and the world did not end.

The integration of the Lobos produced far more whimper than bang. With some irony, Cubans Leyva and McBean were released within the week for failing to understand Haney's instructions in English.[7] A month later, the Lobos handed Wingate his unconditional release, and he was off to the Kansas City Monarchs.[8] In a baseball eulogy doubling as prophecy, Collier Parris penned the following in his column of May 26:

> Lamesa fans, being sturdy, southern home-towners to whom Negroes mean cotton pickers, shine boys, and car-washers, never did give Wingate a chance. Even refused to attend the home games because of his presence in the lineup. This treatment gave Negro baseball prospects quite a setback in Texas, made it difficult for others of his race to "break in" so far as this section of the country is concerned.[9]

How much or little of this history Dallas Eagles owner Dick Burnett, both emboldened and threatened by the impending arrival of the National Football League's integrated Dallas Texans franchise amid hemorrhaging attendance league-wide (see Table 1), was

Table 1. Paid Attendance in Decline, Texas League, 1949–51[11]

Year	BMT	DAL	FTW	HSN	OKC	SAN	SHV	TUL	Total
1949	116,264	404,851	265,982	263,965	287,858	225,500	222,331	221,176	2,007,927
1950	170,536	317,592	233,789	255,809	187,991	180,580	117,854	184,677	1,648,828
1951	109,893	228,263	160,276	333,201	109,181	180,577	76,073	147,907	1,345,371

aware of when he announced in January 1952 his plans to integrate the Double-A Texas League, all White since its establishment in 1888, is unknown.[10] What is known is that reaction around the league, outside of Shreveport, ranged from accepting to intrigued.

- John Reeves, president of the Fort Worth Cats, remarked simply enough that "time marches on," at the same time acknowledging the unlikelihood that any Black players in the Dodgers system were suitable for the Cats.[12]

- Guy Airey, president of the Beaumont Roughnecks (later "Exporters"), expressed qualified support for the idea. "If Mr. Burnett intends to use Negro players to strengthen his Dallas team and also help the Negro race, fine. But if he plans to use Negro players simply for drawing cards, as gate attractions, I do not approve." Airey added, "If Texas League Negro players are introduced in Dallas and other Texas League points, and I get a chance to sign an outstanding player, regardless of his color, I will do so."[13]

- Art Routzong, business manager of the Houston Buffaloes, noted the Buffs had already played against Black players, presumably without incident, in exhibitions against the Brooklyn Dodgers and Milwaukee Braves.[14]

- Jimmy Humphries, president of the Oklahoma City Indians, declined to comment but committed the matter to further study.[15]

- Grayle Howlett, Jr., president of the Tulsa Oilers, recognized the value of Black players but preferred to follow rather than lead: "Negro players have come into organized baseball in recent years and made key contributions to winning clubs in both the major and minor leagues. Certainly we in Tulsa will do nothing less than any other clubs in the Texas League are doing in the quest for the winner which we all seek."[16]

- Joe McShane, president of the San Antonio Missions, understood that integration was unstoppable. "It's coming. The majors, including the Browns, are signing Negro ball players and putting them in their farm systems…" In a statement that could be read two ways, McShane added that "Any Negro who gets into the Texas League should be an outstanding player when he is here."[17]

- Only Bonneau Peters, president of the Shreveport Sports, was openly defiant. He not only doubled down on segregation ("You can quote me as saying that the Shreveport club has no plans for using any Negro players.") but added that even competing against integrated teams could be problematic.[18]

It was against this backdrop that the Dallas Eagles drew nearly 200 Black players, among them J.W. Wingate, to a February 12–15 tryout seeking what Burnett hoped might be "one or two players who can make the grade."[19,20] Remarkably, but perhaps predictably, not a single player impressed the Eagles as good enough for AA ball. Of the tryout's top three players (James Thomson, Johnnie Williams, Bobby Joe Fritz), Burnett stated, "We believe these boys are capable of Class C ball," i.e., the Bakersfield Indians of the California League. "How far they go from there is strictly up to them."[21] (In fact, none of the three even made Bakersfield.[22])

The script was again familiar, but—as in Lamesa—the story was not over. The Eagles ultimately reached agreement with two players who had not been at the tryout—Othello Renfroe and Ray Neil—to train with the club in Daytona Beach. Renfroe proved a no-show and Neil, a former Negro League all-star, was deemed not good enough.[23] Still, Burnett was not one to give up easily. By late March, the Eagles owner had reached agreement with Hank Greenberg, general manager of the Eagles' parent club, the Cleveland Indians, to send Mississippi native Dave Hoskins from camp with Indianapolis to Dallas instead.[24]

Hoskins' baseball credentials to that point had been quite impressive. A member of the Homestead

AUTHOR'S COLLECTION

1952 Globe Printing baseball card of Dave Hoskins.

Homestead Grays Murderers' Row of Sam Bankhead, Josh Gibson, Buck Leonard, Dave Hoskins, and Jerry Benjamin.

"Inside Baseball" cartoon, featuring death threats, on reverse of 1954 Topps Dave Hoskins baseball card.

Grays' fabled Murderers' Row, he had played for two pennant winners and a Negro League World Series champion between 1944 and 1946. Though the Grays blocked him from participating, Hoskins was also one of three Negro Leaguers—along with Jackie Robinson and Sam Jethroe—selected by Wendell Smith to try out with the Braves and Red Sox in 1945.[25] And in 1948, Hoskins batted .393 for the Grand Rapids Jets, integrating the Central League in the process.[26] Were it not for the number of White pitchers throwing at his head, Hoskins might have arrived in Dallas as an outfielder. Instead, self-preservation demanded that he arrive as a pitcher. "I was tired of having pitches thrown at me. I made up my mind that I would start throwing at other guys."[27]

Though Burnett's efforts at integration had fared poorly to this point, his firsthand experience with

Hoskins led him to believe he might prove the "lone star" among so many also-rans. Hoskins had already pitched *against* Dallas that spring and retired all six batters he faced.[28] Burnett's faith in the curve-baller was further affirmed when Hoskins held the Boston Red Sox to two hits across four innings in his Eagles preseason debut.[29] His first regular season start, on April 13, was less sharp but no less successful. Despite walking seven Tulsa Oilers, Hoskins allowed only one earned run in a 4–2 complete game victory. For good measure, he even notched a pair of singles.[30] More significantly, he was the first Black player in the 57-year history of the Texas League.[31]

To say Hoskins gave Burnett everything he could have asked for is a massive understatement. In just over a month, Hoskins established himself as the league's best pitcher, one of its leading hitters, and by far its top box office draw, both at home and on the road.[32] Bolstered by Hoskins' success, the Eagles added Wilkes-Barre (Cleveland Indians Single-A affiliate) ace and former New York Cuban Jose Santiago on May 17.[33]

None of this suggests Hoskins himself had it easy. A Black man in the Jim Crow South, Hoskins could neither eat at the same restaurants nor stay in the same hotels as teammates. Add to that the dependable contingent of White fans at every ballpark ready to greet "the Savior of the Texas League" with name-calling and hostility.[34] The roughest destination was always Shreveport, where just a week after proposed legislation sought to bar integrated athletic competition statewide, even death threats entered the mix.[35]

Regardless, Hoskins kept on pitching, kept on winning, and kept on spinning league turnstiles at breakneck pace. The Oklahoma City club, which in January had relegated the matter of integration to "further study," signed Birmingham Black Barons ace Bill Greason on July 28.[36] As in the Jackie story, Greason's July 31 debut made a team with the Indians nickname second to integrate. When Greason's next start, August 3, paired him against Hoskins, the league witnessed not only its first ever matchup of Black pitchers but a season-high attendance of 11,007 to boot.[37]

As the regular season wound to a close, Hoskins had not one but two nights held in his honor, the first by the Eagles' archrival Fort Worth Cats. On cue, Hoskins obliged by winning his 20th game of the season, and his two hits temporarily raised his batting average to tops in the league, albeit unofficially due to limited at-bats. His numbers at season's end: a 22–10 record, a 2.12 ERA, a .327 batting average, a first place finish for the Eagles, two postseason victories, and a doubling (or more!) of attendance everywhere he pitched, even Shreveport![38] See Table 2.

Not to be outdone, Santiago and Greason finished the season a combined 23–8 with earned run averages of 2.83 and 2.14 respectively, though neither approached Hoskins' numbers at the plate. Either way, the success of the three hurlers left no doubt that Black players were more than capable of success in the Texas League. If there were any question remaining, maybe the players were *too* good...?

Hoping for their own version of Dave Hoskins, two additional teams entered the 1953 season with integrated rosters. Chuck Harmon, who integrated the Cincinnati Reds a year later, integrated the Tulsa Oilers on April 9 and went on to finish sixth in the batting race and third in stolen bases.[39] The very next day, future Milwaukee Brave Charlie White made history for the San Antonio Missions, starting at catcher and tallying a hit, a run, and an RBI.[40] White was again part of history four days later, pairing with pitcher Harry Wilson to form the league's first all-Black battery. As for Wilson, all he did that day was allow one run in 10 innings, collect two hits, and score the game's winning run.[41]

Despite its proven success, integration across the rest of the league proceeded slowly, if at all. The Beaumont Exporters got the ball rolling in January 1954 by trading for Jim "Buster" Clarkson, who had enjoyed a monster season with Dallas in 1953. Clarkson, already 39 years old at the time of his April 9 Beaumont debut, went on to pace the circuit in home runs. Later that month, the Exporters added former Negro League all-star Jesse "Bill" Williams, though he played only eight games.[42]

May 27, 1954, marked the integration of the Houston club when Bob Boyd, acquired from the White Sox, doubled, tripled, and registered eight putouts at first base for the Buffs.[43] He would bat .321 for the season. The Fort Worth Cats, initially dubious that any Black player in the Dodger system could assist them, finally integrated on April 18, 1955, with the insertion of future National League Most Valuable Player Maury Wills into the lineup.[44] Table 3 provides a summary.

Table 2. The "Hoskins Effect" Across the League

Dallas Eagles Road Opponent	Paid Attendance, Season	Per Game Estimate	Hoskins as Starter	Attendance Multiplier
Beaumont	101,717	1,271	4,250	3.3
Fort Worth	180,559	2,257	7,709	3.4
Houston	195,246	2,441	6,207	2.5
Oklahoma City	146,972	1,837	3,748	2.0
San Antonio	110,001	1,375	8,057	5.9
Shreveport	153,127	1,914	7,016	3.7
Tulsa	155,064	1,938	3,879	2.0

Table 3. Texas League Integration by Team

Team	First Black Player	Texas League Debut
Dallas Eagles	Dave Hoskins	April 13, 1952
Oklahoma City Indians	Bill Greason	July 31, 1952
Tulsa Oilers	Chuck Harmon	April 9, 1953
San Antonio Missions	Charlie White	April 10, 1953
Beaumont Exporters	James "Buster" Clarkson	April 9, 1954
Houston Buffaloes	Bob Boyd	May 27, 1954
Fort Worth Cats	Maury Wills	April 18, 1955
Shreveport Sports	N/A	N/A

As for the Shreveport Sports, the team remained segregated all the way through its December 1957 exit from the league, following a last place finish and barely 500 fans per contest.[45] In opting for *disintegration* over integration, team president Bonneau Peters— whom minor league officials anointed "King of Baseball" in 1959—was nothing if not a man of his word. ■

Acknowledgments

The author wishes to thank Jim "Mudcat" Grant, Scott Hodges, and Bruce Adelson for their works that sparked an interest in this topic, as well as Mark Armour and Lou Moore for providing early reviews of this paper.

Notes

1. "Tribe Rookie Hoskins Discloses Death Threats," *The Afro-American*, February 28, 1953.
2. "2 Negro Players Get Lamesa Baseball Trial," *Fort Worth Star-Telegram*, March 20, 1951.
3. "White Texas Loop Team Picks Two Negro Players," *The Call*, March 30, 1951.
4. "Pampa Wins in Lamesa," *San Angelo Standard-Times*, April 2, 1951.
5. A second catcher, Humberto "Yogi" Marti, was described as a "Cuban Negro rookie" in the various season preview articles that appeared on April 19, 1951. However, subsequent sources suggest Marti was neither Cuban nor Black.
6. "Al Maul's Bat Leads Winners in Big Attack," *Albuquerque Journal*, April 22, 1951.
7. "Lobos Release Cubans, Negro Shortstop Stays," *Clovis News-Journal*, April 27, 1951.
8. "Late Lobo Rally Sinks Pioneers," *Clovis News-Journal*, May 23, 1951.
9. Collier Parris, "Sportometer," *Abilene Reporter-News*, May 26, 1951.

10. Burnett may have overestimated the threat posed by the Texans, who went winless (0–7) before being taken over by the league, and then folding. Their final record was 1–11.

11. William B. Ruggles, *Texas League Record Book, 1953 Edition* (The Texas League of Professional Baseball Clubs, Dallas), 43.

12. "Dallas Okays Use of Negroes in TL," *Fort Worth Star-Telegram*, January 27, 1952.

13. "Dallas Okays Use of Negroes in TL."

14. "Dallas Okays Use of Negroes in TL."

15. "Dallas Okays Use of Negroes in TL."

16. "Dallas Okays Use of Negroes in TL."

17. "Dallas Okays Use of Negroes in TL."

18. "Sports Have No Plans to Use Negroes," *The Times* (Shreveport, LA), January 30, 1952.

19. First-day attendance was reported in many sources as 148, however, later reports indicated "nearly 200" or "around 200." It's not clear whether these subsequent reports were rounding generously or if they simply accounted for additional players arriving after the first day.

20. "150 Negroes Show For Eagle Tryout," *Corsicana Daily Sun*, February 13, 1952; "Eagles Set Tryouts for Negro Players," *Waco Tribune-Herald*, February 3, 1952.

21. "Reds Acquire Four Negroes; Tribe Signs 3," *The Tribune* (Scranton, PA), February 16, 1952.

22. "1952 Bakersfield Indians," https://www.baseball-reference.com/register/team.cgi?id=3080da3d, January 22, 2025.

23. Bruce Adelson, *Brushing Back Jim Crow: The Integration of Minor-League Baseball in the American South* (University Press of Virginia, 1999), 54.

24. "Dallas May Sign Negro," *St. Joseph Gazette*, March 26, 1952.

25. "May Get Tryouts," *New Pittsburgh Courier*, April 14, 1945.

26. John J. Watkins, "Dave Hoskins," BioProject, Society for American Baseball Research, March 2023.

27. Jim "Mudcat" Grant (with Tom Sabellico and Pat O'Brien), *The Black Aces* (The Black Aces LLC, 2006), 103.

28. Adelson, 55.

29. "Dallas Ties Bosox," *Pittsburgh Press*, April 4, 1952.

30. "Eagles Stop Tulsa by 4–2," *Fort Worth Star-Telegram*, April 14, 1952.

31. The Texas League began play in 1888 but missed seasons in 1891, 1893, 1894, 1900, 1901, 1943, 1944, and 1945.

32. Jason A. Schwartz, "August 28, 1952: Dave Hoskins wins 20th game for Dallas Eagles on night held in his honor," Games Project, Society for American Baseball Research, June 2023, https://sabr.org/gamesproj/game/august-28-1952-dave-hoskins-wins-20th-game-for-dallas-eagles-on-night-held-in-his-honor/, accessed May 16, 2025.

33. A.S. "Doc" Young, *Great Negro Baseball Stars and How They Made the Major Leagues* (AS Barnes, New York, 1953), 220; "Dallas Purchases Pair of Pitchers," *Tulsa World*, May 18, 1952.

34. "Fort Worth Holds Night for Dave Hoskins," *Jet Magazine*, September 11, 1952: 54.

35. "Seeks To Ban Negro-White Sporting Events In State," *Daily World* (Opelousas, LA), June 4, 1952; "Tribe Rookie Hoskins Discloses Death Threats," *The Afro-American*, February 28, 1953.

36. "Negro Hurler To Make Debut Soon In O.C. Uniform," *Miami News-Record*, July 29, 1952.

37. "Greason Defeats Hoskins In Negro Hurling Contest," *Sun Herald*, August 4, 1952.

38. Schwartz.

39. "Oilers Cop Opener on Stout Varhely's Arm, Harmon's Club," *The Tulsa Tribune*, April 10, 1953.

40. "Missions Trim Exporters, 6–0," *Fort Worth Star-Telegram*, April 11, 1953.

41. "Missions Take Texas Loop Lead," *Tulsa Tribune*, April 15, 1953.

42. "Beaumont Exporters Sign K.C. Infielder," *The Call* (Kansas City, Missouri), April 23, 1954

43. "Buffs 11, Sports 4," *Fort Worth Star-Telegram*, May 28, 1954.

44. "Cats Break Color Line," *Fort Worth Star-Telegram*, April 19, 1955.

45. Bill O'Neal, *The Texas League* (Eakin Press, Austin, Texas, 1987), 123.

Integration Comes to the Texas League

1952–58

Alan Cohen

Most fans of baseball are aware that Jackie Robinson broke the major league color line in 1947. Fewer folks are aware of how slowly integration came to the minor leagues. Whereas Robinson and five others broke into the minors in 1946, most of the minor leagues remained segregated until 1952. In 1951, 27 of the 50 AL/NL affiliated minor leagues were segregated, and in many cases more than half of the teams in the integrated leagues still had no Black players.

As 1951 ended, the situation in the American and National Leagues was not particularly encouraging. Only 20 players had crossed the color line, and ten of the 16 teams remained segregated.[1] There was not a single Black player in Class AA until 1952, and that is where our story begins. The Texas League and the Southern Association were the only two minor leagues with the Class-AA designation. The Southern Association clung to its Jim Crow ways until it ceased to function after the 1961 season with one exception: a brief two-game appearance by Nat Peeples with Atlanta in 1954.

Dallas was the AA affiliate of the Cleveland Indians, the first American League team to integrate. The Eagles held tryouts from February 11 through February 15, 1952, and, according to the *Kansas City Call*, 200 Black players participated.[2] The Indians purportedly awarded contracts to three players, but none of them was assigned to Dallas. One of the three, Bobby Fritz, only played one minor-league game, with Big Spring in the Longhorn League in 1954. The others did not play at all in the minors.

The story of the integration of the Texas League could have begun with Ray Neil. In 1951, Neil played for the Indianapolis Clowns and participated in the East-West All-Star Game. He batted .327 with 102 hits (second most in the league), and, at the beginning of the 1952 season, went to spring training with the Dallas Eagles.[3] He was the first Black player signed by a Texas League team when, on February 23, 1952, owner R. W. (Dick) Burnett of the Class AA Dallas Eagles purchased him conditionally. On March 16, he was the subject of a column by Bill Rives in the *Dallas Morning News*.[4] The ink was barely dry on that article when it was announced that Neil would be released on March 19.[5] Neil returned to the Indianapolis Clowns and remained with them through 1954, batting .397 in 1953. He never had the opportunity to play in AL/NL affiliated ball.

Reportedly signed on March 12 by Dallas was Othello "Chico" Renfroe, who had played for the Kansas City Monarchs and the Cleveland Buckeyes. Renfroe failed to show up when camp got underway in Daytona Beach, because the Union Laguna Baseball Club failed to grant him a release from his pre-existing contract.[6]

As reported elsewhere in this journal, **Dallas** integrated with a player who was already in the Cleveland organization: Dave Hoskins, later joined by Jose Santiago. Willard Brown was with the team in 1953, batting .310 in 138 games. Brown, who was age 38 in 1953, spent four seasons in the Texas League. He batted .302 with Houston in 1955 and was with three teams (San Antonio, Tulsa, and Austin) in 1956. Another veteran of the Negro Leagues, Bus Clarkson, joined Dallas in 1953.

Bill Greason, who had pitched for the Birmingham Black Barons in 1951, began the 1952 season at Camp Lejeune, pitching for the military base team. When he was released, he joined the **Oklahoma City** Indians of the Texas League. His debut was on Thursday, July 31, and he defeated Shreveport, 6–4. He won nine games with only one loss and posted a 2.14 ERA. In 1954, he was acquired by the Cardinals' organization and became the first Black pitcher with St. Louis on May 31, 1954. His time in the National League was brief. He only appeared in three games and registered an 0–1 record. As of this writing, he is the oldest man to have played in the major leagues still alive.

The **San Antonio Missions** integrated in 1953 with Harry Wilson and Charlie White. San Antonio was affiliated with the St. Louis Browns, and White and Wilson had been signed by Bill Veeck.[7] Wilson, a pitcher from Blount County in Tennessee, was signed by the Browns in March 1950 and was assigned to

Gloversville-Johnstown in the Canadian-American League, a league that had first integrated in 1946.[8] He posted an 18–7 record with Stockton in the California League in 1951 and was in the military in 1952. In 1953, he signed on with San Antonio. In his first appearance, on April 14, he won a 10-inning pitching duel, 2–1, and he batted in the winning run.[9]

Joe Durham joined the Missions in 1954, and Lenny Green joined in 1955. Green was signed by Veeck and was one of the first Black stars with Baltimore. Also on the Missions in 1955 were Dave Roberts and Willie Tasby.

Tulsa integrated with Chuck Harmon and Nino Escalera in 1953. Also on the 1953 team was Honey Lott, whose career had begun with the New York Black Yankees in 1948. Harmon and Escalera broke the Cincinnati Reds color line on April 17, 1954. Lott never made it higher than Class AA. Frank Robinson was with Tulsa early in the 1954 season, but spent most of the season one level lower, in the South-Atlantic League.

The other teams were a bit slower to add Black players.[10] The **Houston Buffaloes** added Bob Boyd in 1954. Boyd played with the Memphis Red Sox of the Negro American League before joining the Chicago White Sox organization in 1950. He made his American League debut at the tail end of 1951 with the White Sox and spent all of 1952 and part of 1953 with Chicago minor league affiliates. He played parts of 1953 and 1954 with the White Sox and, at the end of May, was sold to the Cardinals.

The Cardinals, an organization that didn't integrate at all until August A. Busch & Co. acquired the team in 1953, was affiliated with Houston and Boyd, once St. Louis obtained him, was assigned to the Buffaloes. He batted .321 in 94 games with Houston in 1954 and .310 in a full season in 1955. In 1955, Houston added Willard Brown and Bill Greason. Although both Brown (.302 BA) and Greason (17–11) put up good numbers in 1955, neither was destined to return to the majors. Boyd was not protected in the offseason Rule 5 draft and was selected by the Baltimore Orioles. From 1956 through 1960 Boyd, though in his late 30s, batted .301 in 1,795 plate appearances.

Prior to the 1954 season, **Beaumont** traded pitcher Ed Konick to the Dallas Eagles for Bus Clarkson, who had spent the prior season with Dallas, batting .330.[11] Clarkson was a Negro League veteran who broke the Beaumont color line with a flourish. In front of a crowd of 5,114 fans, he went 4-for-5 with a home run and started two double plays from his shortstop position in an 8–5 win over Tulsa on April 9.[12] Through 79 games, he was batting .339 with a league-leading 20

Bill Greason on his 100th birthday, 70 years after becoming the first Black pitcher for the St. Louis Cardinals.

US MARINE CORPS

home runs and 77 RBIs.[13] But Clarkson was 39 and a brief stint in 1952 with the Boston Braves was his only appearance in the AL/NL. On June 23, he was traded to Dallas and finished the season with the Eagles. Overall, in 1954, he batted .324 with 42 homers and 135 RBIs.[14] He played two more minor league seasons.

Beaumont also added Jesse Williams in 1954. He was at the end of his professional career. He first played with the Kansas City Monarchs in 1939. At age 41, he only had six at-bats with Beaumont but registered his only hit in affiliated ball before retiring from the game. Another former Negro League player, Leroy Williams—who had played with the Newark Eagles—began the season at Tulsa.

Fort Worth was the Dodgers affiliate through 1956. Despite the organization's well-documented efforts in integration, Fort Worth remained segregated until April 18, 1955. Breaking the color line in Fort Worth was Maury Wills, whose minor league career had begun in 1951 at Hornell in the PONY League. He finally made it to the National League with the Los Angeles Dodgers in 1959. The man credited by many with having brought the stolen base back to the majors stole only 12 bases with Fort Worth in 1955. It was the only season from 1951 through 1970 in which he stole fewer than 20. Eddie Moore was also with Fort Worth in 1955. After banging 52 homers in his first three seasons in the Dodgers organization, he only had two homers with Fort Worth, the first coming on April 22 in his debut with the team. The Black fans welcomed Wills and Moore. Per the *Fort Worth Star-Telegram*, of the 2,617 fans at the game on April 22, 1,167 were Black.[15]

Dallas became affiliated with the New York Giants in 1955 and some of the players that started with the Giants in the majors passed through Dallas. Bill White, a player who would star with the Cardinals in the 1960s was working his way through the Giants organization when he spent the 1955 season in Dallas, as

Willard Brown debuted with the Kansas City Monarchs at age 22, and was 32 when he appeared in 21 games for the St. Louis Browns of the American League in 1947. When he was 38 he joined Dallas and spent four seasons in the Texas League, 1953–56.

did Ozzie Virgil who, along with White, moved on to the New York Giants the following year. In 1958, Virgil crossed the color line with the Detroit Tigers. In 1956, Andre Rodgers was with the Dallas Eagles. Willie McCovey was one of four Black players with the Eagles in 1957. McCovey slammed 11 homers that season.

Only **Shreveport**, which fought integration to the end, was not integrated as the 1955 season ended. The state of Louisiana was so opposed to integration that visiting teams were told not to bring their Black players to games in Shreveport. This was pursuant to an act signed into law by Governor Earl Long on July 17, 1956, banning inter-racial athletics events held after October 15, 1956.[16] The team ceased operation after the 1957 season.

With the passage of time, the alignment of teams in the Texas League changed. The first change of significance was the movement of the Beaumont team to Austin in 1956. Austin continued the affiliation with the Milwaukee Braves, and there were four Blacks on the 1956 Austin Senators.

By 1957, 10 years after Jackie Robinson debuted with Brooklyn and five years after Dave Hoskins had begun his time with Dallas, the Texas League was far more integrated. There were still players entering the Texas League who had ties to the Negro Leagues. Webbo Clarke joined Dallas that season. But even more players without ties to the Negro Leagues were coming of age and integrating the minors. Tony Taylor, who later starred for the Phillies, was with Dallas in 1957.

Oklahoma City, in 1956, affiliated with the Boston Red Sox. The 1957 roster included Pumpsie Green who, two years later, became the first Black player for Boston at the major league level.

In 1958, each of the teams in the Texas League was integrated (21 players in all), and two new cities joined the league: **Corpus Christi** and **Victoria**. Corpus Christi was the new home for the franchise that had been based in Shreveport. Victoria had been in the Big State League prior to 1958 and replaced Oklahoma City. The Giants switched their affiliation from Dallas to Corpus Christi, and the Dallas team, now called the Rangers, was unaffiliated in 1958. The Dodgers, who had no Texas League affiliate in 1957, affiliated with Victoria in 1958, and shipped prospects including Tommy Davis and Derald Wooton to Victoria.

The Dallas Rangers had two Black players, each with ties to the Negro Leagues. Jim Tugerson pitched for the Dallas Eagles in 1954–56. He had first pitched professionally for the Indianapolis Clowns of the Negro American League in 1951 and 1952. In 1954 with Dallas, he posted a 9–14 record with a 3.98 ERA. He remained with Dallas in 1955 when they affiliated with the Giants. In 1958, Tugerson struck out a league-leading 199 batters. Also returning to Dallas in 1958 was Dave Hoskins. At age 40, he posted a 17–8 record.

The season marked Dallas's final season in the Texas League. The team moved on to the Class AAA American Association in 1959.

Forth Worth also marked 1958 as their last year in the Texas League and they, like Dallas, had a 40-year-old veteran with ties to the Negro Leagues. In 1948, Lorenzo "Piper" Davis had played for Birmingham and posted a .393 batting average while managing the team and its rookie, Willie Mays, to the Negro American League pennant. Davis had first played in affiliated ball with Scranton in 1950, being dismissed by the Red Sox affiliate after 15 games despite batting .333. He was in his last professional season in 1958, batting .282 in 82 games with the Cats. Also with Fort Worth was Leonard "Preacher" Williams, who had first played professionally with the Indianapolis Clowns in 1950.

Houston finished in second place in 1958, and Ellis Burton led the team with 22 homers. Burton was in his fourth minor league season and advanced to the St. Louis Cardinals late in the season. He played in parts of five big-league seasons. Also on the team was George Moton, who hailed from California. Moton was only 2–8 with the team when he was sent to York of the Class A Eastern League in late June.

Austin finished the season in fourth place and lost to Corpus Christi in the playoffs. They had five Black players on their roster during the season, the most of any team in the Texas League. The team finished second in the league in home runs and three Black sluggers were a big part of the picture. Nat Peeples had 21, Dave Roberts had 20, and Lee Maye had 15. Winston Brown led all team pitchers with a 17–10 record, and Chi-Chi Olivo was briefly with the team. Olivo had spent most of the season in the South Atlantic League before being promoted to the Texas League. Of these players, Maye had the most accomplished major-league career, playing 13 seasons, leading the National League in doubles with 44 in 1964 with the Braves.

San Antonio had Jesse Gonder, Jose Santiago, and Sam Hairston on its roster in 1958. Hairston, at age 38, was on loan from the White Sox organization. Gonder, on loan from the Cincinnati organization, batted .328 for San Antonio in 1958, and was promoted to the Pacific Coast League for the last month of the season. He debuted in the majors with the Yankees in 1960 and played parts of eight seasons in the majors, his best year being with the Mets in 1964 when he batted .270 in 131 games. Santiago, who had pitched for Dallas 1952–53, had a 7–5 record. He was in his 11th professional season. He had first played with the New York Cubans in 1948 before joining the Cleveland Indians organization that same year. He played with the Indians in 1954 and 1955 and last played in the majors in 1956 with Kansas City.

Tulsa's roster included John Kennedy and Marvin Williams. Each had played in the Negro Leagues. Kennedy, in 1957, had become the first African American to play with the Philadelphia Phillies. Williams had taken a long and winding trail in professional baseball, beginning in 1943 with the Philadelphia Stars of the Negro National League. He was 38 when he played with Tulsa in 1958. Although he batted .294 in 144 games, he had essentially reached the end of the line, although he continued to play in the minors until he was 41.

Corpus Christi had three Black players in 1958. Although James Miller, Jack "Bo" Bossard, and Cal Dorsey did not make it to the majors, they nevertheless played an important part in the story of the integration of the Texas League. Corpus Christi finished the 1958 season in third place, but by virtue of playoff wins over Houston and Austin earned a place in the Dixie Series against Southern Association champion Birmingham. Bossard's three-run homer in the decisive seventh game against Austin enabled Corpus Christi to win the league championship series. He was honored with a $50 gift certificate.[17]

Segregationist Birmingham, pursuant to Section 597, originally passed in 1944 and updated via a referendum on June 1, 1954 (in the wake of the US Supreme Court's Brown vs. Board of Education ruling), prohibited interracial play at any facility in the city, including

Rickwood Field, home of the Birmingham Barons. Corpus Christi's Black players stayed home when the series started in Birmingham on September 26.[18]

All told 53 Black players integrated the Texas League 1952 through 1958. During the first wave of Texas League integration, the American and National Leagues added 87 players of color, and the stage was set for the final team—the Boston Red Sox—to finally integrate in 1959. In coming years, the Texas League would welcome more cities and build on the foundation laid from 1952 through 1958. ∎

Sources

In addition to the sources shown in the notes, the author used Baseball Reference, and the following:

Adelson, Bruce. *Brushing Back Jim Crow—The Integration of Minor League Baseball in the American South* (University of Virginia Press, 1999).

Jackson, Marion E. "Sports of the World," *Atlanta Daily World*, October 3, 1961: 5.

Tagliabue, Emil. "Tagged Topics: Piper Davis Another Satchel Paige," *Corpus Christi Caller-Times*, September 4, 1958: 37.

Notes

1. Alan Cohen, Team Integration Dates Log compiled by the author. See Appendix 1 online for the complete list of 20 players 1946–51.
2. R.E. Dixon, "Near 200 Report for Baseball Tryout in Dallas," *Kansas City Call*, February 22, 1952: 10.
3. Per the September 8, 1951, issue of the *Baltimore Afro-American*, based on Howe News Bureau statistics and shown on the Center for Negro League Baseball Research website.
4. Bill Rives, "The Sports Scene," *Dallas Morning News*, March 16, 1952: 2:1.
5. Rives, "Eagles to Drop Negro Player," *Dallas Morning News*, March 19, 1952: 14.
6. Joel W. Smith, "Othello Renfroe Rejoins Team in Mexican League," *Alabama Tribune* (Montgomery, Alabama), April 11, 1952: 7.
7. The integration of the Baltimore Orioles began in the minor league system of the St. Louis Browns, of which San Antonio was a part. Veeck, who had pioneered integration in the American League during his time with the Indians, had moved on to the Browns. He signed Black players and assigned them to the minor league teams in the St. Louis organization. Prior to the 1954 season, Veeck sold his interest in the team, and the Browns relocated to Baltimore, becoming the Orioles.
8. "Browns Sign Blount Negro," *Knoxville News Sentinel*, March 30, 1950: 30.
9. "Missions Take Texas Loop Lead," *Tulsa Tribune*, April 15, 1953: 37.
10. The order in which the teams of the Texas League integrated is shown in Table 3 on page 60.
11. "Clarkson Traded by Dallas Eagles," *Longview News-Journal*, January 3, 1954: 7.
12. "Clarkson is Hero at Bat for Shippers," *Shreveport Times*, April 10, 1954: 8.
13. "League Leaders," *The Sporting News*, June 30, 1954: 31.
14. "League Leaders," *The Sporting News*, September 15, 1954: 33.
15. Lorin McMullen, "Cats Homers Nip Indians," *Fort Worth Star-Telegram*, April 23, 1955: 11.
16. "Court Fight Due on Louisiana Bill," and "Shreveport's Future Tops TL Meeting," *Austin American-Statesman*, July 17, 1956: 20.
17. "Bossard Says Thanks," *Corpus Christi Caller-Times*, September 30, 1958: 31.
18. Bob Phillips, "Corpus Christi Arrives…Bearing Gifts," *Birmingham Post-Herald*, September 26, 1958: 8.

Waco Pirates
A Tale of Two Cities

Eric Bynum

This is a Tale of Two Cities. The Big State League was a Class B League from 1947 to 1957. For eleven seasons, teams from around Texas competed for the title. Each team was affiliated with a major-league club who could purchase players from them. The Waco Pirates played 1948–57 as an affiliate of Pittsburgh. The 1953 and 1954 seasons could not have been more different from each other. This is the Waco Pirates' story from tragedy to championship.

1953: A YEAR TO FORGET

The 1952 season for the Pirates was one to forget in many ways as the team lost 118 games. To shake things up, Pittsburgh general manager Branch Rickey brought back former manager Buster Chatham. In 1948, Chatham had led the team to a third-place finish. Buster had his work cut out for him. Heading into the 1953 season only 3 of 32 players were returning, so he would be working with an unfamiliar and untested group.[1] The team spent three weeks at Country Campus, Texas near Huntsville for spring training. Country Campus had four ballfields built on a former prisoner of war camp, and the ballfields were carved out of old Black Angus cow pastures. Perhaps this foreshadowed how the season would go.[2]

Professional teams in Waco never fared very well, winning only three titles despite the large number of different teams and leagues that bounced in and out of Waco over the first half of the twentieth century. Heading into the 1953 season, newspapers were picking the Pirates to finish in fourth place, a rise from the cellar a year before.[3] With optimism high, Big State League President Howard Green anticipated Waco to surpass the 100,000-attendance mark which was a big number for a Class B team. The record-breaking crowd, however, would never make it to the ballpark. Mother Nature had a different plan.[4]

The 1953 season started well for the Pirates. By May 5 the Pirates had already won 11 games. Newspaper reporter Oscar Larnce wrote in the Waco *Tribune* about how the team was nearly halfway to their win total of a year before despite dropping a heartbreaker in the ninth inning to Greenville.[5] "Pirate 'Tornado' Rips Austin 10–5," was an unfortunate headline by Waco sports reporter Jinx Tucker. Unbeknownst to him as he penned this headline, he was foreshadowing one of the most horrific natural disasters in Waco's history.[6]

MOTHER NATURE STRIKES

"8 Killed, Scores Hurt as Twisters Rampage" was the headline of the *Waco News-Tribune* on May 11, 1953, referring to tornadoes in Minnesota. It was the middle of tornado season after all, but nobody in Waco would believe what was headed their way that day. The front-page weather forecast called for "Partly cloudy with mild temperatures today, tonight and Tuesday."[7] That night's matchup had Ed McLish set to pitch versus Greenville hurler Jodie Phipps—but the game never took place.[8]

"37 Die, 300 Hurt in Waco Twister" was the headline in the *Waco News-Tribune* the next day. At 4:36 PM on Monday May 11, 1953, the deadliest tornado in the history of Texas would rip through the heart of Waco, killing 114 people and injuring 600 more. The F5 caused an estimated $10,000,000 in damage.[9] The nearly one-third-mile-wide twister destroyed numerous businesses and homes with winds up to 260 miles per hour.[10] It had been long said that the native population had chosen the area because it was tornado-proof. According to legend, the rim of hills surrounding Waco would prevent a tornado from hitting that spot. Unfortunately, the natives were either misquoted, or wrong.[11]

As for the Pirates, their stadium, Katy Park, was demolished by the storm. Despite three players going missing for around 24 hours, none of the players were hurt. Pitcher Cleo Lewright—the first black player ever on a Waco team[12]—and catcher Marcos Cobos were planning a move that day to the east side of town. Instead, they waited due to the weather looking bad. That decision might have saved them from injury or worse as the area of town they were going to move to was one of the hardest hit.[13]

THE MOVE TO LONGVIEW

After Katy Park was destroyed, the fate of the team was up in the air. While the Pittsburgh Pirates ran the Waco club, the park was owned by local businessman A.H. Kirksey. This left the Pirates scrambling to find a place to play or they would be forced to disband. One option that quickly arose was Longview, which was 176 miles northeast of Waco. Longview had lost their Big State League team to Tyler a year before.[14] The Pirates began their transition period as a road team, and the Temple Eagles offered the use of their field until something could be worked out.[15] On May 23, 1953, Rickey announced that the Waco Pirates would become the Longview Pirates for the remainder of the season.[16]

The 1953 team featured five future major league players, including Dick Hall, who would go on to win 93 games over 16 years in the big leagues. Ironically, he was an infielder/outfielder for Waco/Longview during the 1953 season. He started pitching in 1955.[17]

Despite being hit with the worst tornado in Texas' history and moving 176 miles to a new city, the Longview Pirates played well enough to make the playoffs in 1953, finishing in fourth place with a 77–68 record. They would lose in four games to the leading Wichita Falls Spudders, who would go on to win the 1953 title.[18]

1954: A NEW LEASE ON BASEBALL

A.H. Kirksey rebuilt Katy Park for the 1954 season, and the Pirates looked for good things to happen. Jack Paepke became the new manager when Buster Chatham moved to the front office to help run the club. Paepke was only in his second season as a manager, having managed the club in Brunswick, Georgia, the year before.[19] Many people in the media were picking the Pirates to come out on top.[20] The *Waco News-Tribune* invoked the greatest Big State League team of all-time, the 1948 Sherman-Denison Twins, who had gone 94–51 and won the league by 10½ games.[21] Little did anyone know that the 1954 Pirates would go down as one of the top 25 teams of all time, not just in the Big State League but in the minor leagues.

The season started off rather nondescriptly as the team meandered through the first few games at a .500 clip, before rattling off five straight wins in late April. Then the rain came. Sitting at only 8–7, the Pirates had three straight rainouts.[22] And just as the team was finding a rhythm in early May, manager and catcher Jack Paepke broke his thumb.[23] Paepke batted .348 before he got injured. His replacement, William Phillips, a 23-year-old who only lasted one more minor league season, did not have the hitting ability of Paepke.

Dick Hall was one of five players on the 1953 Waco team who saw major league service time. He would switch to pitching in 1955 and would play through 1971 with Pittsburgh, Kansas City, Philadelphia, and Baltimore.

Phillips finished the season batting just .234, while Paepke came back to finish out the year at a .314 clip.[24]

The Pirates continued to win in May, despite some offensive slumps. "Anybody have a base hit to spare?" was the question Waco sportswriter Dave Campbell asked in a May 31 article. "Just any old kind will do. Mail your offerings to Jack Paepke, in care of the Waco Pirates, Inc., at Katy Park." He even suggested you put a "rush" on that. Despite the bleak outlook that Campbell gives, the team built a 28-17 record with a winning month of May and sat just two games behind the league-leading Tyler Tigers.[25]

A RUN AT THE TITLE

When the calendar turned to June, the Pirates were on the heels of Tyler, but by June 4 they would take the lead and not look back. Two days later, one of the longest hitting streaks in baseball history would begin. On the tenth anniversary of the D-Day landings in France, Roman Mejias started what would become a 55-game hitting streak, the third longest in minor league history.[26]

By the end of June, the Pirates led Tyler by three games, which was not a lot considering Waco ran off an unbeaten streak of 12 games ending on June 30. Mejias' streak was twice the length at 24 games by the end of June.[27] Later in July, with his hitting streak at 46 games, Mejias was awarded a $200 diamond ring and $214 in cash by Waco fans during an intermission of a game against the Corpus Christi Clippers. A few innings later he was able to thank the fans by extending his streak to 47 games, breaking up a no-hitter and starting a rally as Waco went on to win, 5–2.[28]

The Pirates continued to win, and Mejias kept hitting. Waco ran away with the league's regular season title by 13 games over Tyler, and Mejias would finish the season with 198 hits and a .354 batting average. He jumped to the majors the next season and spent parts of nine years in the big leagues with Pittsburgh, Houston, and Boston before finishing his career in Japan.

The team went on to defeat the Austin Pioneers in the semifinals, and then capped the year with a league championship by defeating the Clippers in a close seven-game series.[29]

The journey through the two seasons was marred with disaster and loss, yet ended with a team coming together and building a championship. The Pirates tried to run it back again in 1955, but ran into the Clippers once again in the finals and lost in four games. Nevertheless, the team overcame a tragedy and became champions of the Big State League, and are now regarded as one of the greatest minor league teams of all time. In 2001, in conjunction with the centennial celebration of the National Association of Professional Baseball Leagues, the top 100 minor league teams of all-time were selected by historians Bill Weiss and Marshall Wright. At number 25 on the list were the 1954 Waco Pirates.[30] ∎

Notes

1. Oscar Larnce, "Waco Pirates Begin Job Today of Rebuilding Team," *Waco News-Tribune*, March 20, 1953, 19.
2. Larnce, "Waco Pirates Begin Job Today of Rebuilding Team."
3. Jinx Tucker, "Waco Teams Finish on Top Only 3 Times in History," Baseball Tabloid, *Waco News-Tribune*, April 14, 1954, 7.
4. Oscar Larnce, "In This Corner," *Waco News-Tribune*, March 24, 1953, 11.
5. Oscar Larnce, "In This Corner," *Waco News-Tribune*, May 5, 1953, 10,12.
6. Jinx Tucker, "Pirate 'Tornado' Rips Austin 10–5," *Waco News-Tribune*, April 29, 1953, 12.
7. "8 Killed, Scores Hurt As Twisters Rampage," *Waco News-Tribune*, May 11, 1953, 1.
8. Jinx Tucker, "Bucs Win In Tenth, 9-to-8," *Waco News-Tribune*, May 11, 1953, 8.
9. "Vicious Winds Crumble Buildings, Autos in Business Heart of City," *Waco News-Tribune*, May 12, 1953, 1.
10. Amanda Sawyer, "Waco Tornado," WacoHistory.org, https://wacohistory.org/items/show/53, accessed February 1, 2025,
11. "Old Legend About Waco Blows Away," *Waco News-Tribune*, May 12, 1953, 6.
12. Earl Golding, "Golding Glances," *Waco News-Tribune*, April 17, 1953, 19.
13. "'Missing' Bucs Found Okeh," *Waco News-Tribune*, May 13, 1953, 13.
14. Buster Hale, "Chances Bright for Longview To Get Big State Berth: Officials Here to Study Shift," *Longview News-Journal*, May 14, 1953, 13.
15. "Bucs to Operate as Road Team Until Site Is Picked," *Waco News-Tribune*, May 14, 1953, 11.
16. Buster Hale, "Pirates Will Open Here Thursday Night," *Longview News-Journal*, May 24, 1953, 10.
17. "Dick Hall," Baseball Reference. https://www.baseball-reference.com/players/h/halldi01.shtml, accessed May 16, 2025.
18. "1953 Waco/Longview Pirates," Baseball Reference, https://www.baseball-reference.com/register/team.cgi?id=d121cf02, accessed May 16, 2025.
19. "Pirates Led by Versatile Boss," Baseball Tabloid, *Waco News Tribune*, April 16, 1954, 6.
20. Dave Campbell, "Bucs Open Chase With High Hopes," Baseball Tabloid, *Waco News-Tribune*, April 16, 1954, 2.
21. George Raborn, "'48 Twins Were All-Time Kings," Baseball Tabloid, *Waco News-Tribune*, April 16, 1954, 13.
22. "3rd Straight Rainout for Pirates at Bryan," *Waco News-Tribune*, May 3, 1954, 6.
23. Dave Campbell, "Pirates Win 7 to 1, But Paepke Lost for Month," *Waco News-Tribune*, May 7, 1954, 15.
24. "1954 Waco Pirates," Baseball Reference, https://www.baseball-reference.com/register/team.cgi?id=34db8aa8, accessed May 16, 2025.
25. Dave Campbell, "Pirates Continue Hit Slump, Lose to Austin," *Waco News-Tribune*, May 31, 1954, 4.
26. "Longest Hitting Streaks," Baseball Reference, https://www.baseball-reference.com/bullpen/Longest_Hitting_Streaks, accessed May 16, 2025.
27. "Temple Ends Waco's Streak With 10th Inning Victory, 4–3," *Waco News-Tribune*, July 1, 1954, 21.
28. "Slugging Wacoan Continues Streak," *Corsicana Daily Sun*, July 24, 1954, 8.
29. "1954 Waco Pirates."
30. "100 Best Minor League Baseball Teams," Baseball Reference, https://www.baseball-reference.com/bullpen/100_Best_Minor_League_Baseball_Teams, accessed May 16, 2025.

How the Metroplex Went Major League

John Bauer

"I just want to point out that if you want it, you can have it."[1] Speaking at a Chamber of Commerce luncheon in December 1953, R.W. (Dick) Burnett informed his audience that Dallas could go major league if civic leaders made the requisite commitment to attract a team to North Texas. The oil tycoon and owner of the Texas League's Dallas Eagles believed his city could factor into the remaking of the map of Major League Baseball with upgraded facilities. Burnett added, "If Dallas had a stadium today, it could have a major league team next year."[2] Burnett passed away in 1955 and did not live to see Dallas, alone or in partnership with Fort Worth, achieve that status, but his words spurred the effort to bring big-league baseball to Dallas-Fort Worth.

By the time of Burnett's speech, modern air travel ensured no region of the country was too far from the established big leagues. As the Dodgers and Giants plotted moves westward from New York, the Lone Star State was a potential option for the Giants. Owner Horace Stoneham claimed in 1957 that Dallas had presented an offer in the event San Francisco could not make good on a new stadium.[3] But as is well known, the Giants made the jump to California, leaving Dallas and the Fort Worth Cats as mainstays of the Double-A Texas League.

In late 1957, the Texas legislature passed legislation authorizing counties with populations greater than 350,000 people to issue bonds to support construction of stadiums. Dallas and Tarrant counties met the population threshold and, in May 1958, the counties formed a joint committee to investigate whether local interest justified the issuance of bonds to build a ballpark. Tarrant County included Arlington, a growing city along the new turnpike that connected the two regional hubs. Tom Vandergriff, the Arlington mayor, became an influential voice on the bi-county committee and a champion of efforts to land a major league team. The committee commissioned a survey, which revealed in February 1959 that the area was "ready, willing, and able" to support the drive for the big leagues.[4]

Dallas construction magnate J.W. Bateson purchased the Eagles in 1958 with an eventual eye toward the majors. While Burnett had believed Dallas could go it alone, Bateson thought a regional effort was better, saying, "I had wanted Dallas to have its own team but I realize now that a joint team might be best."[5] To shore up the Fort Worth side of the equation, Bateson partnered with newspaper publisher Amon Carter, Jr. to combine big-league efforts (as well as both local minor-league teams into the Dallas-Fort Worth Rangers).

With Dallas-Fort Worth and other growing cities pushing for major league baseball, the inevitability of expansion became evident. This appetite could only be satisfied by organic growth of the existing leagues or by a third major league. Commissioner Ford Frick convened a meeting of baseball executives in May 1959 to establish criteria under which major league status would be granted to a third league. It did not take long for that pretender to emerge. Partly an offshoot of efforts to reestablish a second team in New York, the Continental League was launched in July 1959. Five cities were on the initial roster: Denver, Houston, Minneapolis-St. Paul, New York, and Toronto. Dallas-Fort Worth was not, but Bateson declared for the Continentals after voters approved an October 1959 referendum to issue $9.5 million in bonds for a stadium to be built near the turnpike in Arlington. In March 1960, the Joint Board of Park Commissioners of Dallas and Tarrant counties selected a 203-acre site near the former Arlington Downs race track on which to build a major league-caliber stadium.

The CL planned to make formal application for major league recognition, but the effort folded when the majors agreed in August 1960 to make room for the pretenders. The AL and NL committed to expand to four CL cities by 1962 with the remainder to follow. To support the effort, the Joint Board revealed plans on August 20 for a domed stadium in Arlington. The stadium could be ready for the 1961 season—but open-air with 31,000 seats, with a roof, air conditioning, and an expanded 60,000 capacity to follow for 1962. Bateson pronounced, "We're ready to go into major league ball the minute we're accepted."[6]

The question of major league acceptance for Dallas-Fort Worth and other CL cities became muddied by the AL's interest in Los Angeles. The CL roster of cities did not include Los Angeles or any Pacific Coast locales, but the AL was eager to rival the NL's presence out west. Yankees owner Dan Topping wanted to extract this price from the NL if the senior circuit reentered the New York area. If Los Angeles moved up the AL list, a CL city would have to yield.

Dallas applied formally to the AL on October 14, 1960, with expectations to begin play in 1962. The tilt toward the AL was driven by the NL's focus on (and eventual selection of) New York and Houston. On the eve of the AL's decision, Allen Russell, general manager of the minor-league Rangers, said, "There is no reason to believe that the league won't expand and it won't take our area."[7]

On October 26, 1960, the AL announced its expansion plans, which were surprisingly brought forward to the 1961 season—fewer than six months away. Those plans did not include Dallas-Fort Worth. Rather, the AL sanctioned the move of the Washington Senators to Minneapolis-St. Paul, while establishing the Angels in Los Angeles and replacing the departed team in DC.

These moves contravened the recommendation of the AL's own expansion committee to take two CL cities, including Dallas-Fort Worth, as had been committed. The result was particularly bitter for Bateson and Carter, who believed they were on the wrong end of a "double-cross." Bateson huffed, "The American League has wrecked our hopes…[and] by its low blow, has ruined baseball here."[8] Carter added, "We just got a good old country beating. We thought Dallas-Fort Worth deserved major league baseball and we did all we could to bring it there."[9] Vandergriff was "heart-sick"[10] and blamed "quite a bit of late scheming and swapouts between some of the owners."[11] Neither Bateson nor Carter was mollified by suggestions that buying and moving the Kansas City Athletics or Cincinnati Reds might offer an alternative. The duo were so upset that they vowed to exit baseball and terminate efforts to land a major league team.

Following the expansion disappointment, Dallas-Fort Worth would become linked with just about every relocation rumor over the next decade. The Athletics ended up in Charlie Finley's hands in December 1960, and it did not take long for him to antagonize Kansas City officials with complaints about his lease, attendance, parking, and the state of Municipal Stadium. Rumors of a potential move to Dallas burst into the open during the 1961 season. After being fired by Finley, former general manager Frank Lane claimed that Finley considered a move to Dallas and the Cotton Bowl had been evaluated for suitability as a temporary venue.[12] In May 1962, Finley put the issue before the AL and, by summer, formalized his request to relocate. The AL tabled the question and Finley withdrew his request before the league could vote it down. As league president Joe Cronin stated, "The American League does not wish to revise its circuit."[13]

In late 1963, Tommy G. Mercer, a young businessman who led a trucking and beer distribution enterprise established by his grandfather, and Lamar Hunt, son of oil tycoon H.L. Hunt and founder of the American Football League, teamed up and acquired the Rangers to renew a big league push. Mercer believed Dallas-Fort Worth had fallen behind cities such as Atlanta, Seattle, and San Diego. To close the gap, Tarrant County voters passed a $16.5 million bond measure in April 1964 to build a convention center and baseball stadium in Arlington. The ballpark would seat 10,000 initially, but could be expanded to 45,000 upon acquisition of a major league team. Construction began that fall on what became Turnpike Stadium.

Dallas-Fort Worth was bypassed with the next franchise shift when the Braves decamped Milwaukee for Atlanta after the 1965 season. New Commissioner William D. Eckert declared upon assuming office that expansion was "a matter of years, not months."[14] Mercer and Hunt submitted expansion applications to both

SABR/RUCKER ARCHIVE

Arlington Stadium before the addition of high walls atop the outfield bleachers to cut down the severe summer winds. Note the "Lone Star State" scoreboard beyond left field.

leagues under the name "North Texas Baseball Club," but with the Angels and Senators struggling to establish themselves, the AL was not considering the issue. Cronin said, "We haven't even talked expansion."[15] The NL, dealing with antitrust litigation in Wisconsin over the Braves' departure, was in no position to do so either.

Potential antitrust issues would lead to major league expansion, but it was a different franchise shift that prompted action. The AL finally allowed Finley to leave Kansas City, in this case for Oakland, after the 1967 season. In doing so, the AL immediately created problems for itself as Missouri's powerful Senator Stuart Symington threatened legislation to revoke baseball's antitrust exemption. On October 19, 1967, the AL agreed to add clubs in Kansas City and Seattle for the 1969 season. Dallas-Fort Worth was barely considered, with the AL too eager to increase its West Coast presence with a Pacific Northwest outpost.

The AL's action forced the NL to consider whether to expand on a similarly expedited timeframe. The NL opened an expansion process in late 1967 that attracted applications from Buffalo, Milwaukee, Montreal, and San Diego, in addition to Dallas-Fort Worth. Having to rely on NL action placed Dallas-Fort Worth in a disadvantageous position given the presence of Houston president Judge Roy Hofheinz on the league expansion committee. The Astros broadcast their games throughout Texas, including the Dallas-Fort Worth area, and Hofheinz placed greater value on monopolizing Texas media revenues than creating an instate rivalry. Mercer analyzed the situation, "It all boils down to Hofheinz. If he relents and goes for us, I'd say we're in."[16] Though Hofheinz denied charges of bias against Dallas-Fort Worth, the NL announced in May 1968 that it would expand to Montreal and San Diego for 1969. Mercer bristled, "This is still a big disappointment, and it still rankles but, in the long run, we might be better off. We're going to start looking and keep looking, and Hofheinz doesn't have an American League veto."[17]

The AL presented numerous possibilities for someone looking to buy and relocate a team. The Senators hit the market in late 1968, and Hunt claimed to have reached out. Both the sellers and the AL preferred to keep the club in Washington, and the league approved the sale of the Senators to Minnesota businessman Bob Short (over entertainer Bob Hope) in December. Hunt observed, "I don't have to tell you that several American League franchises are doing poorly."[18] The Chicago White Sox struggled to draw fans and began playing games in Milwaukee; Hunt inquired, but the

sale of controlling interest in the Artnell Corporation which owned the club, from Arthur Allyn to brother John, shelved immediate prospects of a move. The Cleveland Indians were periodically rumored to be headed to Dallas, and owner Vernon Stouffer periodically denied such plans. Even Finley appeared to develop wanderlust after only a few seasons in Oakland.

One of the AL's newest members was also its most unstable. Under-financed and playing in minor-league Sicks' Stadium, the Seattle Pilots struggled from the start. The team was almost evicted during its inaugural 1969 season, and Pilots officials scouted Dallas-Fort Worth and Milwaukee in case relocation became necessary. Mercer and Hunt declined to seriously pursue the Pilots, with Mercer describing negotiations in October 1969 thus: "We felt like…we had told them a price and they had taken that price to Milwaukee and asked them to beat it and then came back to us and asked us to beat that."[19] Bankruptcy followed for the Pilots ahead of the 1970 season, and the team landed in Milwaukee as the Brewers just before Opening Day.

Despite more than a decade of dashed hopes, patience remained the order of the day. Hunt explained the cautious approach, "We're interested only in making a reasonable deal.…We feel we can afford to wait."[20] Mindful that Milwaukee's major league stadium gave that city a leg up, Vandergriff had urged, "We have to have a bigger stadium, one that can be enlarged to major league standards in a minimum of time."[21] To be ready in May 1970, Arlington voters overwhelmingly approved a $10 million bond issue to expand Turnpike Stadium to 21,000 seats before the 1971 season. The wait was nearly over.

After a winning season in 1969 spurred a surge in attendance, the Senators returned to their losing ways and lower gate numbers followed. Owner Short complained of losing money and argued that if baseball felt compelled to maintain a team in DC to placate Congress, then the other owners should share his losses. He owed money to the Armory Board, his landlord at RFK Stadium, and had loan payments upcoming on his leveraged purchase of the Senators. Selling or moving became Short's only options.

The AL convened on September 21, 1971, to consider the relocation question. Vandergriff and other local officials made their way to the meeting, armed with sweeteners to entice Short and the AL. The promises included a $1 per year lease at Turnpike Stadium on the first million fans, expansion of the ballpark to 35,000 for 1972 and 45,000 for 1973, payment of indemnifications to the Texas League and the Mercer/

Hunt group, and a $7.5 million advance on a decade's worth of broadcast rights. (That final promise would clear Short's debts but handicap cashflow after Short sold the team in 1974.) The AL consented to the move by a 10–2 vote with only Baltimore and Chicago in the negative. Vandergriff cheered, "We started 13 years ago with the Bi-County Sports Committee. It's been a long hard road but now I can say it was well worth it."[22]

Despite earlier promises of a name-the-team contest, the name "Texas Rangers" was revealed at a November 23, 1971, luncheon with hundreds of business leaders. Turnpike Stadium also acquired a new name. Vandergriff rejected calls to name the ballpark to honor his efforts to bring major league baseball to the area and, at his suggestion, "Arlington Stadium" became the name. The Rangers were set to debut on April 6 at home, but a players' strike delayed the season opener by over a week. After going 1–3 in Chicago and Anaheim, the Rangers hosted an announced 20,105 fans for their home opener on Friday, April 21, 1972, which was a 7–6 win over the California Angels. The Metroplex was now major league. ■

Sources

In addition to the notes cited below, the author also consulted the following:

John Helyar, *Lords of the Realm: The Real History of Baseball* (New York: Villard Books, 1994).

Frank P. Jozsa, Jr., *Major League Baseball Expansions and Relocations: A History, 1876–2008* (Jefferson, NC: McFarland and Co., 2010).

Andy McCue, *Stumbling Around the Bases: The American League's Mismanagement in the Expansion Eras* (Lincoln, NE: University of Nebraska Press, 2022).

Bill O'Neal, *The Texas League: A Century of Baseball (1888–1987)* (Austin, TX: Eakin Press, 1987).

Michael Shapiro, *Bottom of the Ninth: Branch Rickey, Casey Stengel, and the Daring Scheme to Save Baseball from Itself* (New York: Times Books, 2009).

Notes

1. Bill Rives, "Big Baseball Stadium Would Bring Majors Here—Burnett," *Dallas Morning-News*, December 16, 1953.
2. Rives, "Big Baseball Stadium."
3. Joe King, "Mayor of 'Frisco Calls Pay-TV Key to Bid for Giants," *The Sporting News*, July 31, 1957, 8.
4. "Dallas-Fort Worth Reported Ready for Majors in Survey," *The Sporting News*, March 11, 1959, 21.
5. Bill Rives, "Texas Neighbors Plan Joint Bid for Major Team," *The Sporting News*, May 28, 1958, 34.
6. Ray Gillespie, "Dallas, Fort Worth Join Hands in Major Bid," *The Sporting News*, September 21, 1960, 15.
7. "Area Baseball Leaders Head for AL Meet," *Dallas Morning-News*, October 25, 1960.
8. Ray Gillespie, "'A.L. Double-Crossed Us,' Claims Angry Dallas Pair," *The Sporting News*, November 2, 1960, 4.
9. Bill Rives, "Berth In Future? Chances Remote," *Dallas Morning News*, October 27, 1960.
10. "Sadness at Arlington, Too," *Dallas Morning News*, October 27, 1960.
11. "Disappointed Backers Blast League Owners," *Fort Worth Star-Telegram*, October 27, 1960.
12. Ernest Mehl, "Frankie Fires Fast Reply to Finley Fusillade," *The Sporting News*, August 30, 1961, 5.
13. Dan Daniel, "Finley Backs Off—Fails to Seek Approval for Shift," *The Sporting News*, September 29, 1962, 16.
14. Clifford Kachline, "Expansion 'Years Away,' Majors Insist," *The Sporting News*, December 18, 1965, 1.
15. Kachline, "Expansion."
16. Merle Heryford, "Buffalo Dome No Worry," *Dallas Morning News*, May 11, 1968.
17. Merle Heryford, "Dallas-FW Search Not Ended," *Dallas Morning News*, May 29, 1968.
18. "'Dallas Will Step Up Bid For A.L. Team'—Hunt," *The Sporting News*, February 28, 1970, 24.
19. Sam Blair, "A Trip Worth Missing," *Dallas Morning News*, April 1, 1970.
20. Wells Twombly, "Lamar Hunt—Facts and Fiction," *The Sporting News*, December 5, 1970, 20.
21. Merle Heryford, "18 Years, Dreams, and Vandergriff, *Dallas Morning News*, September 26, 1971.
22. Harold McKinney, "Short Set to 'Pitch Tent' in Arlington," *Fort Worth Star-Telegram*, September 22, 1971, E1.

An Encounter with Cliff Gustafson

Charlie Grassl

Attend most high school baseball games in Texas today, and you will encounter a beautiful stadium with a staffed food shack. The walled outfield is most likely carpeted with neatly trimmed artificial turf, and a warning track encircles a carefully manicured infield. The helmeted players are impeccably dressed in ultra-clean uniforms that appear to have been individually sized and fitted to each player by elite tailors.

Such was not the case for those of us who were privileged to play high school baseball in the late 1950s. Most games were played in city parks, on baseball diamonds also used for family games, picnics, and parking cars. Dugouts and backstops were made from chainlink fence. The backstop was not there to protect spectators, but to stop errant pitches or overthrows to the catcher. Most fields had no outfield fences. Players wore baggy, ill-fitted flannel uniforms, batted without helmets, and played the whole season with a team supply of only five or so wooden bats. A broken bat was viewed as worse than a strikeout. During most at bats, the coach's usual shout was, "Keep the trademark up." Foul balls not captured by the backstop were hastily hunted down, usually by a bench player or someone's little brother, who quickly returned them to the umpire.

Despite the contrasts in uniforms, facilities, and equipment, all eras of baseball share the joys of exciting one-run games, key game-winning hits, difficult balls caught, and speedy runners stealing bases. I attended Central Catholic High School in San Antonio, Texas, 1954–58.

At that time Central Catholic was a member of the Texas Catholic Interscholastic League (TCIL) along with other Texas Catholic schools.[1] This organization functioned much like the Texas University Interscholastic League (UIL), conducting athletic championship playoffs and regulating sport competition between its member schools. Though not eligible to pursue a UIL Baseball Championship, Central Catholic scheduled games with San Antonio's major high schools, February through May. In the 1958 high school season, Central played Alamo Heights, Harlandale, South San Antonio (known as South San), Northside, and Edgewood high schools, going 9–6 against this competition. We were also fortunate to be eligible to play as a team in a second season: a summer of American Legion baseball.

In the summer, Central was sponsored by American Legion Post 420 and played in San Antonio's District 28 American Legion League. Members of District 28 were Central, Jefferson, Breckenridge, Alamo Heights, South San, and Burbank high schools. Despite the organizational separation of parochial and public schools, significant interplay was made possible by the cooperation of each of the coaches and the openness of the American Legion.

The Central Catholic team matured that summer of 1957, learning to compete with the best high-school competition San Antonio could offer. The American Legion summer season ended with a three-game series between Central and Jefferson High School for the District 28 title. After a split in the first two games, a third game was necessary to determine the champion.

Falling behind, 8–3, early, Central rallied for four runs in the sixth and seventh innings to close the gap, 8–7. With two outs and the tying run on base, Jefferson pitcher Garret Steubing got the strikeout and the victory for a very deserving Jefferson team. Though we were disappointed by the heartbreaking loss, we were consoled when our roster dominated the postseason All-Star team, with six of the sixteen players chosen coming from Central.

The exciting summer of 1957 passed into fall and my senior year in high school began. It would be a long wait until February and the start of the 1958 high school baseball season, but a world event deflected my focus from baseball. The event on October 4, 1957, was the Russian space launch of a tiny satellite that circled the globe, going "beep-beep" periodically. Influenced by the panic within the United States over the technological gap between the US and Russia, my dream of a baseball career changed to a career in engineering. A huge factor also was realizing I might not be good enough for the next level of baseball. Engineering might perhaps be better suited for my gifts and talents. This may have been my first measured and mature thought in high school. Nevertheless, I remained very excited about the 1958 high school baseball season.

Eventually mid-February workouts began. Our 1958 season began March 12, on a cold and wet afternoon at East Central High School, giving up a five-run lead in the bottom of the seventh inning to lose, 9–8. Winning ten of the next eleven, however, eased the pain of that first loss. Our overall record for the 1958 season, including the playoffs, was 21–8.

We were blessed to receive excellent coaching from William Kennealy. A World War II veteran, he had left the military for the religious life, becoming a Brother within the Society of Mary. He was my math teacher as well as our baseball coach. From St. Louis, Missouri, he was a fanatical fan of the St. Louis Cardinals. His World War II experiences of "flying the hump" shaped his life and all of us on the baseball team were the undeserving recipients of a man who rededicated his life to serve others.[2] When I was a sophomore aspiring to play shortstop, Brother Bill many times stayed after practice to help me become unafraid of a ground ball, hitting grounders to me until I did not raise my eyes from the ball. His comment to me was always, "Good shortstops do not have sunburned eyeballs." He taught me to watch the ball go into my glove. He was always firm yet encouraging to each of us as we developed into better baseball players and mature young men under his influence.

The highlights of the 1958 season were many, but one was to play South San, coached at that time by one Cliff Gustafson. Though we could not have known Gustafson would later be inducted into the College Baseball Hall of Fame, 1958 was South San's first of seven UIL Texas State Championships under his leadership.[3] We played them twice that year and beat them both times. Our first game, on March 26, was most memorable for me as I drove in three of the four runs in our 4–2 victory, including a home run in the sixth inning, breaking a 2–2 tie. It was my only high school home run. After the game, Gustafson took the time to tell me, "Nice game, kid."

A month later, on April 28, we beat South San a second time, 9–5. Gustafson went on to coach another nine years at South San, capping off his time there in 1967 with a perfect 39–0 that season. He left South San to accept Darrel Royal's job offer of to become head baseball coach at the University of Texas in Austin.[4] As the Longhorn baseball coach until 1996, Gustafson's teams won 79.2% of their games, twenty-two Southwest Conference (SWC) titles, made seventeen College World Series appearances, and won two national championships.

The irony of the 1958 season was that Central also won a baseball championship: the 1958 Texas Catholic Interscholastic League (TCIL) championship.[5] The tournament was held at Keefe Field at St. Mary's University over the weekend of May 9–11. Entering the double-elimination tournament with a 15–7 record gave us confidence that we could win the whole thing, but perhaps overconfidence was in play. Our first game, at noon Friday, was an easy, 7–3, win. Our second game was at three o'clock, against St. Joseph of Victoria, Texas. They were the 1957 TCIL champions, the ones who had defeated us in the championship game by one run.

I remembered that 1957 championship game well. I had been the one who struck out to end the game with the tying run on third base, swinging and missing a very slow change-up for the third strike. Emotionally crushed by my failure, unable to leave the batter's box, I saw Brother Bill running toward me from his third base coaching position, He put his arm around me and told me, "That was just one of twenty-one

The 1957 American Legion Central Catholic Team. The author is in the front row, furthest to the left.

outs, Charlie. We had many opportunities to win this game. This was just one of those opportunities." It was a healing moment to be given that perspective of my strikeout. Always to see disappointments in a larger context of life.

In our second tournament game, our play was sloppy and careless, and we lost once again to the same St. Joseph team, 8–7.

Brother Bill was not pleased with our performance and clearly expressed those feelings to us in the postgame dugout briefing. In a most unfeeling tone, he informed us our next game, in the loser-bracket, was Saturday at nine o'clock in the morning. The meeting ended with his admonition: "Show up tomorrow only if you want to play like you know you can." Saturday at 8:00 AM sharp, everyone showed up for warm-ups. We went about our routines quietly, without much chatter. What lay before us seemed too much to comprehend, causing us to focus on only the game immediately in front of us. That attitude prevailed throughout the whole of Saturday: play one game at a time. By the end of the day, we had won three games (one of them a 1–0 victory over St. Joseph), making us eligible to play the tournament's only undefeated team, St. Thomas High School of Houston. We would play them Sunday at 1:00 PM.

The "one game at a time" attitude carried over from the previous day. We didn't even think about having to play two games to win the championship. The 1:00 game was all there was. My own interpretation of my personal attitude was that we had screwed up by losing that second game, and we were being punished by having to play as many baseball games as you could fit into a weekend. It was Saturday night before we realized we had played five baseball games in two days.

When the game arrived, Central jumped out to a 7–0 lead after one inning and then padded that lead in the latter innings, resulting in an easy, 13–3 win. Central pitchers held St. Thomas to two hits. That put us in the position to play in the championship game. In the deciding game, once again, Central jumped to a lead after the first inning, this time 3–0, and adding another two runs in the bottom of the sixth. St. Thomas rallied for two runs in the top of the seventh, but that was all. The last out of the game was a pop-up to shortstop, and we won the tournament.

It was an exhausting experience to play seven games in three days. We discovered what the term "grind" meant. But soon I was rested, and the numbness of the "grind" had been overcome. Next was a celebration banquet for the team. A graduation ceremony. Then a seventy-two-mile drive to Austin, where I began my engineering studies at the University of Texas summer school session.

As the spring of 1959 came around, I thought about how much I would love to play for the Longhorns. Without a scholarship, I would have to be a walk-on. There was a high chance that I would not make the team. One of my Central teammates, Jeff Nesrsta, did make the Longhorn team. Bill Sebera, our catcher, signed a minor league contract with the Dodgers, eventually reaching as high as A-Ball. In the end, I chose to be an engineering nerd with a slide rule on my belt. Over the years I experienced a few moments of sadness over ending my baseball life at eighteen years old. But playing church-league softball and slow-pitch beer league games until the age of fifty-five, plus a wonderful engineering career, has proved adequate for a happy and satisfying life. I have been blessed. ∎

Notes

1. The TCIL ceased operation in 1978 and its members joined the Texas Association of Private and Parochial Schools (TAPPS).
2. "Flying the Hump During World War II," Lyon Air Museum, https://lyonairmuseum.org/blog/flying-hump-during-world-war-ii/, accessed February 17, 2025.
3. University Interscholastic League, https://www.uiltexas.org/history/timeline, accessed February 17, 2025.
4. "Coach Cliff Gustafson 1," Texas Legacy Support Network: The History of Longhorn Sports, October 13, 2021. https://texaslsn.org/new-page-cliff/, accessed November 27, 2024.
5. The Central Catholic varsity sports teams were known as the Buttons. The high school and St. Mary's University (the Rattlers) were founded and managed by the same order of religion, The Society of Mary. The name "Buttons" referred to the part of a rattlesnake's tail that rattles, thus linking the two schools. Unfortunately, we were often demeaned by linking the "buttons" name to the round plastic objects that hold garments closed.

AUTHOR'S COLLECTION

Central Catholic Team Autographed Ball presented to Team Captains, Bill Sebera and Charlie Grassl.

All-Stars and Orphans

Over A Half Century of Rangers Relief Pitching

Wayne M. Towers, PhD

Through 2024, Texas Rangers fans have enjoyed quality relief pitching for over a half century. A look at the careers of the team's Top Ten career saves leaders reveals both memories and surprises.[1]

Texas Rangers Top Ten Career Saves

PITCHER	SAVES	TEAM	YEARS
John Wetteland	150	Texas	1997–2000
Jeff Russell	134	Texas	1985–92, 1995–96
Francisco Cordero	117	Texas	2000–06
Neftali Feliz	93	Texas	2009–15
Ron Kline	83	Washington	1963–66
Joe Nathan	80	Texas	2012–13
Darold Knowles	64	Washington	1967–71
		Texas	1977
Tom Henke	58	Texas	1982–84, 1993–94
C.J. Wilson	52	Texas	2005–11
Shawn Tolleson	46	Texas	2014–16

Four of them combined for five All-Star appearances while with the Rangers (and 12 total, Wetteland 2, Cordero 2, Nathan 6, Henke 2) while adding to their 300 + career save resumes:[2]

- **John Wetteland** (150 of 330 career saves were with the Rangers) led the way with two All-Star appearances (1998–99) as a Texas Ranger. A premier reliever of the 1990s, he is often remembered as saving all four Yankee victories in the 1996 World Series, and for retiring prematurely.[3,4]

- **Francisco Cordero** (117 of 329) had his All-Star nod in 2004, but is often remembered as the subject of a viral video of being robbed at gunpoint in the Dominican Republic.[5,6]

- **Joe Nathan** (80 of 377) was a converted shortstop with two All-Star appearances (2012–13) during his stay in Texas.[7]

- **Tom Henke** (58 of 311) could have been a fourth, but his All-Star nods came with the Blue Jays (1987) and Cardinals (1995).[8,9]

The 300 + career save leaders are joined by another three All-Stars on the list:

- **Jeff Russell** (134 of 186) appeared as a Rangers All-Star twice (1988-89), but mainly figured in two key Rangers trades: from Cincinnati in 1985 with Duane Walker for Buddy Bell, and in 1992 to Oakland with Ruben Sierra and Bobby Witt for Jose Canseco.[10]

- **Neftali Feliz** (93 of 107) became both an All-Star and Rookie of the Year in 2010.[11]

- **C.J. Wilson** (all 52 of 52 career), another home-grown All-Star (2011) and auto racing enthusiast, was converted to a starter just before moving on to the Los Angeles Angels.[12]

Shawn Tolleson earned all 46 of his career saves with Texas, but was never accorded All-Star honors, and became an advocate for health-and-fitness lifestyles based on baseball training techniques.[13]

The other two pitchers on the list have their numbers split between the Rangers and their previous incarnation, the second Washington Senators (1961–71).[14] Despite a brief appearance in Texas (four saves in 1977), peripatetic left-hander Darold Knowles (seven franchises, 1965–80), is most known for his

Ron Kline   Darold Knowles

World Series heroics, helping the Oakland A's to three consecutive championships, 1973–75.[15] Knowles earns a spot in Rangers lore through 60 saves (1967–71). When the Senators became the Rangers in 1972, it creating a record-keeping conundrum with Knowles.[16] Sixty of his saves were as a Senator, but he added another four as a Ranger. Also, his franchise-related All-Star appearance (1969) was in a Washington uniform. Instead of a Texas fixture, he became a franchise mixture, orphaned by a decisive split in franchise history.

The other relief orphan is Ron Kline, with 83 of 108 career saves coming with Washington (1963–66). Kline was never an All-Star, but led the American League in 1965 with a respectable 29 saves.[17] (Ted Abernathy led the NL with 31, the first time 30 + saves led MLB.[18]) Despite the orphan status, Kline was a notable contributor to the franchise's relief-pitching history.

While orphans like Knowles and Kline can be easily overlooked by forward-looking fans, they were a part, albeit a peculiar part, of the franchise's ancestry, and part of its living relief history as well. ∎

Notes

1. Player data from Baseball Reference unless otherwise noted; "Texas Rangers Top 10 Career Pitching Leaders," https://www.baseball-reference.com/teams/TEX/leaders_pitch.shtml.
2. "Rangers All-Stars," http://www.mlb.com/rangers/history/all-star-players.
3. Mark Armour, "SABR 50 at 50: Record Setting Events [October 26, 1996: John Wetteland's fourth save in a World Series], https://sabr.org/50at50/records. Aaron Frisch, The History of the Texas Rangers (Mankato, MN: Creative Education, 2003), 21. Scott Nelson, "Individual Records by Decades: Wagner, Cobb, Williams, Ruth Lead the Way," Baseball Research Journal, 2000, https://sabr.org/journal/article/individual-records-by-decades-wagner-cobb-williams-ruth-lead-the-way/.
4. David Hooley, John Daniels and Sara Andrasik, "The Specialized Bullpen: History, Analysis, and Strategic Models for Success," Baseball Research Journal, Fall 2018, https://sabr.org/journal/article/the-specialized-bullpen-history-analysis-and-strategic-models-for-success/. Andrew Mearns, "Happy birthday, John Wetteland: A tribute to a 1996 Yankees hero," Pinstripe Alley, August 21, 2015, https://www.pinstripealley.com/2015/8/21/9188655/john-wetteland-yankees-biography-closer-world-series-mvp-mariano-rivera; John Pakutka and Elaina Pakutka, "More Relief Pitchers Belong in the Hall of Fame: Which Ones?" Baseball Research Journal, https://sabr.org/journal/article/more-relief-pitchers-belong-in-the-hall-of-fame-which-ones/.
5. "Francisco Cordero," BR Bullpen, https://www.baseball-reference.com/bullpen/ Francisco_Cordero; Pakutka, "More Relief Pitchers Belong in the Hall of Fame."
6. "Former MLB pitcher Francisco Cordero Reportedly a Victim of Armed Robbery in Dominican Republic," MARCA, https://www.marca.com/en/mlb/texas-rangers/2024/10/29/67214446ca4741ba628b45ce.html;

7. Erich Richter, "Ex-MLB Closer Francisco Cordero Robbed at Gunpoint in Stunning Video" New York Post, October 30, 2024. https://nypost.com/2024/10/30/ex-mlb-closer-francisco-cordero-robbed-at-gunpoint-video/.
8. David Bilmes, "Joe Nathan," SABR Bioproject, https://sabr.org/bioproj/person/joe-nathan/. Larry DeFillipo, "April 21, 1999: Joe Nathan's Famous: Converted Shortstop Brings the Mustard in Impressive Giants Debut," SABR Games Project, https://sabr.org/gamesproj/game/april-21-1999-joe-nathans-famous-converted-shortstop-brings-the-mustard-in-impressive-giants-debut/; Pakutka, "More Relief Pitchers Belong in the Hall of Fame."
9. "Tom Henke," https://www.baseball-reference.com/players/h/henketo01.shtml.
10. Eric Nadel, Texas Rangers: The Authorized History (Dallas, TX: Taylor Publishing Company, 1997), 135, 148, 189, 191, 193, 203. Pakutka, "More Relief Pitchers Belong in the Hall of Fame;" Jamie Seiko, "A Tale of Two Seasons: Bob Veale in 1971 and Tom Henke in 1987," 2001 Baseball Research Journal, https://sabr.org/journal/article/a-tale-of-two-seasons-bob-veale-in-1971-and-tom-henke-in-1987/, accessed February 1, 2025. "Tom Henke," Canadian Baseball Hall of Fame and Museum, https://baseballhalloffame.ca/hall-of-famer/tom-henke/. "Tom Henke." Missouri Sports Hall of Fame, https://mosportshalloffame.com/inductees/tom-henke-2/. Eric Vickrey, "Tom Henke," SABR Bio Project, https://sabr.org/bioproj/person/tom-henke/.
11. "Jeff Russell," BR Bullpen, https://www.baseball-reference.com/bullpen/Jeff_Russell; Nadel, Texas Rangers, 7, 152, 166, 209, 211.
12. Bilmes, "Joe Nathan."; Clay Coppedge, A Lone Star Diamond History from Town Teams to the Big Leagues (Charleston, SC: The Hickory Press, 2012), 164, 167, 169, 171, 177. "Rangers' closer Neftali Feliz Wins AL Jackie Robinson Rookie of the Year," BBWAA, November 15, 2010, https://bbwaa.com/10-al-roy/. Jim Reeves, Dugouts and Diamonds: Heartaches and Triumphs with the Texas Rangers (Fort Worth, TX: Berkeley Place Books, 2022), 136. Kevin Sutton, The Fall and Rise of the Texas Rangers (Dallas, TX: OKF Books, 2015), 45, 87, 112, 129, 132, 138, 198. Texas Rangers Shock the World (Englewood Cliffs, NJ: A360MEDIA, 2014), 63. Noah Wright, "Forgotten Pittsburgh Pirates: Neftali Feliz," Rumbunter, https://rumbunter.com/2020/05/19/forgotten-pittsburgh-pirates-neftali-feliz/.
13. "CJ Wilson," Speed Secrets, https://speedsecrets.com/137-cj-wilson-pro-baseball-player-to-race-driver/.
14. Larry Hagner, "Health Is Wealth With Shawn Tolleson," The Dad Edge, May 16, 2021, https://thedadedge.com/health-is-wealth/.
15. Conor Buckley, Texas Rangers: Stars, Stats, History, and More! (Mankato, MN: The Child's World, 2019), 9; Coppedge, A Lone Star Diamond History, 68, 91; James R. Hartley, Washington's Expansion Senators (1961–1971) (Germantown, MD: Corduroy Press, 1997;1998), iii; Ethan Olson, Rangers All-Time Greats (Mendota Heights, MN: Press Box Books, 2024), 5.
16. Austin Gisriel, "Darold Knowles," SABR Bio Project, https://sabr.org/bioproj/person/darold-knowles; "Darold Knowles," Missouri Sports Hall of Fame, https://mosportshalloffame.com/inductees/darold-knowles/.
17. Josh Anderson, The Texas Rangers (Parker, CO: The Child's World, 2025), 7. Nadel, Texas Rangers, 50–59; Reeves, Dugouts and Diamonds, 193; Texas Rangers Shock the World, 58.
18. Bill Nowlin, "Ron Kline," SABR Bio Project. https://sabr.org/bioproj/person/ron-kline.
19. "Year-by-Year Top-Tens Leaders & Records for Saves," https://baseball-reference.com/leaders/SV_top_ten.shtml.

Jack Allen

Baseball in the Land of "Gushers" and Cowboys

Jarrod D. Schenewark, PhD

Jack Allen, former head coach at Ranger College and Tarleton State University, is a member of the National Junior College Baseball Coaches Hall of Fame (inducted 1986) and the American Baseball Coaches Association Hall of Fame (inducted 2000). Allen served as head coach for 23 years at Ranger College (1963–85) and an additional 13 seasons (1990–2002) as head coach at Tarleton State University. He coached at the National Junior College Athletic Association (NJCAA), National Association of Intercollegiate Athletics (NAIA), and the National Collegiate Athletic Association (NCAA) levels in Texas. By highlighting the life of Coach Allen, this paper seeks to spotlight intercollegiate baseball in Texas from the 1960s to the end of the twentieth century, especially at Ranger College and Tarleton State University.

EARLY LIFE AND INFLUENCES

Jack Allen was born and raised in Ranger, Texas, about 85 miles west of Fort Worth. The town derived its name when members of the Texas Rangers law enforcement agency camped nearby sometime in the 1870s. By 1879, a tent city had been created, which was gradually replaced with wooden and brick houses and business buildings until it had a population of nearly a thousand. The town drastically changed in October 1917 when the oil well known as McClesky No. 1 came in as a "gusher" and brought about an oil boom. With other oil wells producing, an estimated 30,000 residents called Ranger home by the early 1920s.[1] With such an energetic population, a minor league baseball team—the Ranger Nitros—was formed to compete in the Class D West Texas League, 1920–22.[2] However, the oil soon dried up and the population rapidly declined to 6,208 by the 1930 census.

Jack Allen was born July 28, 1935. He played baseball at Ranger High School, from which he graduated in 1953, and then pitched for the local American Legion team known as the Eagles. He graduated from Ranger Junior College in 1956 and then signed a professional contract to play in Mexico. He stated that "after three years of that league, I decided I better go back and finish my education." He finished his undergraduate degree in Physical Education at Sam Houston State in 1963.[3]

Immediately upon graduation, he became the first baseball coach at Ranger College. His salary of $3,014 a year required him to also serve as an assistant for football and basketball, and teach five classes.[4]

Reflecting back on his career, Allen stated that the three most influential figures to teach him about life and baseball were his father, his high school coach Stubby Warden, and college coach Andy Cohen.[5] Cohen played for the New York Giants 1926–29, managed the Philadelphia Phillies for one game in 1960, and became the head coach at the Texas Western College in 1963.[6]

RANGER COLLEGE

Ranger Junior College opened in 1926 and remained a small junior college offering two-year degrees. It became known as an athlete's college. Allen coached at Ranger College for a total of 23 seasons, compiling an 814–399 record, winning nine conference championships, seven regional championships, and four state championships. The peak of his tenure came during the mid-1970s when he took his team to the NJCAA World Series in 1973, 1975, 1976, and 1978.[7]

Ranger defeated Gulf Coast Community College of Panama City, Florida, to win the national championship in 1973. The team's star, Donnie Moore of Lubbock, Texas, pitched thirty innings with an ERA of 1.20. He also set a tournament record for pitching victories, going 4–0 during the series, and finished the season with an 18–1 record. Moore was named the most valuable player and would go on to have a 13-year career in the majors.[8]

Allen's team would once again travel to Grand Junction, Colorado, in 1978 and win a championship. But the trip to Grand Junction would not be solely about baseball. The day before the championship game against Yavapai College from Prescott, Arizona, it was expected the team would take batting and infield practice. Jack, however took his team up into the mountains and had a picnic. He did not want them even thinking about baseball. He said that "you can grind the players every day, but you have to give them a break every once in a while."[9]

He had high hopes for returning to the NJCAA World Series in 1983. Players slated for the squad included Jim Morris, future pitcher for the Tampa Bay Rays, and Ellis Burks, who went on to have an eighteen-year major league career. Both were taken in first rounds of the 1983 MLB amateur drafts, Burks in the regular draft and Morris in the secondary draft.[10]

During this period of winning championships, Allen was also busy with other endeavors. Beginning in 1973, he worked as a part-time scout for the Philadelphia Phillies, Chicago Cubs, and San Diego Padres. He was elected mayor of Ranger and served a four-year term starting in 1977.[11] Also in 1977, he managed the McAllen Dusters of the Lone Star League (Class A) during the second half of the season, which lasted from June through August.[12]

Jack retired from Ranger College in 1985. He was elected to the NJCAA Baseball Coaches Association Hall of Fame in 1986. Reflecting back on his retirement, he stated that "retiring was the stupidest thing I've ever done." However, Allen's retirement would not last for long because he "missed the association with the kids and [he] missed the competition."[13]

PERSONALITY AND REPUTATION

Jack had developed a stellar reputation as a "baseball guy," with contacts throughout Texas and the United States.[14] How respected was Jack? "If he told scouts, 'There is a kid who had the ability to play major league baseball,' somewhere in the draft that kid would get drafted."[15] "If he gave you a recommendation, you could guarantee that athlete would be able to play somewhere."[16]

Even though he was known as being ornery, tough, and crusty, he was offered the opportunity to work in professional baseball where he also had developed many friendships. One afternoon in the 1970s, Chip Davis, a local umpire, received a call to come over to Jack's home. When Davis arrived, Allen was sitting on the front porch with Whitey Herzog and Billy Martin, talking baseball.[17] Another longtime friend was Bobby Bragan, the former Brooklyn Dodger, and manager of the Fort Worth Cats and the Atlanta Braves, among other teams. Bragan in the early 1990s established a foundation to encourage youth to stay in school and go to college. In the years that Allen coached at Tarleton State, Bragan would drive to home games and set up a tent with memorabilia for a silent auction in order to raise funds for his foundation.[18]

While he may have been "tough and crusty," Allen was a very talented speaker who had the ability to get an audience to relax, blending his messages with humor that allowed listeners to feel a bond with him. He received various invitations to speak to local groups: After winning national junior college coach of the year in 1973, he was invited to speak before the Rotary Club in Nocona, Texas.[19]

A common remembrance of all who knew him was his love of cigars and chewing tobacco, which he would smoke and chew at the same time. When Jim Morris (the ballplayer portrayed in the Disney movie, *The Rookie*) first met Coach Allen, he described him as "short [with] a cigar in one cheek and a wad of chew in the other."[20] During Allen's tenure as a coach, the NJCAA and NAIA had no rules against tobacco use. However, in 1994 the NCAA prohibition of tobacco products came into effect while Allen was at Tarleton. While the rules changed, he did not.[21]

TARLETON STATE UNIVERSITY

Tarleton State University is located 40 miles southeast of Ranger in Stephenville. Stephenville is the self-proclaimed "Cowboy Capital of the World." The university traces its history back to 1899 when it opened as John Tarleton College. Baseball was one of the earliest sports at the college, with intramural games starting in 1899 and the first intercollegiate season in 1904.[22] The sport was dropped in 1928. Jesse "T-Bone" Winters was the most prominent player during this period. Winters was a right-handed pitcher who totaled five years in the major leagues playing for the New York Giants and the Philadelphia Phillies, compiling a record of 13–24.[23]

Baseball made a comeback in 1950 and was led by Cecil Ballow, a former all-conference shortstop at Texas A&M and member of the Southwest Conference

Jack Allen

79

championship team of 1942. Ballow was the Dean of Men at Tarleton when he was tasked with resurrecting the baseball program in 1950. Ballow coached until 1960 when he led Tarleton to the second-place finish at the 1960 National Junior College Finals in Grand Junction, Colorado. The following year, Tarleton was designated a four-year college and changed its nickname from the "Plowboys" to the "Texans." In 1969, baseball was once again discontinued for "financial considerations."[24]

BASEBALL IS REBORN AND ALLEN COACHES ONCE AGAIN

Baseball remained absent from Tarleton until 1988. The rebirth of the intercollegiate game was part of the guiding vision of Dr. Barry B. Thompson who, with increasing enrollment and new infrastructure, decided that baseball should be brought back for the 1988 season. He had in mind Jack Allen as coach. But this was not to be, as Lee Driggers was hired to be the new coach.[25]

Athletic director Joe Gillespie had interviewed Allen, but he also interviewed Driggers, who was coming off a second state high school championship at Brenham High School. Knowing that a new program would require hands-on work with facilities, he felt that Driggers had more energy to accomplish the task versus the recently retired Allen. Gillespie recalled that "We were looking for someone to do it themselves. My mentality was that I am the head coach—you do it yourself. I was head coach of track and field, when we had a cinder track, and it was up to me to line the track for the meets. I expected it would be the same for the baseball coach."[26]

Driggers did a great job the first year. A new field, named after Cecil Ballow, was built and dedicated on March 5, 1988. However, after the first year, Driggers received an offer from a Division I institution and left. Bill Clay was brought in to place him, but for a number of reasons, he was let go after one year.[27]

Two years after the initial interview, Allen was hired with 60% of his responsibility allocated to coaching baseball and 40% to teaching activity courses such as golf. Upon being hired, Gillespie recalled that Allen "was very gracious, calling and thanking" him for the opportunity. Gillespie acknowledged that he had made a mistake, but Allen was not a man to hold a grudge. As to the upkeep, building, and improvements needed on the field, Allen explained that "I'm not going to do it myself, but I'm going to get it done."[28] He did so with the hiring of his assistant Trey Felan, who would weld fencing, maintain the field, and create a locker room from an old chicken coop that was on site.[29]

Allen guided the team through becoming a member of the NAIA and qualifying for the national tournament in his second season in 1992.[30] One member of this team was Chad Fox, whom Allen converted from a third baseman to a pitcher. Fox was invited to the 1992 Olympic trials and went on to win a World Series ring with the Florida Marlins.[31]

Allen also led the Texans into the NCAA era and to the top of the conference with the school's first NCAA regional tournament appearance in 1998, and the first Lone Star Conference division championship the following season. He went 418–309–3 and won two Lone Star Conference South Division titles and two outright conference championships. He garnered his 1,200th overall collegiate coaching victory against Eastern New Mexico University.[32]

Following Allen's thirteen years at Tarleton as head coach, his assistant Trey Felan held the post for six years, and then his former pitcher Bryan Conger for ten. Allen assisted Conger for two years. Thus he made a direct impact on the program for 29 out of his last 37 years.

Allen passed away on May 27, 2016. Dozens of former players attended his funeral and honored him, each placing a baseball in his casket. Said Lonn Reisman, "Jack Allen was a great baseball coach and just an outstanding gentleman, and in every area of his life demonstrated that he was a true hall of famer."[33] ∎

Acknowledgment

The author wishes to thank Steve Simpson for providing the inspiration for the topic and valuable support in the various interviews that made this paper possible.

Notes

1. Noel Wiggins, "The History of Ranger, Texas: From Oil Boom to Modern Day," Texas State Historical Association. https://www.tshaonline.org/handbook/entries/ranger-tx, accessed January 12, 2025.
2. Mark Presswood, "Professional Baseball Had an Early Start in Small Towns," *Texas Almanac 2008–2009*, 189–91. https://www.texasalmanac.com/drupal-backup/images/almanac-feature/Minor_League_in_Texas-TxAlm0809.pdf, accessed January 20, 2025.
3. Jeromya Beltman, "Allen Celebrates 30 Years of Coaching Baseball," *The J-TAC*, November 2, 1995. https://texashistory.unt.edu/ark:/67531/metapth141862/m1/6/, acessed January 12, 2025.
4. Beltman.
5. Beltman.
6. Gary Gillette and Pete Palmer, *The 2006 ESPN Baseball Encyclopedia* (New York: Sterling Press, 2006) 916–17.
7. "RHS Class of 1953," Ranger Exes Memorial. http://www.rangerexesmemorial.com/yrs50-77.htm#1953, accessed May 16 2025.
8. *1974 NJCAA Baseball World Series Official Program*. https://jucogj.org/documents/2018/2/22//1974.pdf?id=33, accessed January 15, 2025.
9. Lonn Reisman, personal interview, January 17, 2025.

10. Morris was the fourth pick, Burks the 20th. *Jim Morris, The Oldest Rookie: Big Leagues Dreams from a Small-Town Guy* (Boston: Little, Brown, and Company, 2001).

11. "RHS Class of 1953."

12. "McAllen Dusters," Baseball Reference. https://www.baseball-reference.com/bullpen/McAllen_Dusters, accessed January 16, 2025.

13. Beltman.

14. Joe Gillespie, personal interview, January 28, 2025.

15. Reisman interview.

16. Victor Sauceda, personal interview, January 28, 2025.

17. Byron Anderson, personal interview, January 27, 2025.

18. Reisman interview.

19. Edgar Hays, "Jack Allen, Ranger College Ball Coach, Will Speak at Rotary Club," *Nocona News*, December 27, 1973. https://texashistory.unt.edu/ark:/67531/metapth1493621/m1/3/. Accessed January 12, 2025.

20. *Jim Morris, The Oldest Rookie: Big Leagues Dreams from a Small-Town Guy* (Boston: Little, Brown, and Company, 2001).

21. Steve Simpson, personal interview, January 28, 2025.

22. Christopher Guthrie, *John Tarleton and His Legacy: The History of Tarleton State University, 1899–1999* (Tapestry Press: Acton, MA).

23. *2022 Tarleton Texan Baseball Media Guide.* https://tarletonsports.com/documents/2022/2/25//Tarleton___Baseball_Media_Guide_2022_small.pdf?id=4593, accessed January 28, 2025.

24. Christopher Guthrie, *John Tarleton and His Legacy: The History of Tarleton State University, 1899–1999* (Tapestry Press: Acton, MA).

25. Gillespie interview.

26. Gillespie interview.

27. Gillespie interview.

28. Gillespie interview.

29. Trey Felan, personal interview, January 20, 2025.

30. Michael Marbach, "Fox Selected for 1992 U.S. Olympic Tryouts," *The J-TAC*, September 26, 1991. https://texashistory.unt.edu/ark:/67531/metapth141757/m1/5/, accessed January 28, 2025.

31. *2022 Tarleton Texan Baseball Media Guide.*

32. Jacob Withee, Correspondence with Author, January 28, 2025.

33. Brad Keith, "Tarleton Hall of Fame Baseball Coach Jack Allen Passes Away," *The Flash Today Erath County*, May 28, 2016, https://theflashtoday.com/2016/05/28/tarleton-hall-of-fame-baseball-coach-jack-allen-passes-away/. Accessed January 12, 2025.

A Day from Hell at the Office

Lenny Randle's Attack on Frank Lucchesi Created Wounds That Never Healed

Daniel VanDeMortel

WHAT WOULD HAPPEN TO YOU?

Reality check: Playing professional baseball is a job. It requires supreme skill, demanding hours, cultural fit, and a balancing act to win approval from demanding, unpredictable bosses who control when you play, even if you'll be traded. The pressure can become overwhelming.

When you feel the walls closing in at your job have you ever considered letting some rage fly? Maybe even escalating things physically with a higher authority or a subordinate? What would be your breaking point? What would happen if you crossed it?

Texas Rangers manager Frank Lucchesi and utility player Lenny Randle once had a heated dispute over who would be the team's starting second baseman. Violence, litigation, and acrimony followed.

A LONG CLIMB

Frank Lucchesi paid heavy dues. Born just before the Depression into the consummate Italian-American neighborhood of San Francisco's North Beach, he was raised by his mother after his father died when Frank was only one. He worked at produce markets at 5:00 AM before reporting to high school at 9:00. Baseball skills were likewise honed the hard way: Speed and guile advanced his 5'8" stocky frame toward a career. During 13 years as a player buried in the minors, off-season delivery and bartending gigs supplemented scant baseball earnings. Brain surgery removed a blood clot suffered from being hit on the head by a line drive. "I started as a player in Triple-A and went backward," he once quipped.[1]

Luck arrived in 1956 when the Philadelphia Phillies hired Lucchesi to manage in their farm system, which he did for 14 seasons. He earned a colorful, fiery reputation with a track record of fines and suspensions. He won six pennants and was a five-time manager of the year. In 1970, fate smiled again when he was promoted to manage the Phillies, to the delight of the city's Italian-American population. No awards were forthcoming. The rebuilding 63-win team improved to

73–88 in his first year, then retreated. A 26–50 start in 1972 led to his dismissal.

Lucchesi managed Triple-A Oklahoma City in 1973 before becoming third base coach for the Rangers' volatile manager, Billy Martin. Martin guided the team to second place in the AL West. The following year, though, brought regression and conflict with owner Brad Corbett and general manager Dan O'Brien. After 95 games, Martin was fired. Lucchesi took over, despite Martin's warning not to take the job.

GLUE GUY

Lenny Randle was raised in the 1950s and 1960s in the then middle-class Black Compton neighborhood south of Los Angeles. His longshoreman father and seamstress mother taught their eight children to value education, which Randle achieved as an All-American baseball player at Arizona State, where he earned a BS. Drafted by the Washington Senators in 1970, the 5'10", 175-pound first-round pick straddled the minors and majors before flowering under Martin in 1974, batting .302 and stealing 26 bases as a switch-hitting, multi-position glue guy integral to the team's success. He credited his dedication and sacrifice to Martin and former manager Ted Williams. "Those guys played baseball as if it was war. Each game brought the intensity of combat....It was about the team and winning the game."[2]

Randle repeated another strong campaign at second and wherever-else-you-need-me, even catcher, in 1975. He aided managerial flexibility, was rarely injured, and was the team's fourth-best player in WAR over the two seasons.[3] Low key and friendly, he became one of the most popular Rangers and was rewarded with a two-year, $80,000/year contract.

Martin's departure, though, meant the loss of Randle's ideal boss. His contributions over 142 games during the 1976 season—primarily but not exclusively at second—delivered .224/.286/273, a negative WAR, shaky fielding, and an unproductive stolen base success rate.[4] The Rangers experienced another losing campaign. Despite versatility at seven positions, Randle's role was precarious.

A NEW EMPLOYEE ARRIVES

A phenom waited in the wings: Bump Wills, son of legendary shortstop and base-stealing king Maury Wills of the 1960s Los Angeles Dodgers.[5] Like Randle, Wills was a switch-hitting infielder who starred at Arizona State. Unlike Randle, he zoomed through the minors and was tabbed during the winter by Corbett, Lucchesi, and media prognosticators as the club's 1977 second baseman, confirmed by a *Sports Illustrated* cover story touting him among baseball's exciting rookie crop.

Upon arrival to camp in Pompano Beach, Florida, Randle expressed anxiety. "No more Mr. Nice Guy. No more turning the other cheek. I'm not going to hold it in anymore. If they don't want to play me, I'll ask to be traded. I'm not going to be a bench warmer or a cheerleader."[6]

Lucchesi played Wills twice as often as Randle, eventually officially naming him the starter. With all-star Toby Harrah at third and free agent Bert Campaneris at shortstop, Randle had no infield position to regularly play. "I am the Phantom Ranger….If I wanted to be a reserve, I'd have joined the National Guard…. Too bad I'm not Jackie Robinson's nephew, maybe I'd get more respect around here," he icily observed.[7] Lucchesi salved the wound, praising Randle's work ethic and admitting he should have said Wills could earn the spot rather than appointing him prematurely based solely on scouting reports. Nonetheless, the die was cast.

"PUNK"

On March 24, Randle arrived at Municipal Park before an exhibition game against the Kansas City Royals and packed up his gear, ready to confront Lucchesi and leave camp to potentially force a trade. Teammates Bert Blyleven, Gaylord Perry, and Mike Hargrove intervened, successfully convincing him to stay and to avoid Lucchesi.

Frank Lucchesi

Sportswriters smelled a story. After a 5–3 loss, they informed Lucchesi about Randle's intended departure. Little salve was applied. "If Lenny Randle, or any other player for that matter, wants to come in with his bags packed and tell me he's leaving, then I reach over and shake his hand, ask him what time his plane leaves and wish him luck," he offered. "There's no way that Frank Lucchesi is going to kiss anybody's ass or ask them to stay in camp," he colorfully emphasized.[8] Then a headline quotation: "I'm sick and tired of some punks making $80,000 a year moaning and groaning about their situation."[9]

Lucchesi did not apologize for these intemperate remarks but privately told team officials he wished he had used a different word than "punk." The next day, O'Brien met with Randle to talk him off the ledge. The following day, Randle met privately with Lucchesi, maintaining he'd been lied to and wanted out. According to Randle, he asked what Lucchesi meant by "punk"—considered an insult in Black vernacular that implied homosexuality. Lucchesi replied it had not been meant in a derogatory manner. Some press accounts indicated Randle joked with players and the media about the term and didn't seem upset about it. Yet, on March 27, Randle warned, allegedly while smiling, "I'm a volcano ready to erupt."[10]

FLURRY

Lucchesi arrived in street clothes during batting practice at Orlando's Tinker Field before the Rangers March 28 preseason game against the Minnesota Twins. As he talked with a scout near the grandstand, Randle approached to start a conversation. Per Randle, Lucchesi said, "What do you want to talk to me about, punk?"[11] Lucchesi later claimed to have never said "punk" but rather, responding to Randle's beef over not being given a fair shake, indicated they should move near the visitor's dugout along the third base line to talk. Their conversation lasted a minute, tops, with no outward indication of trouble. Until…

Whack! Randle swung, landing a right-hand punch solidly under Lucchesi's right eye. Then a left hit the right cheekbone. Lucchesi landed on his right hip while lifting his left arm to block further blows.[12] The 28-year-old Randle hovered over his 50-year-old manager, swinging wildly, landing body shots. Most players were 10 yards away with their backs turned. Campaneris arrived belatedly to break things up. Lucchesi was bleeding, in pain. Randle backed off, screaming an obscenity at anyone and no one. Outfielder Ken Henderson had to be restrained from attacking him. As other players and personnel swarmed, Randle grabbed a bat from the rack, trotted to third, dropped it, then ran to the outfield to do wind sprints. O'Brien escorted him off the field and suspended him later that day, pending an investigation.

Lucchesi's right eye turned black and blue, and blood trickled from his mouth. An equipment manager drove him to nearby Mercy Hospital, where he was diagnosed with a right-cheekbone triple fracture, cerebral concussion, lip laceration, back pain, a damaged rib, and dental injuries.[13]

Meanwhile, observers assessed the ferocious event. One reporter wrote the five-second flurry of Randle's punches, "hung there suspended in time, like slow motion or instant replay or the old newsreel films of the Hindenburg breaking apart in the dark Jersey skies."[14]

"All I wanted to do was talk....I hate that this had to happen, but I guess he took my passiveness for granted. All a man wants is respect. It was just impulsive. I'm not Judas and he's not Jesus Christ," Randle theorized.[15] He insisted "punk" provoked the attack and apologized to O'Brien, who remained unsatisfied.

Harrah, who dined with Randle later that evening, believed Randle's apology was sincere. But his support had limitations. "All of us on the club agreed that you don't hit an older person like that."[16]

Blyleven's recollection pointed toward premeditation. He claimed Randle asked him that morning what would happen if he hit someone. "I told him if he hit a player, he would be suspended and if he hit the manager, he'd probably never play again," he replied. "Lenny said he told Frank to protect himself and then he went at it....He told me that when he goes to bed at night now he won't have any trouble sleeping. He feels he did the right thing."[17]

As for Lucchesi, he later insisted that he was "Sunday sucker punched" by "a sneak attack—worse than Pearl Harbor."[18] He claimed he was staring at the ground, hands in his hip pockets, when he was attacked. Randle clapped back that Lucchesi couldn't talk without using his hands.

Ode to irony: Post-attack accounts revealed Lucchesi had selected Randle to start the game.

SURGERY, FINGER-POINTING, SUSPENSION

While coach Connie Ryan managed the team, Lucchesi underwent cheekbone surgery and facial plastic surgery. Recovery was slow and painful during five days of hospitalization. Blackness persisted around his right eye. Sleep proved difficult because of the facial surgery and back and chest pain.

Randle flew to Phoenix to meet with his agent, attorney, and MLB Players Association counsel Dick

Lenny Randle

Moss. "I'm a religious person. I've never done anything like this before....I am a very proud and sensitive person, and felt I was being lied to," he explained to a reporter.[19] He wired an apology to Lucchesi and his teammates, which Lucchesi refused to accept: "My only wish is that I was 10 years younger so I could handle this situation myself."[20] Some of Lucchesi's San Francisco and Philadelphia Italian-American friends also charitably volunteered to assist with the handling.

The Rangers ramped up damage control. Corbett expressed his displeasure to executive vice president Eddie Robinson and O'Brien. "I told them that I wanted to get rid of Randle. I knew there was a boiling point. I think we made a terrible mistake."[21] On April 4 in Arlington, Dallas reporters "Blackie" Sherrod and Alan Stone, and players Tom Grieve, Dave May, Sandy Alomar, and Blyleven testified at a private investigative hearing. Neither Lucchesi nor Randle appeared. Findings were to be forwarded to a three-man arbitration panel on April 8 charged to evaluate a grievance Randle filed regarding his suspension. On April 5, the Rangers suspended Randle for 30 days, retroactive to March 28, and fined him $10,000—then a record for baseball—and $13,407.90 in lost wages.[22]

Efforts to trade Randle faltered before the season's start on April 7, a 10-inning victory against the Orioles in Baltimore. Lucchesi was back managing the team. Wills drove in the winning run and would produce at a .287/.361/.410 clip, finishing third in Rookie of the Year balloting.[23]

Hours before the game, Randle dropped his appeal and accepted his fine. He also offered to have Lucchesi receive the $10,000 owed to the Rangers. "He could apologize from the Golden Gate Bridge with the fog rolling in and I wouldn't accept it," Lucchesi snarled back.[24]

HELLO NEW YORK, GOODBYE TEXAS

On April 26, just before his suspension expired, Randle

was traded to the New York Mets for $50,000 and a player to be named later.[25] The Mets quickly signed him to a five-year, $85,000/year deal with annual increases eventually escalating to over $100,000/per year. "The Lord gives a second chance, so should we....He lost his head once, and I don't think it will ever happen again," Mets chairman of the board Donald Grant predicted.[26] Randle proved Grant correct that season, behaving like a model citizen, excelling at third, and posting .304/.383/.404 and the team's highest WAR. "I think they liked my bat, my glove, my legs, and the fact that I get my uniform dirty. I'd be perfect for a Tide commercial," he joked.[27]

Later that day, Randle surrendered to police on an aggravated battery charge brought in Orange County, Florida, carrying a potential 15-year prison term and/or $10,000 fine. In July, the charge was reduced to misdemeanor battery since Lucchesi had suffered no permanent damage. Incarceration was waived. Randle pleaded no contest and received the maximum $1,050 fine, provided he covered Lucchesi's medical expenses. "You should change your profession to boxing and get in the ring and give your opponent an equal opportunity," Circuit Judge Maurice Paul scolded. "Not only organized baseball but organized sports has suffered as a result of your action."[28]

Lucchesi's role also suffered. The Rangers started 31–31, after which, facilitated by a clash with Robinson, he was fired, a move he attributed partly to Randle's attack. Managerial musical chairs led to the dysfunctional shuffling of two managers within a week before coach Billy Hunter piloted the club to a surprising 94–68 finish.[29]

TRIAL

Disappointed with Randle's minimal punishment, Lucchesi filed a civil suit in state circuit court in Orlando, seeking approximately $200,000 in compensation and to make an example of Randle to support baseball's integrity and prevent future similar attacks.[30] "I'm not a bitter guy, but he's been on easy street ever since," he complained.[31]

Five days before the case began on December 5, 1978, Randle fired attorney E. Thom Rumberger. Randle regarded the case as a civil rights matter and feared being tried by a Southern judge and jury. Rumberger disagreed, considering it a matter of provoked alleged assault and battery. As trial commenced, Judge Bernard Muszynski denied Randle's delay request to obtain new counsel. A jury of three men, three women—all White and middle-aged—was selected from a pool of 21 while Randle watched two potential

Black jurors get stricken by Lucchesi's attorneys. A 15-minute recess was called. A desperate situation certainly called for a relief specialist. Randle's wife, Jackie, saved the day, acting upon a last-minute referral to cross the street to request J. Cheney Mason.[32] Mason was in his first decade of practice that would eventually make him an unconventional but renowned criminal defense attorney. He did not regularly wear a suit, so he learned case details from Jackie while driving home to don one. Once at the courthouse, he hurried into court, 10 minutes late, with co-counsel Donald Lykkebak and Randle, who carried a cardboard box of papers and files.

Cheney arrived as treating plastic surgeon Dr. Richard Nazareth testified about Lucchesi's injuries. Shortly thereafter, a Rangers team dentist described damage to Lucchesi's teeth.

Sherrod later confirmed "punk" was an uncomplimentary term directed at Randle but was unaware of its homosexual implications. Recalling Lucchesi's provocative March 24 remarks, he correctly mentioned Lucchesi had also said, "I don't blame Lenny. He just wants to play"—sentiments ignored in most news coverage.[33] He agreed Randle was a peaceful and law-abiding individual who had never previously lost his temper.

For the defense, Blyleven repeated his previous accounts implying premeditation although admitted there was pre-fight questioning around camp whether Randle was being treated fairly. Harrah added that being called a "punk" disturbed Randle, and that teammates maliciously ribbed him for it. Grieve countered that the ribbing was lighthearted, designed to relieve building tension.

Lucchesi testified for two hours. He swore that "punk" meant "wise guy" and did not refer to Randle. He denied racial tension with Randle and explained away his comments as occurring the day he returned some players to the minors. "Here's a bunch of kids making five, six thousand a year and they'd stay and play in the big league for nothing," which is why he said he was tired of "$80,000 punks who say play me or trade me. Give me $80,000 a year for the next 10 years, I'll sit on the bench and keep my mouth shut."[34]

Randle's legal team portrayed Lucchesi as racist, noting the club's decline from 13 Black players to four during his tenure. They claimed Lucchesi was "famous for antics, hysterics, and being an aggressive and hot-tempered man," and called former Rangers third baseman Roy Howell to testify that on May 7 the recuperating Lucchesi had been ejected for his participation in a Royals-Rangers brawl.[35]

Randle took the stand for an hour to give an itemized accounting of his assets and liabilities, and how his mounting legal bills had hampered his ability to monetarily assist his siblings. He was supported by a Who's Who of baseball stars, including St. Louis Cardinals legendary speedster Lou Brock and recently retired home run king Henry Aaron. Brock explained "punk" meant "queer, sissy, unfit" with a homosexual connotation.[36] Lucchesi's reputation was "an explosive type of personality," he added.[37] Aaron offered advice but did not take the stand. Martin was also present, scheduled to testify.

Civil rights activist Jesse Jackson appeared, too, determined to ensure Randle received fair legal treatment in the nationally publicized case. Mason warned Jackson about excessive interference. "I'm not a racist. We're doing a great job and we're going to win this goddamn case. But if you go out there…in downtown Orlando and start parading and stuff, I'm gonna lose."[38] Oh, what chutzpah for a newly-minted attorney to request a prominent civil rights leader to relinquish his First Amendment right! But trial is theater, with roaming, sensitive jurors always on the alert. Perhaps sensing that, Jackson supported Randle with court attendance, not public demonstrations amidst camera-toting spectators.[39]

During trial, Mason received a telephone request to meet baseball commissioner Bowie Kuhn and two associates at a nearby hotel. He warily agreed. The encounter proved aggressively canine: "One of these giants, alongside him is another giant, they're there protecting [Kuhn] against me. I looked at them and they were not friendly, they were not welcoming, they were not anything. I just looked at one guy and I said, you know, I don't know what your job is, but it is clear to every one of you all that you can beat me up, easily. But here's one thing, I will fucking leave bite marks on you."[40] Kuhn tried to convince Mason to have Randle pay damages to avoid further negative publicity. Mason told Kuhn to pay them and exited.

Lucchesi received a phone request, too, from an unidentified caller who threatened his family and suggested he drop the suit. Before the trial's fourth day began on December 8, a $20,000 settlement was reached in Muszynski's chambers: significantly less than Lucchesi's desired outcome due to Randle's effective counsel and, perhaps, the telephone warning. The Court forbade discussion of the terms. Martin, who partially blamed Lucchesi for his dismissal from the Rangers, reportedly contributed $10,000 while Randle's mother-in-law offered to pay the rest.

Lucchesi and Randle, shedding tears, read prepared statements admitting their legal ordeal had been trying. "I want you to know I don't wish him bad luck in the future. I'm sorry it happened, for his family and mine. I only hope something like this never happens again in baseball," Lucchesi said.[41] "Now we can return to the game we've dedicated our lives to," Randle responded. "I think this proves people of all colors and from all walks of life can settle their differences." He turned to Lucchesi, offering, "I guess there is nothing to do now but shake hands so I can go hide my tears and you can hide yours."[42] They did and shared a quick embrace.

AN AWKWARD REUNION

In 1992, Lucchesi and Randle met at an Old-Timers Game at Comiskey Park before a Rangers game against the Chicago White Sox. They shook hands, exchanged pleasantries, and kneeled next to each other for a team photo. During the game, Randle hit a triple, slid, and hugged Lucchesi as he was coaching third. "I guess if [Soviet Prime Minister Mikhail] Gorbachev can come to America and make peace, we can too," Randle reckoned.[43]

Lucchesi paused the happy ending. "I'm a forgiving person, a second-chance kind of guy. If he were insane, or on drugs or drunk or something, I can understand. But not when it was premeditated. I'm not vindictive. I'd forgive anybody, but this…this was too hard on my family."[44] His son, in attendance, concurred, vividly recalling the day at age 12 when he learned of the assault upon arriving home and seeing O'Brien's wife and another woman comforting his weeping mother.

EXITING THE STAGE

Randle's 1977 Mets success proved fleeting. He was released the following year, then bounced around with the Yankees, Cubs, and Mariners. He became the first American to play in Italy and later joined the Senior Professional Baseball Association. He mastered five languages, conducted a baseball academy, practiced yoga and karate, and dabbled in comedy and hip-hop. *Rolling Stone* named him baseball's version of "The Most Interesting Man in the World" and the MLB Network produced a television special calling him the "Forrest Gump of Baseball."[45] Boundless energy and survival on little sleep earned him the nickname "Cappuccino." "After I die there will be plenty of time to sleep," he reasoned.[46] That time arrived in December 2024.

Lucchesi filled various minor and major league roles managing and scouting, and even briefly returned to coach the Rangers in 1979–80. He retired from baseball in 1989 and, except for the 1992 encounter, refrained from publicly obsessing about the 1977 event. He died in 2019.

SCORECARD

The Lucchesi-Randle conflict was a tragic sequence of bad decisions by both parties, occurring during a rapidly changing baseball landscape. Race and free agency underpinned the dispute. Even if the evidence supporting Lucchesi's racism was not as definitive as Randle's legal team argued, certainly cultural understanding was lacking over how his words would be perceived by a Black man. This awareness deficit, cutting both ways between the races, still exists. Free agency-induced salaries do, too. But free agency was in its infancy in the mid-1970s, quickly propelling compensation, including Randle's, to previously unknown heights. An average $44,676 salary in 1975 jumped to $76,066 in 1977—a 70% increase that dwarfed Lucchesi's own earnings history. By March 28, 1977, Randle and Lucchesi—two proud warrior-types who succeeded through challenging journeys—did not share similarities across shifting monetary trajectories, let alone ones across static age and racial lines. It took Lucchesi a lifetime and a top-level managerial position to land a $70,000 salary, which plummeted to $30,000 when he became a coach. Randle's utility role at age 28 rewarded $80,000, with significant boosts to come.[47]

How would you react if your employer failed to adequately inform you of your job status and then dismissively insulted your reputation to the press? How would you feel if someone pummeled you at work only to be transferred to another company and given a raise, an extended contract, and public acclaim?

"You hope such a thing will happen to you only once in a lifetime and I wouldn't want to be scarred by it," Randle once reflected.[48] Yet neither he nor Lucchesi ever completely escaped the horrible experience they shared during one simultaneously brief but ever-lingering moment. How could they? How would you? ∎

Acknowledgment

Appreciation is extended to Ken Manyin for his affection for baseball history and helpful editorial suggestions.

Notes

1. "Time-for-All Plan Paying Off for Lucchesi," *The Sporting News*, August 28, 1971.
2. Charlie Grassl, "Lenny Randle," Society for American Baseball Research Bio Project, https://sabr.org/bioproj/person/lenny-randle/. Randle's father, a World War II veteran, was also influential.
3. Wins Above Replacement (WAR) measures a player's value in all phases of the game, calculating how many more wins he's worth than a replacement-level player at his position (e.g., a minor league replacement or fill-in free agent).
4. Randle's 30 stolen bases were valuable by 1977 standards. Using a modern statistical lens, his 57% success rate over 1971–76 was harmful and would earn a managerial STOP sign in most circumstances.
5. While playing for the Triple-A Spokane Indians in 1973, Randle credited a mid-season talk with Maury Wills for his blossoming base-stealing success.
6. T.R. Sullivan, "Boys of Arlington: Lenny Randle vs. Frank Lucchesi—Jeff Wilson's Texas Rangers Today," Rangers Today, June 27, 2024, https://rangerstoday.com/boys-of-arlington-lenny-randle-vs-frank-lucchesi/.
7. Randy Galloway, "Randle Frustration Explodes in Fistic Fury," *The Sporting* News, April 16, 1977.
8. Sullivan.
9. Galloway.
10. Sullivan.
11. Galloway.
12. Sullivan. Press accounts vary regarding the sequence of punches and how many were thrown before Lucchesi fell. This version seems the most reliable.
13. Press accounts disagree whether his ribs were bruised or broken.
14. Sullivan.
15. "Manager Hospitalized by Player's Punches," *The New York Times*, March 29, 1977.
16. Milton Richman, "Leonard Randle Gets New Lease on Life," *Los Angeles Sentinel*, May 5, 1977.
17. "Randle Leaves Rangers Camp," *Chicago Defender*, March 30, 1977.
18. Galloway; "Hunt Randle for Aggravated Battery," *Chicago Defender*, April 26, 1977.
19. Sullivan.
20. Sullivan.
21. "Manager Hospitalized by Player's Punches."
22. Jonathan Fraser Leight, *A Cultural History of Baseball* (Jefferson: McFarland & Company, Inc.) 2005, 330. The Rangers relied on Major League Uniform Baseball Contract terms requiring a player maintain the highest standards of personal conduct and good sportsmanship.
23. Wills played six years for the Rangers and Chicago Cubs, then signed a four-year contract to play for the Japan Pacific League's Hankyu Braves. Stress from balancing baseball and family made him consistently ill. After playing 78 games in 1984, he was bought out of his contract and returned home. He took a few years off from baseball and never played professionally again.
24. "Lucchesi Unreceptive To Randle Apology," *The New York Times*, April 8, 1977.
25. The player to be named later was utility infielder Rick Auerbach, a player below Randle's value who was subsequently sold to the Reds.
26. Sullivan.
27. Kent Hannon, "One Mindless Moment," *Sports Illustrated*, June 6, 1977. The news media also enjoyed the story, frequently concocting all sorts of fight-related puns and references to their headlines. Jack Lang, "Mets Add Randle For Um-m-m Punch," *The Sporting News*, May 14, 1977.
28. Pam Schwartz, "Major League Drama at Tinker Field," *Reflections from Central Florida*, Fall 2023, https://www.thehistorycenter.org/major-league-drama-at-tinker-field/.
29. University of Southern Alabama baseball coach Eddie Stanky succeeded Lucchesi. He managed one game before deciding to return to his family and job in Mobile. Ryan took over while Corbett attempted to convince Stanky to return, and Robinson and O'Brien sought out recently retired Twins slugger Harmon Killebrew for the position. A week later, management handed the keys to Hunter. This insanity coupled with voluminous dog-chasing-its-tail trades and free agent signings during Corbett's five-year ownership reign gave proof to longtime baseball executive and compulsive trader Frank Lane's observation: "Having Corbett run a baseball team is like giving a three-year-old a handful of razors." Donald Dewey and Nicholas Acocella, *Total Ballclubs* (Toronto: Sport Media Publishing, Inc.) 2005, 599.

30. Unconfirmed reports suggested Los Angeles Dodgers and Boston Red Sox managers Tommy Lasorda and Don Zimmer, respectively, encouraged Lucchesi to sue.

31. "Lucchesi's Still After Randle," *Chicago Defender*, September 22, 1977.

32. Randle met Jackie Coor, a former airline stewardess from Detroit, while on a Rangers charter in 1973.

33. "Fight Helped Take Pressure Off Randle," *Boca Raton News*, December 7, 1978.

34. "Lucchesi Tells in Court Of 'Punk' Remark Context," *The New York Times*, December 8, 1978.

35. A bench-clearing flare-up of heated words, but no fists, was ignited on April 27 at Royals Stadium when Lucchesi allegedly ordered Blyleven to deliberately hit catcher Darrell Porter with a pitch. Bad vibes returned in Arlington as Porter taunted Wills after tagging him out and knocking him to the ground on a rundown play along the third base line. A battle royal commenced. The game was delayed 20 minutes, with 12 consecutive televised minutes of "nothing but good ol' street fighting action," as graded by *The Sporting News*. Police entered the field to restore order. Lucchesi and coach Pat Corrales were ejected, along with three Rangers players and two Royals. Randy Galloway, "Horton Proving a Ranger Bearcat With Bat and Fists," *The Sporting News*, May 28, 1977.

36. "Attorneys Call Lucchesi 'Hot Tempered Man,'" *Rushville Republican*, December 8, 1978.

37. "Len Randle, Ex-Manager Settle Suit," *Afro-American*, December 16, 1978.

38. Schwartz.

39. Perhaps Jackson likewise sensed that Florida's 1978 population demographics of 85% White, 14% Black, and less than 1% "other" did not make for fertile ground for demonstrations on Randle's behalf.

40. Schwartz.

41. Sullivan.

42. Sullivan.

43. Jim Reeves, "Scar in Rangers' Past Resurfaces at Old-Timers Game," *Fort Worth Star-Telegram*, May 4, 1992.

44. Reeves.

45. This label referred to the innocent, childlike movie character, played by Tom Hanks, who is exposed to, influences, and is controlled by life's circumstances. Indeed, Randle seemingly appeared everywhere. He played in two games in 1971 that ended in forfeit, including the Senators last game in Washington when fans, angry over the team's move to Texas, stormed the field. In 1974, he played in the infamous Ten Cent Beer Night game in Cleveland when drunken fans invaded the field, leading to a forfeited game. He was at bat with the Mets in 1977 when the lights in New York City and Shea Stadium went out. In 1979, he joined the New York Yankees, taking the roster spot of catcher Thurman Munson after his tragic death in a plane crash. And he comically blew a baseball across the third base foul line during a game at the Kingdome while playing for the Mariners in 1981.

46. Grassl.

47. Bob Lindley, "Lucchesi Wounded Again—This Time By The Legal System," *Fort Worth Star-Telegram*, December 10, 1978.

48. "Lenny Randle Cleans Up His Old Image," *Chicago Defender*, March 18, 1978.

DON'T MISS THESE BOOKS PUBLISHED BY SABR

THE 1972 TEXAS RANGERS: THE TEAM THAT COULDN'T HIT

The 1972 Texas Rangers were a culmination of decades of trying to get a major-league team in Dallas-Fort Worth. Just how bad were those early Rangers teams? When reporter Mike Shropshire wrote a book about them, he titled it *Seasons In Hell*. So why write a book about the 1972 Texas Rangers, perhaps the worst team in club history? Because they're the start of that history. Articles in this book cover the story of Tom Vandergriff ("the father of the Rangers") and biographies of every man to play or coach for the 1972 team, including Frank Howard, Larry Bittner, Horacio Pina and Tom Grieve, and broadcasters Don Drysdale and Bill Mercer. Owner Bob Short and Arlington Stadium itself are given full write-ups as well.

Edited by Steve West and Bill Nowlin
Associate Editors: Len Levin and Carl Riechers
ISBN (ebook): 978-1-943816-92-7, $9.99
ISBN (paperback): 978-1-943816-93-4, $29.95
8.5″ x 11″, 404 pages

DOME SWEET DOME: HISTORY AND HIGHLIGHTS FROM 35 YEARS OF THE HOUSTON ASTRODOME

Heralded as the "Eighth Wonder of the World" when it opened in 1965, the Astrodome was the world's first domed stadium. Detailed recaps of games played there join insightful feature essays about the ballpark. Nolan Ryan's record-breaking fifth no-hitter, the Astros' 22-inning victory and the Astros' heartbreaking losses in post-season games and other games mingle with essays on the stadium's history, the Astrodome's engineering, movers and shakers in the stadium's creation (including Roy Hofheinz, George Kirksey, and Craig Cullinan), and an in-depth historical review of the Astrodome itself. Astrodome icons, pitcher Larry Dierker and longtime team executive Tal Smith, wrote introductions.

Edited by Gregory H. Wolf
Associate Editors: Frederick H. Bush, James Forr, Len Levin and Bill Nowlin
ISBN (ebook): 978-1-943816-32-3, $9.99
ISBN (paperback): 978-1-943816-33-0, $29.95
8.5″ x 11″, 306 pages

SANDY KOUFAX

SABR's book on Sandy Koufax explores what made him so special in baseball and American society through 17 insightful essays and recaps of 36 key games in his career. Touching on subjects from Koufax's potential basketball (!) career, his relationship with manager Walt Alston, celebrity culture in LA, and his effect on the hurlers who came after him, to analyses of Koufax's stats and records, SANDY KOUFAX takes a deep dive into one of baseball's true greats. Many pitchers enjoyed longer careers than Sandy Koufax. Few, however, reached the glorious heights of this Dodgers left-hander.

Edited by Marc Z Aaron, Bill Nowlin, and Glen Sparks
Associate Editors: Len Levin and Carl Riechers
ISBN (ebook): 978-1-960819-26-0, $9.99
ISBN (paperback): 978-1-960819-27-7, $24.95
8.5″ x 11″, 186 pages

NOT AN EASY TALE TO TELL: JACKIE ROBINSON ON THE PAGE, STAGE, AND SCREEN

Few athletes have sparked the creative imaginations of artists more than Jackie Robinson. His presence can be seen in cinema, on television and on stages, big and small; even tucked within the pages of written fiction. As we celebrate the seventy-fifth anniversary of Robinson's integration of the Dodgers, he continues to inspire, including a recent appearance in HBO's groundbreaking *Lovecraft Country*. Artists keep returning to Robinson because he is one of the most inspirational figures of the twentieth century not in spite of, but because of his complexities. He did more than change the game of baseball—he changed America.

Edited by Ralph Carhart
Associate Editors: Bill Nowlin, Carl Riechers, and Kate Nachman
ISBN (paperback): 978-1-970159-72-1, $19.95 US
ISBN (ebook): 978-1-970159-71-4, $9.99
128 pages, 8.5″ x 11″

SABR members can purchase the paperbacks for half price and access the ebooks for free as a member benefit.
Visit SABR.org to learn more about becoming a member of SABR today!

Oklahoma State Cowboy Baseball

The Remarkable Gary Ward Years

Ronald Elliott, PhD, and Wade McWhorter

Founded in Stillwater, Oklahoma, in 1890, Oklahoma A&M College (OAMC) became Oklahoma State University (OSU) in 1957. The school fielded its first baseball team in 1909 and from then through the 1977 season, 11 head coaches combined for a record of 823–538–3 (.605 winning average).[1] OSU joined the Big 8 conference in 1958.[2] Over the 15 seasons from 1954 through 1968, the Aggies/Cowboys went to eight College World Series, winning the national championship in 1959 and finishing 2nd (twice), 3rd (twice), 4th, 5th, and 7th. However in five of the next nine seasons (1969–77), the Cowboys' record was below .500.[3]

Gary Ward grew up on a farm and ranch near Ramona, Oklahoma, learning the value of hard work from his father. Ward played basketball (on scholarship) and baseball at New Mexico State University.[4] From 1971 to 1977 he was the head baseball coach at Yavapai Junior College in Prescott, Arizona. Ward enjoyed considerable success, compiling a record of 240–83 (.743) and winning national championships in 1975 and 1977. He was twice named the NJCAA Coach of the Year.[5]

In May 1977 OSU hired Ward to be its head baseball coach.[6] He hit the ground running. Rex Holt, radio voice of the Cowboys, commented: "When we heard him at the press conference, he blew everyone away. You believed everything he said."[7] Ward recruited Tom Holliday, one of his players at Yavapai and then on the staff at Arizona State, to be the pitching coach and recruiting coordinator. That was the beginning of a fruitful, 19-year coaching partnership.

Coach Ward inherited a very subpar playing field. Per Holt, "the University Park was not as good as most small high school stadiums."[8] Ward immediately saw the need for, and value of, a new, modern facility. He was "the driving force behind the planning, funding, design and construction of Allie P. Reynolds Stadium."[9] Ward later said "everything that we saw follow got its genesis in the collective power and emotion and inspiration created around Reynolds Stadium and the building of it."[10] OSU played its first game in Reynolds Stadium on April 4, 1981, and the official dedication was held on April 24, 1982.[11] Those attending included not only Allie Reynolds himself but also Mickey Mantle, Bill Dickey, Warren Spahn, and Henry Iba (Reynolds' baseball coach at OAMC and legendary college and Olympic basketball coach).

TEAM ACCOMPLISHMENTS

Over the 19 seasons from 1978 through 1996, Gary Ward's teams had an overall record of 953–313–1 (.753).[12] The Cowboys averaged just over 50 wins per season and were 61–15 in 1984 and an outstanding 61–8 (.884) in 1988.[13] In the decade of the 1980s, OSU had the second highest winning average among all Division I teams.[14] Their 30 consecutive wins in 1986 set a Big 8 record.[15]

Ward's tutelage helped to make OSU baseball an offensive juggernaut. Over 19 seasons and more than 41,000 at bats, the Cowboys posted a slash line of .321/.444/.531.[16] The NCAA has compiled annual "statistical trends" for all Division I teams reporting.[17] This includes well over 200 teams in each of the years 1978 through 1996. On a year-by-year basis, Figure 1 compares the average runs scored per game by: OSU, their opponents, and Division I teams. The differences are striking. OSU averaged an amazing 11 + runs per game in 1987, 1988, and 1996. In 1988 the Cowboys

Figure 1. Timeline of Average Runs Scored per Game by Osu, Its Opponents, and Division I as a Whole

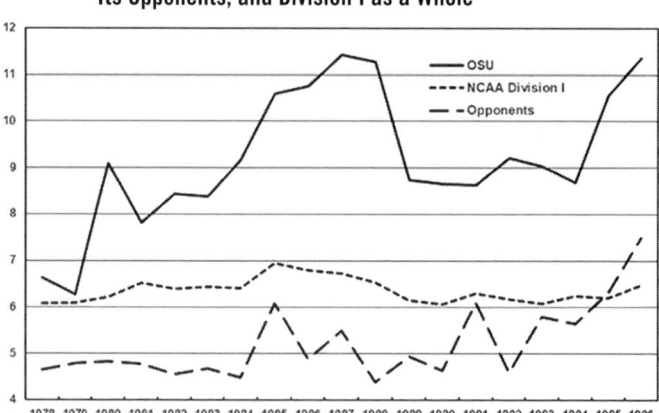

Coach Gary Ward

outscored their opponents by an average of 6.9 runs per game. Over the 19 years that Ward served as head coach, the average score of the 1267 games was 9.3 (OSU) to 5.2 (opponent).[18] The Cowboys led the nation in runs scored per game for four consecutive seasons (1985–88) and again in 1995 and 1996.[19]

In 1986 the Cowboys set the NCAA record for walks in a season (607). They also hold the 3rd, 4th, and 5th spots in that list (1985, 1996, 1987).[20] Throughout Ward's tenure, the walk rate was .172 per plate appearance.[21] Ward's hitters were known for being very selective at the plate, waiting for a pitch in their "zone." But the Cowboys also hit for power, as evidenced by their .531 slugging average over the 19 seasons. Not surprisingly, OSU set many Big 8 offensive records during the Ward years. These include hits, runs, and home runs in a season, and consecutive games played without being shut out (269).[22]

Although not as heralded as the offense, Cowboy pitchers more than held their own during the Ward/Holliday era. For example, Figure 2 looks at season-by-season data on strikeouts per nine innings. Cowboy hurlers bested the Division I average in 18 of the 19 years and in five of those, the difference was more than two strikeouts per nine innings pitched. Reynolds Stadium had the reputation of being a hitters park, but in 14 of the 19 seasons OSU's team ERA was less than the Division I average.[23]

Postseason success further cemented the Cowboys' profile of dominance during the Ward era. OSU won the Big 8 tournament and became the conference's automatic qualifier for NCAA Regional play in Ward's first year (1978) and then in each of his last 16 years (1981–96). This incredible run of 16 straight conference championships is a national record.[24] During that span the Cowboys posted an overall record of 56–10 (.848) in the conference tournaments.[25] Ward's teams advanced to the College World Series ten times, with an NCAA record seven consecutive appearances from 1981–87.[26] The Cowboys played in three CWS championship games (1981, 1987, 1990), each time falling short of the elusive prize. The 1990 scenario was perhaps the most heartbreaking. Two years earlier a format change had led to two four-team double-elimination brackets, with the winners appearing in a one-game championship. After sailing through its bracket undefeated, winning by scores of 14–4, 7–1, and 14–3, OSU lost the championship to a once-defeated Georgia team by a score of 2–1.[27]

Using *Collegiate Baseball*'s final poll from each season, the Cowboys were the only school in the country to be ranked in the top 15 in each season from 1981 through 1996.[28] The same was true for *Baseball America*'s final polls over those 16 seasons.[29] For both *Collegiate Baseball* and *Baseball America*, eight of the 16 final rankings were top 5 and four more were top 10. Clearly, OSU was consistently in the upper echelon of college baseball for an extended period of time.

PLAYER ACCOMPLISHMENTS

Reflecting back, Coach Ward said: "I did not get a base hit; I did not strike anybody out; players win championships."[30] Ward coached many nationally elite players, as indicated by the program's prominence in All-American selections. (See Table 1.)

From 1978 through 1996, a total of 86 different Cowboy players were picked in a major league draft, and nine of those were first-round selections (Greg Pastors, Darren Dilks, Robbie Wine, Dennis Livingston, Gary Green, Pete Incaviglia, Monty Fariss, Robin Ventura, Jeromy Burnitz). Additional players signed with major league teams as free agents.[31] Twenty-three Cowboys who played one or more years under Ward went on to play major league baseball.[32] John Farrell and Ventura also managed in the major leagues. Ryan Folmar and Josh Holliday both played for Ward in the 1996 College World Series and later were head coaches for CWS teams (Oral Roberts and OSU, respectively). Ward's sons Rocky and Roger played for their father and went on to college coaching careers.

Figure 2. Timeline of Strikeouts per Nine Innings Pitched by Osu and Division I as a Whole

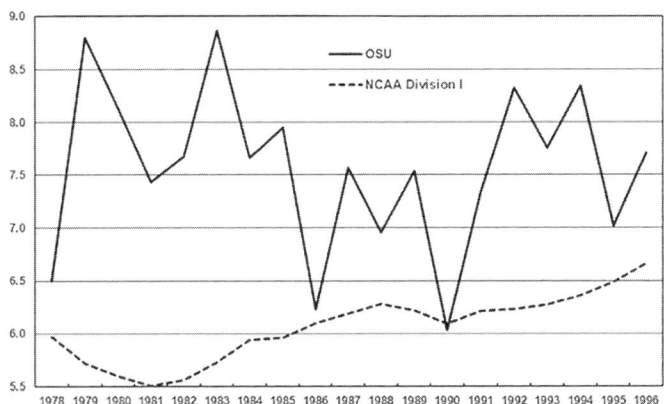

There are many additional indicators of Cowboy excellence. For example, seven times over an eight-year period (1984–91), four different OSU players led the nation in RBIs (Incaviglia, Ventura, Fariss, Daniel).[33] Three Cowboys were named to the 11-member CWS

Table 1. OSU All-Americans in the Gary Ward era*

	American Baseball Coaches Association	Baseball America
	7	9
1st team	Robbie Wine, Pete Incaviglia (twice), Robin Ventura (twice), Jim Ifland, Jeff Guiel	Dennis Livingston, Incaviglia (twice), Ventura (3 times), Monty Fariss, Michael Daniel, Jason Bell
2nd team	6	5
3rd team	8	6

*All came during the last 15 years of Ward's tenure (1982–96).

Allie P. Reynolds Stadium

Robin Ventura at the plate.

The classic home run swing of Pete Incaviglia.

1980s All-Decade Team (Mike Day, Ventura, Incaviglia).[34] From 1984 through 1990, four different Cowboys recorded the highest batting average in the CWS (Day, Ventura, Jimmy Barragan, Bobby Carlsen), with Ventura batting .600 in the 1986 Series.[35]

LEGENDS

Among the many outstanding players, two—Pete Incaviglia and Robin Ventura—stand out as true legends, not only in the Ward era but throughout the entire history of Cowboy and NCAA baseball. Current head coach Josh Holliday said: "I always tell people that, over a six-year window of time, Oklahoma State had the two greatest hitters in college baseball history."[36] Both were recruited to OSU out of California, three years apart, so their college careers did not overlap.

Incaviglia played three seasons (1983–85) as a right-handed hitting left fielder and designated hitter. He is considered by many to be the greatest power hitter in NCAA history. His OSU career slash line was .398/.527/.915 with an amazing OPS of 1.442.[37] He holds the NCAA career record for home runs (100) and is second in slugging average (.915) and RBIs (324).[38] *Baseball America* named Incaviglia as its College Player of the Year in 1985.[39] In that season he had 48 home runs, 143 RBIs, 285 total bases, and a slugging average of 1.140. All these are NCAA records that still stand 40 years later.[40] In 1999 *Baseball America* named Incaviglia its Player of the Century.[41]

Ventura also played in Stillwater for three seasons (1986–88). He was a left-handed hitting third baseman for the Cowboys. Ventura's career slash line was .428/.533/.792 with an OPS of 1.324. As a freshman, Ventura slashed .469/.563/.846 and led the nation in runs (107), RBIs (96), and total bases (204).[42] *Baseball America* named him Freshman of the Year in 1986, College Player of the Year in 1987, and Player of the Decade for the 1980s.[43] In his 1987 sophomore season, Ventura posted the amazing, highly publicized, 58-game hitting streak.[44] As a junior (1988), he was awarded the Dick Howser Trophy and USA Baseball's Golden Spikes Award.[45] Ventura won *The Sporting News* College Baseball Player of the Year Award in 1987 and 1988.[46]

Ventura (2006), Incaviglia (2007), and Ward (2008) were inducted into the College Baseball Hall of Fame in its first three years of existence. All three have had their uniform numbers retired at OSU.[48]

Robin Ventura (58 games) and Joe DiMaggio (56 games) at the 1998 Golden Spikes Award ceremony.

Gary Ward with the Big 8 conference championship trophy in 1995 (the 15th of 16 consecutive league championships).

CLOSING PERSPECTIVES

Gary Ward announced his retirement from OSU on October 23, 1996. At the news conference he said, "It is a time to celebrate what has transpired the last 19 years, celebrate one tremendous run. It's been a labor of love. All we did was put some numbers up, and they handed me the keys and I pass them on."[49]

Coach Ward was a program builder and sustainer, and an exemplary leader and molder of young men. He not only could teach hitting at the highest level, but he was also a cerebral coach, a gifted communicator, and a tremendous motivator. In 2009 Incaviglia said: "We took on the identity of the guy who was in charge, Gary Ward. We never thought we wouldn't win a Big Eight Tournament, that we wouldn't win a Regional or that we wouldn't be in the World Series. We went out and competed every day, every pitch. That's a tribute to Gary. We just played the game really, really hard."[50] Just before managing in the 2013 World Series, Farrell said: "He was so relentless, how could we not be. He was so far ahead of his time for the way he coached our minds. He was light years ahead."[51] In his Hall of Fame induction speech, Ward said: "Scoreboards take care of themselves if you do everything right. What I wanted out of my players: you be here, you be on time, you go to class, you be kind to people, courteous, accountable, responsible. No alibis, no excuses."[52]

As a member of the Big 12 Conference, OSU has had an overall winning average of .637 since Ward's retirement, well above the 1909–77 period (.605) but considerably below the .753 posted in the Ward era. Looking at the program's entire history, OSU is the 4th all-time winningest Division I program (.661).[53] Gary Ward's legendary teams contributed significantly to that record and OSU fans and former players remember the Ward years with great appreciation and even reverence.

A final piece of wisdom from Coach: "Those that look back should never say 'remember when.' They should say 'remember how.'"[54] ■

Acknowledgment

The authors acknowledge with great appreciation the database contributions of Howard Johnson, founding president of SABR-Oklahoma.

Notes

1. Wade McWhorter, *2024 Oklahoma State Baseball Guide*, https://okstate.com/documents/2024/2/9/2024_OSU_Cowboy_Baseball_Media_Guide_-_WEB.pdf, 115.
2. "Baseball Guide," McWhorter, 81.
3. "Baseball Guide," McWhorter, 115.
4. Gary Ward, College Baseball Hall of Fame induction speech, July 3, 2008, https://www.mlb.com/video/gary-ward-induction-speech-c15716731.

5. Gary Ward, College Baseball Hall of Fame inductee bio, https://www.mlb.com/college-baseball-hall-of-fame/class-of-2008#ward.

6. "Oklahoma State Baseball - The Gary Ward Era," OSU Athletics video, https://www.youtube.com/watch?v=wyt9Nn5_-XE.

7. Rex Holt interview with Oklahoma State Athletics, Orange Power Studios, April 2019.

8. Holt interview.

9. Ward, Hall of Fame inductee bio.

10. Gary Ward interview with Oklahoma State Athletics, Orange Power Studios, April 2019.

11. "Allie P. Reynolds Stadium," Cowboy Baseball, March 2, 2009. https://okstate.com/news/2009/3/2/Allie_P_Reynolds_Stadium.

12. "Baseball Guide," McWhorter, 115.

13. "Baseball Guide," McWhorter, 68–70.

14. "Division I Baseball Records," http://fs.ncaa.org/Docs/stats/baseball_RB/2023/D1.pdf, 58.

15. "Baseball Guide," McWhorter, 48.

16. Compiled from yearly statistical summaries, "Statistical Archive: OSU Baseball," Cowboy Baseball, https://okstate.com/sports/2017/6/26/BSB_0821151355.

17. "Division I Baseball Records," 78.

18. Yearly statistical summaries.

19. "Division I Baseball Records," 48.

20. "Division I Baseball Records," 44.

21. Yearly statistical summaries.

22. "Baseball Guide," McWhorter, 48.

23. Yearly statistical summaries; "Division I Baseball Records," 78.

24. "Baseball Guide," McWhorter, 132.

25. "Baseball Guide," McWhorter, 67–72.

26. "General CWS Records," 14, 21–22. http://fs.ncaa.org/Docs/stats/baseball_cws_RB/2023/1-CWSGeneral.pdf.

27. "General CWS Records," 7.

28. "Division I Baseball Records," 63–64.

29. "Division I Baseball Records," 68–69.

30. Ward interview.

31. "Baseball Guide," McWhorter, 117–19.

32. "Baseball Guide," McWhorter, 116.

33. "Division I Baseball Records," 24.

34. "General CWS Records," 39.

35. "General CWS Records," 31.

36. Josh Holliday interview with Oklahoma State Athletics, Orange Power Studios, April 2019.

37. Yearly statistical summaries.

38. "Division I Baseball Records," 14–15.

39. Matt Eddy, "The 12 Most Decorated College All-Americans of the Last 40 Years," Baseball America, February 4, 2020, https://www.baseballamerica.com/stories/the-12-most-decorated-college-all-americans-of-the-last-40-years/.

40. "Division I Baseball Records," 2.

41. "Pete Incaviglia Named College Baseball's Player of the Century," Cowboy Baseball, April 3, 2003, https://okstate.com/news/2003/4/3/Pete_Incaviglia_Named_College_Baseball_s_Player_of_the_Century.

42. Yearly statistical summaries; "Division I Baseball Records," 20, 24, 25.

43. Eddy, "The 12 Most Decorated College All-Americans." Mike Baldwin, "The Hit of the '80s Former Pokes' Star Ventura Named College Baseball's Player of the Decade," The Oklahoman, February 6, 1990, https://www.oklahoman.com/story/news/1990/02/06/the-hit-of-the-80s-former-pokes-star-ventura-named-college-baseballs-player-of-the-decade/62575975007/.

44. Wayne Cavadi, "College Baseball's Most Unbreakable Records," NCAA.com, June 11, 2024, https://www.ncaa.com/news/baseball/article/2023-06-26/college-baseballs-most-unbreakable-records.

45. "Dick Howser Trophy Winners," MLB, https://www.mlb.com/howser-trophy/winners; "Golden Spikes Award Winners," USA Baseball, https://www.usabaseball.com/golden-spikes-award/history/winners.

46. "Baseball Guide," McWhorter, 103.

47. "College Baseball Hall of Fame Inductees," MLB, https://www.mlb.com/college-baseball-hall-of-fame/inductees.

48. "Baseball Guide," McWhorter, 122.

49. Berry Tramel, "'Tremendous Run' Ward Ends Era as OSU Baseball Coach," The Oklahoman, October 24, 1996, https://www.oklahoman.com/story/news/1996/10/24/tremendous-run-ward-ends-era-as-osu-baseball-coach/62339175007/.

50. John Helsley, "Collected Wisdom: Pete Incaviglia," The Oklahoman, June 7, 2009, https://www.oklahoman.com/story/sports/college/cowboys/2009/06/07/collected-wisdom-pete-incaviglia/61402541007/.

51. Berry Tramel, "World Series: John Farrell talks Gary Ward," The Oklahoman, October 23, 2013, https://www.oklahoman.com/story/sports/columns/berry-tramel/2013/10/23/world-series-john-farrell-talks-gary-ward/60872512007/.

52. Ward, Hall of Fame induction speech.

53. "Division I Baseball Records," 56.

54. Ward interview.

Boos to Cheers

Darrell Porter and the 1982 World Series

Doug Wedge

Darrell Porter's second season as a St. Louis Cardinal was difficult. He was playing on an incredibly talented team with great fielding at every position, solid starting pitching, and a future Hall of Famer as a closer. But the alumnus of Southeast High School in Oklahoma City batted only .231, a significant step down from 1979 when he had played for Kansas City and became one of the few players in baseball history to have 100 runs, RBIs, and walks in a season.[1] As the catching successor to the popular Ted Simmons, a six-time All-Star who had spent thirteen seasons behind the plate in St. Louis, Porter was the target of fans' boos. "[Darrell] took some heat in St. Louis during that 1982 season because he did not hit particularly well and had replaced a Cardinal favorite in Ted Simmons," Mike Ramsey, a versatile infielder who played second base, shortstop, and third for St. Louis in 1982, says.[2]

"Everybody expected Darrell to do what he did in Kansas City," pitcher Jim Kaat explains. "Well, St. Louis is a little bigger ballpark, and some of those fly balls that might have been home runs in Kansas City were warning track outs in St. Louis."[3] After one of those warning track outs, Porter would return to the dugout frustrated. Placing his bat in the rack, he would say something along the lines of "You turkey turd! You flew out again to left field!"

"The strongest language he would use was 'turkey turd,'" Kaat says.

Porter had found sobriety after struggling with alcohol and drugs in Kansas City.[4] Staying clean was a constant effort and priority for him.[5] Despite his difficult journey of recovery from addiction, one coach jabbed Porter with a low blow after Porter lofted a fly ball for an out and leaving men stranded on base: "Darrell, I liked you better when you were drinking."

"That was really mean-spirited," Kaat says. "And, it got real quiet in the dugout, and nobody knew exactly what to say, but, you know, that's the kind of stuff Darrell was going through early in the season because he just wasn't producing."

Despite the struggles and the negativity, Porter persevered. John Stuper, a rookie pitcher who worked with Porter in seventeen games in 1982, was impressed with how unflappable Porter was. "When Darrell struggled during that year, they let him know it, but it didn't bother him. He never said anything. He would just come out and hit extra, work hard. Things rolled off his back."[6]

Porter also took the time to make Stuper, a right-handed starter who joined the Cardinals from the minor leagues that June, feel welcomed. "You were comfortable around Darrell, always," Stuper says. "You ever been around somebody, even if you don't know them that well, they're just so friendly and so easygoing that you're instantly comfortable around them? That's the Darrell I remember."

Ramsey echoes the sentiment. "Darrell was great. One of my favorite teammates. Tough physically and a very good catcher."

Behind the plate, Porter offered multiple qualities. He called an excellent game, presented a good target, blocked the ball well, and, with his strong and accurate arm, threw out baserunners. He also noticed when his young pitcher Stuper started to deviate from his usual mechanics. When that happened, Porter trotted out to the mound. "Hey, you're dropping your arm a little bit," Porter pointed out. "Be sure to keep it up at the exact same release point as where your fastball is."

Stuper was receptive to Porter's observations, recalibrated, and returned to his original form. "He didn't force himself on you," Stuper says. "He just made suggestions. You thought to yourself, 'Heck, that's an All Star catcher. I'm a rookie. He probably knows a little bit more than I do. So, I'll go with it.' But, he didn't force himself on you. He was a quiet leader." If Stuper struggled during a game, Porter visited the mound and shared a kind and encouraging word with his young pitcher. "Come on, John!" he would say. "You can do this!"

Porter worked well with veteran pitchers, too. By 1982, Kaat was pitching in his twenty-fourth season in the major leagues. At 43-years-old, Kaat knew how to pitch and understood what he could do effectively. So did Porter. And, the two of them kept their approach

SABR/RUCKER ARCHIVE

Darrell Porter got hot in 1982's postseason, but his work with the pitching staff may have also been crucial to the championship.

direct and uncomplicated. "When I came in, it was pretty simple," Kaat says. "I side-armed left-handers. I threw a fastball that I'd try to run inside, and I threw a curveball that I tried to sweep outside. We kept it pretty simple."

While working effectively with pitchers and taking extra batting practice to get on track in the batter's box, Porter maintained a clubhouse routine he developed to protect his sobriety. After a game, players might gather around, open a cold beer, and rehash what went well during the game and what didn't. Porter needed to distance himself from that atmosphere.

"He was one of the quick into the shower, quick out," Kaat says. "My locker was right near the shower. He'd practically be in and out before I ever had my uniform off. He explained to me one day, he said, 'You know, I just can't stick around with you guys and do that anymore.' We all respected his personality from that standpoint."

When looking back on his experiences with Porter, Kaat recalls their non-baseball conversations about Porter realigning his life and his priorities. Kaat cheered Porter on and supported him. "Off the field, he changed his life and had to discipline himself," Kaat says. "He said he was so shy when he was a younger player, and so he found out if he went out and had a couple beers that would relax him. Or, when he'd have too many and then the next day he had to take something to bring him up. He was on that roller coaster. So, my talks with him were about encouragement, how I was proud of the fact that he got his life in order and was conducting himself the way he needed to."

Meanwhile, Porter helped Stuper adjust to pitching at the highest level. Individually, Stuper had a great year, winning nine games and maintaining a 3.36 ERA in twenty-three appearances. Likewise, the team had a terrific year as the Cardinals won the National

League Eastern Division to face the Atlanta Braves in the Championship Series. As the Cardinals swept the Championship Series to claim the National League pennant, Porter caught fire.

"Maybe he felt weight lifted off his shoulders because people couldn't say, 'Oh, we couldn't make it to the World Series because of him,'" Stuper says. "He turned into Reggie Jackson for us. He's like Mr. Clutch. If there was a chance for a big hit, he seemed to get it every time."

Indeed, in the Championship Series, Porter batted .556. He also got on base with his keen eye: he had five walks. He scored a run in every game. He threw out baserunners. And he handled the pitching staff effectively. Cardinals pitchers gave up only five runs over three games.[7]

With the sweep, the Cardinals advanced to the World Series to face the Milwaukee Brewers. Porter continued his hot hitting, and he continued mentoring Stuper who started Game Two in St. Louis against future Hall of Famer Don Sutton. "We compared every Brewer hitter to a hitter in the National League," Stuper says. "That's how we did it then. Now, they'll have fifteen hours of film on every hitter. But, that's the way we did it. Hey, this guy's kind of like Bill Madlock. This guy's kind of like…And, so, it gave you a point of reference."

Even though he was on baseball's biggest stage, Stuper maintained his composure. He kept things in perspective, telling himself it was still a baseball game, just like any other. He would be throwing a ball to his catcher. An umpire would be calling balls and strikes. Stuper needed three outs every half inning. "I tried to divvy the game up into little segments so that it wouldn't overwhelm me," Stuper says. Augmenting this approach was Porter who, as he had been all season, was an illustration of calm and ease. "He looked like he was preparing to go on a picnic."

Stuper pitched four innings and gave up four runs when Cardinals manager Whitey Herzog called in Kaat from the bullpen in the top of the fifth. As Stuper watched the rest of the game from the bench, with the score at 4–2 he knew he would be tagged with the loss unless the Cardinals rallied.

They did, courtesy of Darrell Porter. In the bottom of the sixth, with Cardinal baserunners on first and third, Porter stepped to the plate to face Sutton. Porter ripped a two-run double to tie the game.[8] "Darrell comes up and hits an opposite-field double," Stuper remembers. "He hadn't hit a ball to left field in like six years."

With the game tied, Stuper was off the hook. Porter wasn't finished yet, though. In the bottom of the eighth, he hit a single to contribute to a rally that loaded the bases and set the stage for Brewers pitcher Pete Ladd to walk Steve Braun. George Hendrick scored, and the Cardinals took the lead, and ultimately won Game Two, 5–4.

Over the next three games, the Series see-sawed back and forth. By the time Stuper's turn in the rotation rolled around again, the Cardinals were in a must-win situation. Going into Game Six, the Brewers led the series, 3–2. Stuper and Porter shared a couple of goals: 1) Win the game to force a decisive Game Seven. 2) Pitch a complete game to save the bullpen, so that all arms would be available for that final game.

The battery achieved their goals and delivered a gem. They had a great rhythm with Stuper retiring fifteen consecutive hitters between the third and eighth innings. Stuper nearly had a shutout, and the Cardinals won, 13–1, to force Game Seven. Again, Porter was a force at the plate, hitting a home run in the fourth.

In Game Seven, Porter again delivered, this time with an RBI in the bottom of the eighth to add to St. Louis's lead. And, the game ended with relief maestro Bruce Sutter striking out Gorman Thomas and the Cardinals winning the team's ninth World Series championship.

Stuper points to that moment and notes something interesting and miraculous. "If you see the end of the game when Bruce strikes the last guy out, Darrell takes his mask off. And, he throws it up in the air. You don't see it come back to earth. Nobody knows where that mask went," Stuper says. "Just watch it. He'll throw his mask up in the air. It's an angle of the camera where you could see it if it came back down, and it didn't. I don't know if God took it or what, but it didn't come back down."

As the Cardinals celebrated their championship and learned that Porter was named the World Series Most Valuable Player, Stuper was happy for his batterymate.

"I remember just the sense of relief that Darrell had. Just this sense of relief he had that we won. He was a big reason that we won. Just a relief. I could feel this huge weight just coming off his shoulders. And, I was so happy for him."

Ramsey agrees: "It was extremely exciting for all of his teammates when he turned it on during the '82 playoffs and the World Series."

Stuper played for St. Louis for another two seasons, and he compares the organization to a family. The team prides itself on staying connected with and celebrating its alumni and their contributions throughout the team's history. Reunions are common, and Stuper attends. He enjoys seeing former teammate Kaat who, like Porter, made him feel welcomed as a rookie in 1982, but he misses his catcher. Porter died in 2002 at age fifty.

"He's a member of the Cardinal family, and I'm just very very sad that he's gone and that he can't come back to the reunions. He can't come to the fantasy camps. He can't do any of that," Stuper says. "He was such a fine gentleman. A great player. Clutch player. I have a ring because of him. I miss him. I just miss him." ∎

Notes

1. "Darrell Porter," Baseball Reference, https://www.baseball-reference.com/players/p/porteda02.shtml. References to statistics are to this source unless otherwise noted.
2. Mike Ramsey, Letter to author, September 2020. All quotations attributed to Mr. Ramsey are from this letter unless otherwise noted.
3. Jim Kaat, Interview with author, September 3, 2020. All quotations attributed to Mr. Kaat are from this interview unless otherwise noted.
4. Will Grimsley, "World Series MVP Porter Recalls Personal Struggle," *Oklahoman*, October 27, 1982.
5. Darrell Porter with William Deerfield, *Snap Me Perfect* (Thomas Nelson Publishers, 1984).
6. John Stuper, Interview with author, May 12, 2020. All quotations attributed to Mr. Stuper are from this interview unless otherwise noted.
7. Jim Lassiter, "World Series Starts out Like 1960's Classic," *Oklahoman*, October 15, 1982.
8. Steve Wulf, "A Hopping Good Series," *Sports Illustrated*, October 25, 1982, https://vault.si.com/vault/1982/10/25/a-hopping-good-series.

Jimmy Porter

A Man or a Legend?

Steve West

In the 1950s Dallas and Fort Worth stood apart, and scattered small towns surrounded the big cities. Since then, the cities have spread, the towns have filled in, and the outskirts have been transformed into suburbs. Today you can exit Interstate 635 in Dallas—the loop which was the boundary of the old city—and drive about five miles up Josey Lane without ever leaving built-up areas. If you do, you'll come to a small park in the city of Carrollton, an area which used to be wide open fields. That park on Josey is named Jimmy Porter Park, for a longtime resident who made his name in baseball.

Jimmy Porter died in 1984, and the oft-repeated tale of his life focused on how he gave up his career in the Negro Leagues, where he faced the likes of Satchel Paige and Ty Cobb, to return home to Carrollton.[1] The abiding story is of the hundreds of kids Jimmy played pickup ball with, encouraging legions of young people in the game.[2]

But did Jimmy Porter ever actually play in the Negro Leagues?

Stories prior to and contemporary with his death, often encouraged by his own comments, specifically mention Jimmy Porter having played on the 1926–27 St. Louis Stars in the Negro American League. But there's a problem: The Stars were in the Negro National League, and current research doesn't show his name on any Negro League roster, Stars or otherwise.[3]

There are numerous major league players we have little information on. The further back you go, the less there is. In the White major leagues, we aren't even sure of the real names of some players from the nineteenth century. For many who played in the Negro Leagues, basic documentation such as a birth certificate may never have existed. Thus, for someone like Jimmy Porter, we have to rely on the stories told about him. As time goes by those stories naturally get stretched, and someone's slightly made-up detail becomes a fact, passed down until the truth is lost.

We know that Jimmy Porter was born on September 2, 1900, in Jacksonville, Texas, a little over a hundred miles southeast of Dallas.[4] The widely reported story is that his family moved from East Texas to Carrollton when Jimmy was young, and he lived there the rest of his life, with a brief break while he was in St. Louis with the Stars. Even this part of his story is disputed: some stories suggest he came to Carrollton when he was 18, and others say he didn't move there until after his baseball career ended.[5]

Most of the stories about Jimmy agree that he took up baseball when he was six, encouraged by his father, and he eventually became good enough to go to St. Louis to play in the 1926 and 1927 seasons, where he played catcher, infield, and center field, after which he returned to Carrollton because he was homesick.

It is reasonable to think the best young player in the area would go to St. Louis to try out for the Stars, even if he was already in his mid-20s. There were a

Jimmy Porter, pictured third from left seated on the bleachers, was known for advocating for youth baseball.

few options for a player in Texas, but the mighty Kansas City Monarchs may have seemed out of reach. Still, the romantic idea of a young man going off to seek his fortune is so common it is something of a trope in early twentieth century stories.

In 1926 and 1927 the Black team in St. Louis was the Stars of the Negro National League. In each of those seasons researchers have uncovered more than 90 box scores, and Jimmy Porter doesn't appear in any of them. It is believed the team played as many as twice that number of games. So what are the chances of Porter playing in some of the missing games? It's possible, especially if he only played in a few games.

One odd thing is how he described the team he played for. In multiple stories Porter called them the St. Louis Cardinals, which of course was the name of the White major league team.[6] When asked, he could not remember the name of his manager (to be fair, the Stars had four managers over those two seasons), and he even called it the Negro American League, a league which didn't exist until 1937. Are these simply technical details, the signs of a fading memory, or the words of someone telling a tale which wasn't quite true?

Another question is whether a player would really quit after two seasons because they were homesick. It's certainly possible, although in those days there weren't necessarily many opportunities for a young Black man to make as much money as he might have made in baseball.[7] In one story, he says he had a lifetime .338 batting average, which doesn't seem like a player you would let go for being homesick.[8] It seems far more likely that Jimmy tried and tried to get on the team, perhaps even playing on a local semi-pro team, and eventually gave up, or ran out of money to stay in St. Louis.

There are also conflicting reports about what Jimmy did after leaving St. Louis. Some say he returned directly to Carrollton because he was homesick. Others say he went to Corsicana, Texas (50 miles south of Dallas), where he played and coached for a Black minor league team for four years. Still others say he moved to the family farm near Dallas and worked to help the family avoid failure. Any of these could be true, although if he was truly homesick, would he have gone to Corsicana for four years? If he was staying in baseball anyway, why not stay at the highest level?

When Satchel Paige died in 1982, Jimmy was interviewed for his thoughts on Paige.[9] He told several tales about playing against Paige, none with great detail other than that Porter hit well against him. In the story we learn he also played against Babe Ruth (who apparently pitched to Porter), Willie Mays (born in 1931, so even if

a teenage Mays played an exhibition in Texas, Porter would have been close to 50), and other stories mention him playing against both Ty Cobb and Joe DiMaggio. If any of these were true for the White players, at best they were in exhibition games due to the color barrier in baseball at the time. In fact research has shown that Cobb did not play against any Black players after 1916, so this story must be false.

Regardless of his playing career in baseball, we do know that Jimmy Porter was important in helping to found the Carrollton Little League in the 1950s and 1960s. How involved is difficult to know (he was, after all, a Black man in 1950s Texas), but in the late 1960s and 1970s he received several awards for his efforts in helping to start the league. To this day the Carrollton Parks and Recreation Department gives the Jimmy Porter Award for an outstanding volunteer in youth sports.

Many older citizens have remembered Jimmy in blog and Facebook posts over the years. They talk about him having just one rule: everyone gets to play. He was regularly seen on the streets of Carrollton, bat and ball in hand, heading somewhere to coach young ballplayers. Jimmy Porter was, in his time, the most famous person in Carrollton.

So who was Jimmy Porter? Was he one of the hundreds or perhaps thousands of men who have claimed to have been pro ballplayers, only to have that claim refuted as research proved them wrong? Everyone has heard a story of someone, perhaps even a relative, digging into the claims of an uncle or grandfather, only to discover they didn't do what they said they did.

These claims harm no one. This is not a case of stolen valor, after all. A little stretching of a story here and there to inspire the local kids doesn't really matter.

Jimmy Porter will be remembered for his tall tales and by a youth baseball field that bears his name.

COURTESY OF THE CITY OF CARROLLTON

Jimmy Porter might be the perfect example of an obscure old-time ballplayer. His story could be completely made up, or it might simply be waiting for a baseball researcher to dig up some old newspaper. It's entirely plausible that Jimmy's name will pop up somewhere in a year or a decade, and we'll learn a little more truth about his life.

An article from 1975 may have gotten to the heart of the Jimmy Porter story without even realizing it. One paragraph may tell you all you need to know:

> Jimmy Porter is a 75-year-old toothless black man who may or may not have done all that he says. No one really cares. Fact is, no one should care. At first the tendency is to try sorting truth from fiction, but after awhile you realize that in some cases truth and fiction blend in such a way you hardly care which is which.[10]

In the final reckoning, we know that at the very least Jimmy Porter was a very good man who was heavily involved in youth baseball, and influenced many people throughout his life. Some parts of his story are surely true, some completely false, and some embellished, but none take away from his legacy.

And that may be enough. ■

Acknowlegments

The author is grateful for the assistance of the City of Carrollton Parks and Recreation Department.

Notes

1. Most stories called him Jimmy, and that is how the park is named, but in autographs he wrote it as Jimmie, and that is how it is spelled on his gravestone. For the sake of continuity this article will refer to the way he was commonly known.
2. Much of the information in this article was based on old newspaper clippings found in archival boxes owned by the City of Carrollton. Some of them included sources, which are listed here when available, but most did not.
3. There is no record of Jimmy Porter in Negro League statistics on Baseball Reference or Seamheads.com, and Negro League experts consulted were unaware of his existence.
4. "Carrollton Youths Call Themselves 'Lucky To Have Friend Like Jimmy,'" undated article.
5. Steve Pate, "A Legend in his Own Town," *Dallas Morning News*, 1975.
6. Pate.
7. "Although most Negro leaguers were paid less than their White counterparts in the major leagues they were much better off than their black contemporaries outside baseball." Robert Gardner & Dennis Shortelle, *The Forgotten Players: The Story of Black Baseball in America* (NY: Walker and Company, 1993). https://nlbemuseum.com/nlbm/player2.html.
8. Dean Glazer, "Satchel Paige: Porter Reflects on Legend," undated article. However, the Stars were the best-hitting team in the Negro National League for both those seasons, and with a batting average of .338 Porter would have only been about fifth on the team.
9. Glazer.
10. Pate.

Southwest Conference Baseball History

Bo Carter

The Southwest Conference (SWC) was an NCAA Division I conference, 1914–96, which included colleges from Texas, Oklahoma, and Arkansas. With the way Texas Longhorns baseball has dominated the SWC diamond throughout much of the conference's existence, with 64 baseball championships over 82 seasons, one might think that's the whole story of the SWC. However, programs such as Texas A&M, Baylor, TCU, Texas Tech (in the 1987–96 final years), Arkansas (which dropped varsity baseball from 1931–47 due to financial and weather considerations, but roared back), and even outmanned Rice have had their moments.

In fact, then-seventh-seeded Rice, led by future Hall of Fame head coach Wayne Graham, figured largely in the final days of the SWC.[1] In May 1996 at Lubbock, Texas, fireballing right-handed reliever David Aardsma blew a 97-mile-per-hour fastball by a Texas hitter to seal a 16–8 win in the SWC postseason championship finals and an NCAA Championship berth. Rice began its ascent to college baseball's elite in the conference's final years under Graham, head coach of the Owls 1992–2018.[2]

Intercollegiate baseball in the Lone Star State traces its roots back 112 years to 1884, when traditional arch-rivals Texas and Texas A&M first met in Austin sometime in March or April (the exact date is not known). That rivalry has continued beyond the SWC days into competition in the Big 12, Western Athletic, American Athletic Conferences as well as Conference USA. Before it was dissolved in July 1996, the famed SWC was a major factor in college baseball, with dozens of major league players listed among its alumni and solid representation in the NCAA trophy room and NCAA World Series.

Despite the outsized score, 16–8, of the final game of any SWC sport in 1996, the SWC was regarded as a solid, pitching-dominated circuit for nine decades.

The Texas Longhorns baseball program under Hall of Fame coach Cliff Gustafson won national titles in 1975 and 1983, as well as titles under Bibb Falk in 1949 and 1950 with Gustafson playing on those teams as an infielder. The SWC Arkansas Razorbacks also fielded fine teams that advanced to the College World Series in 1979, 1985, 1987, and 1989, before leaving for the Southeastern Conference in July 1991 in all sports (except football during the '91 campaign).

Behind Texas, Texas A&M was a factor in the next most conference races, with 15 regular-season crowns 1931–93 and three visits to the NCAA World Series in 1951, 1964 and 1993. The Aggies won a combined 1,536 contests 1959–2005 under coaches Tom Chandler (660 victories from 1959–84) and Hall of Fame coach Mark Johnson (school-record 876 wins from 1985–2005) with 20 NCAA tournament bids during those years.

TCU made its presence known with seven SWC crowns 1933–94 but advanced into NCAA postseason play just twice, in 1956 and 1994.

Baylor also had its heyday with a pair of SWC tournament titles in the first two years of the postseason meet in 1977 and '78, and eventual treks during those seasons to the NCAA World Series.

Texas Tech made its late run into SWC competition (after dropping baseball 1930–53) with NCAA appearances in both 1995 and 1996 and near-misses at at-large NCAA bids in the early 1990s under Hall of Fame coach Larry Hays.

Wally Moon played college ball at Texas A&M.

Who would be crowned SWC champion, and receive the automatic berth into the NCAA Championship since it began in 1947, has not always been clear-cut. A prime example came in the 1966 season when Baylor, TCU, Texas, and Texas A&M all closed with 9–6 league records. There was no playoff plan or SWC postseason tournament at that time, so a conference call was arranged with the four teams' head coaches and directors of athletics, and SWC commissioner Cliff Speegle. They used a series of coin flips to determine the circuit's NCAA representative.

As fate would have it, the ever-present Longhorns won the tosses, advanced to the NCAA District 8 tournament, and eventually to the NCAA World Series where they finished 1–2 and tied for fifth nationally.

Yet another peculiar instance was the tenth SWC postseason tourney in 1986 at College Station, Texas, with the top four teams competing for the meet title and the league's automatic NCAA bid. Weather and fate played major roles in the final decision. The tournament began on Friday, May 16. The number 4 seed Baylor upset number 1 Texas, 13–5, and 2 seed Texas A&M edged Arkansas, 4–0.

Then came the deluges Saturday and Sunday. Play was impossible. Conference officials, including tournament director and SWC coordinator of umpires Art Blair, conferred Sunday night as rain continued. Gustafson and fellow Hall of Fame coach Norm De-Briyn of Arkansas spoke by phone with members of the NCAA Baseball Selection Committee. They were told that both of their teams were in line for two of the 15 at-large berths in the 40-team NCAA field (with 25

Eddie Dyer pitched a no-hitter for Rice and made All-SWC 1919–21, but left college just shy of graduation to sign with the St. Louis Cardinals. He would later manage the Cardinals 1946–50.

automatic conference winners) due to NCAA Rating Percentages Indices among the top nationally.

Both teams packed their gear and headed back to campus despite pleas from Blair, and Baylor and Texas A&M coaches and administrators. The semifinals and loser's bracket games were canceled and Baylor and Texas A&M would have to play each other for the guaranteed slot. Texas A&M officials began working on the diamond at A&M's Olsen Field, and gasoline burn-off and local helicopters were arranged to get the field playable. The result was a two-game sweep by the homestanding Aggies over the Bears, 8–0 and 7–6.

And both Arkansas and Texas made the NCAA field, tying the record (3) for the most SWC representatives among the 40-team NCAA bracket. None of the trio advanced to the World Series, though. It was the middle season for Arkansas' three CWS appearances in five years.

SWC-based and SWC legacy program college baseball players also have been prominent in winning the Dick Howser Trophy, voted upon by the National Collegiate Baseball Writers Association, as well as the Golden Spikes Award given annually since 1978 by USA Baseball.

Dick Howser Trophy winners with Texas ties include: Scott Bryant (Texas, 1989), Brooks Kieschnick (only two-time winner of the Howser Trophy, Texas 1992–93), Jason Jennings (Baylor, 1999), Brad Lincoln (Houston, 2006), Anthony Rendon (Rice, 2010), Taylor Jungmann (Texas, 2011) (also Big 12 Conference Male Athlete of the Year), and Ivan Melendez (Texas, 2022). Jennings and Melendez doubled with the Golden Spikes Awards in those years.

Former TCU head coach and pitching star Lance Brown also had the distinction of becoming the only person in SWC history to earn Player of the Year (1963),

(L to R) Coach Buck Bailey of Washington State, Umpire Jim Tobin of National Association of Professional Baseball, Umpire Lon Warneke of National League, Coach Bibb Falk of Texas, and Umpire Hank Soar of American League.

Coach of the Year (1991 and '94), pitch on a SWC championship team (1963), and coach a SWC title team (TCU 1994).

Many other notables wore SWC uniforms in the Lone Star State or Arkansas. They include Texas's Roger Clemens, Greg Swindell, Keith Moreland, national championship quarterback James Street, two-sport star Bobby Layne, Burt Hooton, and the Howser Trophy winners from the UT program, Baylor's famed player and coach Mickey Sullivan and National Baseball Hall of Fame pitcher Teddy Lyons, Houston's Doug Drabek, Rice's Lance Berkman and Eddie Dyer, Texas A&M's Wally Moon, Chuck Knoblauch, Doug Rau, and Michael Wacha, TCU's Jim Busby, Carl Warwick and Jake Arrieta, and Texas Tech's Josh Jung, Mike Humphreys, and Stubby Clapp.[3]

1948 Heisman Trophy winner Doak Walker and teammate Kyle Rote also starred on the diamond and gridiron for SMU, while record-setting TCU and NFL quarterback Sam Baugh originally attended Texas on a baseball scholarship before transferring to TCU to star in two sports.

Gustafson as both player and coach helped the Longhorns to an NCAA-record 63 appearances in the NCAA Championship (which began in 1947) and 38 College World Series treks prior to 2025. He became the NCAA Division's winningest head coach with 1,332 victories, all at UT. He was eventually passed for this record by coaches Mike Martin of Florida State and Augie Garrido, who finished his career with 20 seasons (1997–2016) at Texas and NCAA championships in 2002 and 2005. Current Texas Longhorns head coach Jim Schlossnagle just recently guided Texas A&M to its highest finish in school history, coming in as runner-up to Tennessee at the CWS in 2024.

Interestingly, despite the many seasons of SWC national college prominence and the many future major-leaguers who honed their skills in the SWC's competitive environment, only Baylor's Lyons has a place in the National Baseball Hall of Fame in Cooperstown, though UT's Clemens has garnered multiple votes through the years with his MLB lifetime record of 354–184, 4,672 strikeouts, and seven Cy Young Awards.[4] This pitching-rich (with occasional home run power) history continues to be celebrated as fans recall the glory days of the Southwest Conference. ∎

Sources

Stats and scores from Baseball Reference, Southwest Conference Baseball Media Guides (1987–96), SWC Facebook History Page (1914–96), and University of Texas Baseball Guides, (1982–97).

Notes

1. The term Hall of Fame in this paper refers to the College Baseball Hall of Fame unless otherwise specified. The National College Baseball Hall of Fame is located in Lubbock, Texas.

2. Rice would eventually reach the CWS in 1997 for the first time and win the NCAA crown in 2003.

3. "Associated Press 1969 College Football Polls," Sports Reference, https://www.sports-reference.com/cfb/years/1969-polls.html, accessed May 19, 2024.

4. It is largely understood that Clemens has not been voted into the National Baseball Hall of Fame because BBWAA voters are reluctant to vote for any player implicated in the Mitchell Report or performance enhancing drug scandals, although Clemens never tested positive for PEDs and was found not guilty of false testimony to Congress.

Abigail Moore

Breaking Barriers

Leslie Heaphy and Cecilia M. Tan

Abby Moore has played baseball in her hometown of Arlington, Texas, since she was four years old, and now the high school student is making a splash on the national stage in women's baseball. Moore got her start with the North Arlington Little League and loved the experience from day one. She took one swing of the bat and said she was hooked, and she stuck with baseball over the years, even when many of her friends made the switch to softball. This led to her playing baseball at Arlington High School, where she also plays basketball. Baseball coach Brian Womack had never had a girl try out for his team, but as a father of two daughters was willing to give the idea a try when Moore showed up before she entered ninth grade.[1]

Moore's hard work paid off and she made the JV baseball team her freshman year, where she caught and played the outfield.[2] Making the JV team made her the first woman to ever play baseball at her school. She did not play her sophomore year after tearing her ACL playing basketball. Moore says she loves the strategy of the game. "It's a slow game. I feel like you're really in control," she said. "Especially as a catcher, you control the game. Everything is always in your hands. The scales can flip at any time. Nothing's ever too far out of reach."[3]

Moore's baseball career until 2024 had all been played with boys. She never really let that bother her; she acknowledged she has received lots of negative comments from opposing teams, but has always had the support of her own teammates. Often the reaction of other teams is initially just surprise, especially when she is catching. Being behind the plate puts her at the center of all the action.

Moore had the opportunity to attend a catcher's clinic put on by Anna Kimbrell, catcher for the USA Women's National (baseball) Team. Even there, Moore was the only girl who attended, but that connection to Kimbrell opened up the door for her to be selected to play in the All-American Women's Baseball Classic, an annual tournament organized by American Girls Baseball, a Florida-based organization promoting baseball

for girls and women that was founded by Sue Zipay, who played in the All-American Girls Professional Baseball League for the Rockford Peaches, 1953–54.[4]

Moore also had another chance to connect with women's baseball history when she was introduced by a neighbor to another former Rockford Peach, Gloria McCloskey Rogers, who played in 1953.[5] Rogers, who grew up in Missouri, now lives in North Texas and has become a big supporter of Moore, even attending her high school baseball games when she can.[6] Rogers, who is almost 90, still travels around to help promote the game for girls and women.

The All-American Women's Baseball Classic became Moore's first chance to play on an all-women's team. The event—which was hosted by the Baltimore Orioles at their spring training facility in 2022 and 2023[7]—was held in 2024 in Durham, North Carolina, at the Durham Bulls Athletic Park. She was chosen as one of 60 players taking part, and one of only a few

(L to R) Arlington High School baseball head coach Brian Womack, Abby Moore, and Gloria Rogers.

high school players in the tournament. The rest were in college or beyond, including 13 who have played for the USWNT.[8]

Moore played for the Belles in four games, catching one game and playing the outfield for the other three, tallying five hits and six RBIs. The Belles finished with a 2–2 record in the tournament (won by the Comets, 3–1).[9] All four teams carried the names of the early clubs in the AAGPBL from the 1940s: Belles, Comets, Peaches, and Blue Sox.[10] Moore got the chance to play and learn from some of the best women playing the game today, many of whom play for the USA National team, such as pitcher Elise Berger, infielder Valerie Perez, pitcher/outfielder Kelsie Whitmore, and catcher Beth Greenwood.

Moore is playing varsity girls basketball again in 2025, as a starting guard, and has set her sights on college baseball next. Moore, who ranked second in her junior class, hopes to be able to study engineering and play baseball in college at Texas A & M, but understands that the scholarships currently are for softball.[11] Perhaps in the future there might even be a women's professional team that Moore can aspire to, as the WPBL, Women's Pro Baseball League, is currently set to launch in 2026.[12] "I think it's time for a change," said Rogers about the new league. "I don't have to worry about Abby. She's not gonna quit!"[13]

Moore says her parents have been her greatest support, making all the sacrifices needed for her to be able to continue to follow her dream of playing baseball at the highest levels she can reach. Her advice for any young girl wanting to play baseball, is this: "Don't let negativity get to you, and surround yourself with people who will support you and lift you up."[14] ∎

Notes

1. "Arlington High School Student Abby Moore Plays in All-American Women's Baseball Classic," Arlington Independent School District website, District News, October 29, 2024, https://www.aisd.net/district-news/arlington-high-student-abby-moore-plays-in-all-american-womens-baseball-classic/, accessed February 25, 2025.
2. Sylvia Gutierrez, "Baseball for All: Female Joins JV2 Baseball Team," *The Colt* (Arlington high school newspaper), April 5, 2023, https://www.coltnews.com/2023/04/baseball-for-all-female-joins-jv2-baseball-team/, accessed April 26, 2022.
3. "Arlington High School Student Abby Moore Plays in All-American Women's Baseball Classic."
4. Sue Zipay Player Profile, AAGBPL website, https://www.aagpbl.org/profiles/sue-parsons-zipay/472, accessed April 26, 2025; American Girls Baseball, "About American Girls Baseball," https://americangirlsbaseball.org/about/, accessed April 26, 2025.
5. Gloria McCloskey Rogers Player Profile, AAGBPL website, https://www.aagpbl.org/profiles/gloria-mccloskey-rogers-mac/207, accessed April 26, 2025.
6. Katherine Lusby, "Baseball Player to Play in All-American Women's Baseball Classic," *The Colt*, October 1, 2024, https://www.colt-news.com/2024/10/baseball-player-to-play-in-all-american-womens-baseball-classic/, accessed March 1, 2025.
7. "All American Women's Baseball Classic at Ed Smith Stadium, MLB.com, https://www.mlb.com/orioles/spring-training/all-american-womens-baseball-classic, accessed April 26, 2024.
8. Melanie Martinez-Lopes, "All-American Women's Baseball Classic honors—and Makes—History," MLB.com, October 31, 2024, https://www.mlb.com/news/all-american-womens-baseball-classic-2024, accessed April 26, 2025.
9. "Third Annual All-American Women's Baseball Classic Results," American Girls Baseball, https://americangirlsbaseball.org/third-annual-all-american-womens-baseball-classic/, accessed April 28, 2025.
10. Martinez-Lopes, "All-American Women's Baseball Classic honors—and Makes—History."
11. Lusby, "Baseball Player to Play in All-American Women's Baseball Classic."
12. Alanis Thames, "Women's Baseball Players Could Soon Have a League of Their Own Again," AP News, November 13, 2024, https://apnews.com/article/womens-pro-baseball-league-2026-e572ee8481c4e0ba3f2b611eaf47f9cd, accessed April 26, 2025.
13. Noelle Walker, "Arlington High School Baseball Players Hopes for a 'League of Her Own' One Day" NBC DFW 5, October 23, 2024, https://www.nbcdfw.com/news/local/arlington-hs-baseball-player-hopes-for-a-league-of-her-own-one-day/, accessed April 26, 2025.
14. Lusby, "Baseball Player to Play in All-American Women's Baseball Classic."

Did the Texas Rangers Buy a World Series?

Josh West

On December 1, 2021, the Texas Rangers spent half a billion dollars on two players. Two years later they were world champions. This series of events prompts the inquiry: Did the Rangers buy a World Series? Well, what does it mean to "buy" a World Series? Every team pays all of their players whether they finish as world champions or as the first team eliminated from playoff contention. This article will analyze the contributions of the ten most influential players (based on Wins Above Replacement) on a roster to answer that question in a sensible way. While the definition of "buying" a championship is foggy, within this article I will go with a rule of thumb: If a player was acquired at the MLB level within the last three years, they were a piece that was "bought." If they came up through the minors, they are a part of the team's farm system. Finally, if a player has been on the team for the previous three seasons, no matter how they entered the organization, we can classify them as pre-existing. To categorize a team as a whole, we take whichever category—Bought, Farm, or Existing—the majority of the top ten contributors to the team's success (based on WAR) fall under and apply that label. To fully understand the financial process that led to the creation of the 2023 championship team, we will break the Rangers' recent history in eras, weighing the positives and negatives of each period.

Figure 1. Texas Ranger Spending Pattern (2000–24)*

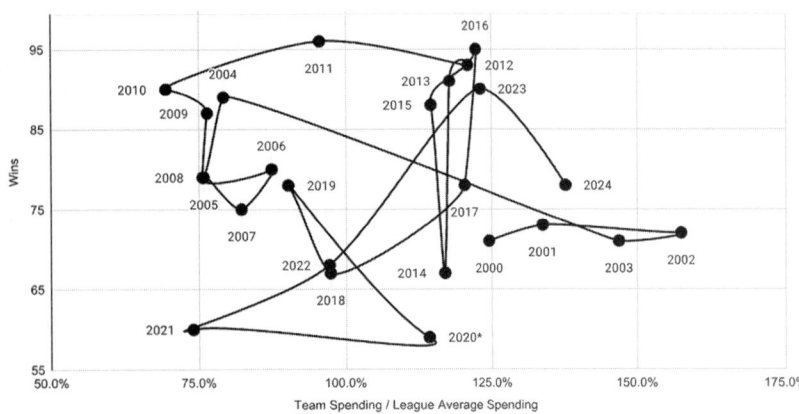

*2020 is extrapolated to 162-game season.

THE A-ROD YEARS (2001–03)

For most of the twenty-first century, the Rangers had fewer wins the more they spent, when compared to league average spending (LAS). This is mostly due to the A-Rod Years, where the team spent the highest for the franchise in all of the 2000s, at over 130% LAS each of those three years. During this time the team went through three managers in as many seasons. Despite having one of the best batters in the league (top five in league WAR each year), they never had more than 73 wins in a season. These teams lacked consistent pitching, with none having more than two pitchers with a WAR above 2.0.[1] These Rangers teams each finished in the top ten in runs scored, but bottom four in runs allowed in the league each year.

- **Notable Bought Players**: Alex Rodriguez, Frank Catalanotto

- **Notable Farm Players**: Hank Blalock, Michael Young

- **Notable Existing Players**: Ivan Rodriguez, Rafael Palmeiro

POST A-ROD ERA (2004–06)

In spring 2004, the team traded Alex Rodriguez to the Yankees for second baseman Alfonso Soriano. That season the team jumped up to 89 wins, while reducing payroll by nearly $50 million from the year prior.[2] The lowered payroll was partly due to having a young, arbitration eligible infield, all four of whom would be All-Stars by 2005: Hank Blalock 3B, Michael Young SS, Soriano 2B, and Mark Teixeira 1B. However, the biggest factor to this single-season turnaround was the pitching. The Rangers stayed at the same level of runs scored, but lowered their runs allowed. They still

106

did not make the playoffs, because both the Angels and Athletics won more than 90 games. The following two seasons were both let-downs compared to the 2004 campaign, with the pitching to blame in 2005, and the batting to blame in 2006.

- **Notable Bought Players**: Alfonso Soriano, Gary Matthews

- **Notable Farm Players**: Mark Teixeira, Chris Young

- **Notable Existing Players**: Michael Young, Kenny Rogers

RON WASHINGTON HIRING (2007–09)

The Rangers decided they needed new management, which led to the hiring of Ron Washington. With a young, talented team, they felt they were poised for a big breakthrough in the next few seasons. After finishing in the bottom three in farm systems in 2007,[3] the Rangers flipped the script and climbed into the top five farm systems 2008 through 2010. The acquisitions of young outfielders David Murphy, Josh Hamilton, and Nelson Cruz, along with farm players Ian Kinsler and Elvis Andrus, created one of the best young cores the Rangers have had. The 2008 and 2009 seasons both improved on the previous year, getting them 79 and 87 wins respectively. The 2009 season would be the first time since 2004 they finished with a winning record. The team did not make the playoffs, but they were heading in the right direction. During this span the team spent in the bottom third of the league, staying between $65 and $70 million in payroll for each of these three years.

- **Notable Bought Players**: Marlon Byrd, Josh Hamilton

- **Notable Farm Players**: Ian Kinsler, Elvis Andrus

- **Notable Existing Players**: Michael Young, Scott Feldman

WORLD SERIES RUNS (2010–11)

In 2010, after having the fifth-most runs scored and 11th in fewest runs allowed—the Rangers reached the World Series for the first time in club history. The improvement mostly came from players on the roster reaching new heights. CJ Wilson finished second in WAR for the team, with six pitchers in the top ten. Of these top ten players, six were existing on the Rangers,

two were farm players, and only two were bought—and bought as bargains. One was Colby Lewis, a player who had been with the Rangers for several years in the past, but had injuries and spent time overseas, and the other was Darren O'Day, a player the Rangers got off waivers a year before. The team had the fifth-lowest payroll in MLB due to the majority of their players being so young.

Going into the 2011 season, the Rangers signed two players who immediately made an impact: Catcher Mike Napoli and future Hall of Fame third baseman Adrian Beltre were signed for a combined $19 million. They were the only players that were bought and made the top ten that year. The team also relied heavily on their pitching, with the entire starting rotation finishing in the top 11 players. The team again made it to the World Series and again fell short, finishing with the third most runs scored and 13th fewest runs allowed. With the new signings and the young stars starting to grow older, the team ended up paying roughly $30 million more this season than the year before. This ended up making the overall payroll roughly $90 million, the highest since A-Rod's last year (2003) and the first time since then that the team spent over $70 million in a single year.

- **Notable Bought Players**: Adrian Beltre, Mike Napoli

- **Notable Farm Players**: Alexi Ogando, Neftali Feliz

- **Notable Existing Players**: CJ Wilson, Josh Hamilton

DISAPPOINTMENTS (2012–14)

After back-to-back World Series trips, the 2012 season gave hope the team could go one step further and nail down a championship. The farm system made the top five and they won the bid for Japanese star Yu Darvish, putting the payroll at $120 million (seventh in MLB). But the team ended up losing in the wildcard round, and faced a tough offseason financially.

That winter the team traded Michael Young and did not re-sign Josh Hamilton. After finishing first in runs scored but 18th in runs allowed in 2012, they improved pitching to get tenth in runs allowed, but fell to eighth in runs scored in 2013. This team ended up spending $125 million (ninth in MLB) and missing the playoffs. Because of the poor performance and high payroll, the Rangers traded Ian Kinsler and decided to let Nelson Cruz leave as well.

The 2014 season ended with the team finishing last in the division with only 67 wins and manager Ron Washington resigning with 22 games left. The team spent over $130 million (tenth in MLB) and had their worst record in 29 years. This season was the biggest disappointment, and it fully closed the window that the team had opened only five years prior.

- **Notable Bought Players**: Yu Darvish, Adrian Beltre

- **Notable Farm Players**: Leonys Martin, Robinson Chirinos

- **Notable Existing Players**: Elvis Andrus, Craig Gentry

BANNISTER ERA (2015–18)

The next two years bounced back nicely in the win columns, while the Rangers continued to spend more each year. New manager Jeff Bannister was able to take his team to 88 and 95 wins while payroll stood at $140 and $150 million in 2015 and 2016, respectively. Both of these teams made the playoffs, losing in the divisional round both times. These teams, like many previous Rangers teams, had top-tier run-producing teams, but were bottom tier when it came to giving up runs.

The 2017 and 2018 years failed to hit the previous mark with only 78 and 67 wins, while spending $165 and $133 million each. These teams both missed the playoffs, finishing third and fifth in the division. During this time several players finished their time with the Rangers, including Adrian Beltre, who retired after the 2018 season, and Yu Darvish, who was traded to the Dodgers in 2017. These years also saw the farm system fall from hovering around the top ten to bottom ten in the league.

- **Notable Bought Players**: Cole Hamels, Shin-Soo Choo

- **Notable Farm Players**: Joey Gallo, Rougned Odor

- **Notable Existing Players**: Yu Darvish, Adrian Beltre

WOODWARD ERA (2019–22)

After frustrating seasons of overspending and not producing, the team moved on to new manager Chris Woodward in 2019. The team lowered their total budget, and did nothing to improve their farm system, which also stayed in the bottom-third of the league. Despite glimpses of above-average play, these teams could not reach a winning record. The 2021 season ended with 60 wins, the lowest in a full length season since 1973.

After three abysmal years, the team decided to spend in free agency, and in a single night signed two players to huge long-term contracts: 2021 Gold Glove and Silver Slugger second baseman Marcus Semien to a seven-year, $175 million deal, and two-time Silver Slugger Corey Seager to a ten-year $325 million deal. These signings, as well as a farm system in the top ten for the first time since 2016, helped kickstart the upward trajectory for this franchise. Despite both of the big free agents performing at the level the team was hoping for in their first year, the team performed poorly overall, as 2022 finished with only 68 wins, despite a $140 million payroll.

- **Notable Bought Players**: Mike Minor, Lance Lynn

- **Notable Farm Players**: Adolis Garcia, Isiah Kiner-Falefa

- **Notable Existing Players**: Joey Gallo, Jose Leclerc

WORLD SERIES CHAMPIONS (2023)

The Rangers started the push for a title by hiring Bruce Bochy to be their manager in October 2022. Looking to improve from 12th in runs scored and 23rd in runs allowed, the team spent more—120% of LAS—to add a few key players. With a farm system now in the top half of the league, and these new additions, the team took a huge leap forward. This team went on to finish with the 13th fewest runs allowed, the highest ranking since 2013, and the third most runs scored. Semien and Seager ended up combining for 14.9 WAR. The Rangers made their third World Series, and won their first title in franchise history.

Looking at the top ten contributors to the team's success in 2023, only one was from their farm, with two already existing. The other seven in the top ten were Bought. Of these players, only one joined in 2023, while three were on the team for the first time in 2022, including both Semien and Seager, and three more joined the team for the 2021 season. Compared to the previous trips in 2010 and 2011 (two Farm, six Existing, and two Bought players), this is almost the opposite makeup for a team.

- **Notable Bought Players**: Marcus Semien, Corey Seager

- **Notable Farm Players**: Josh Jung, Evan Carter

- **Notable Existing Players**: Adolis Garcia, Leody Taveras

Table 1. Texas Rangers Teams, 2000–24

Year	Bought	Farm	Existing	Classification
2000	5	2	3	Bought
2001	5	3	2	Bought
2002	5	3	2	Bought
2003	5	2	3	Bought
2004	5	3	2	Bought
2005	4	2	4	Bought/Existing
2006	5	2	3	Bought
2007	4	2	4	Bought/Existing
2008	6	1	3	Bought
2009	2	2	6	Existing
2010	3	3	4	Existing
2011	2	3	5	Existing
2012	4	0	6	Existing
2013	4	2	4	Bought/Existing
2014	3	3	4	Existing
2015	5	2	3	Bought
2016	3	3	4	Existing
2017	2	2	6	Existing
2018	1	2	7	Existing
2019	5	1	4	Bought
2020	2	7	1	Farm
2021	4	4	2	Bought/Farm
2022	8	2	0	Bought
2023	7	1	2	Bought
2024	6	3	1	Bought

CONCLUSION

When asking the question "Did the Rangers buy a World Series?" the answer must be Yes. With the biggest contributions coming from players that were mostly brought in through trades and free agency less than three full years before the team won it all, this Championship was bought, not grown.

Examining how the Rangers constructed their three World Series rosters shows how teams should prioritize player acquisition based on spending. A team can spend less by building through their farm system and acquiring players early in their career. However, if a team can afford to go all out and spend, adding multiple high-level players with proven talent can get results. The Rangers going through different philosophies over the last 25 years proves that there is not one singular way to win, but the team must be well rounded and firing on all cylinders no matter whether the players were bought or not. ■

Notes

1 "Texas Rangers Team History & Encyclopedia." Baseball Reference. Accessed April 22, 2025. https://www.baseball-reference.com/teams/TEX/.

2. "Cot's Baseball Contracts." Cots Baseball Contracts. Accessed April 22, 2025. https://legacy.baseballprospectus.com/compensation/cots/al-west/texas-rangers/.

3. J.J. Cooper "MLB Farm System Rankings for Every Team in the 21st Century." Baseball America, March 5, 2024. https://www.baseballamerica.com/stories/mlb-farm-system-rankings-for-every-team-in-the-21st-century/.

CONTRIBUTORS

JOHN BAUER resides with his wife and two children (with one now at college) in Bedford, New Hampshire. By day, he is general counsel of an insurance group headquartered in Manchester, New Hampshire with specialties in corporate and regulatory law. By night, he spends many spring and summer evenings staying up too late to watch the San Francisco Giants, and he is a year-round avid reader of baseball, history, and baseball history. He is a past and ongoing contributor to various SABR projects.

ERIC BYNUM has been a die-hard Atlanta Braves fan since the early 1980s thanks to WTBS. A history teacher by day, he tried to immerse himself in baseball as much as possible by night. For years he has run a baseball blog on international baseball, BaseballdeWorld, and is taking a break from working on his history PhD to write more about baseball.

BO CARTER joined SABR in 1993 and was the media relations director for the Southwest Conference from 1986–96 and Big 12 Conference from 1996–2006. He also has served on the SABR College Baseball Committee for 20-plus years and is a member of the College Sports Communicators Hall of Fame. He has been executive director of the National Collegiate Baseball Writers Association since 1998.

MONTE CELY is a member of the Society for American Baseball Research, and has previously written articles about baseball's Cy Young Award, as well as co-authored a research study on SABR's baseball reminiscence programs. He grew up playing baseball in Staunton, Illinois, a town about the size of Marlin, Texas. He is a fan of the St. Louis Cardinals, having attended his first game with his Dad in 1959 (against the Giants!) Monte and his wife Linda reside in Round Rock, Texas, about 90 miles southwest of Marlin.

JIM CHAPMAN is a Waxahachie native, Judge of the Ellis County Court at Law No. 1, and the winner of SABR's 2024 Larry Ritter Book Award for *Baseball Photography of the Deadball Era*.

ALAN COHEN has been a SABR member since 2011. He chairs the BioProject factchecking team, is Vice President-Treasurer of the Connecticut Smoky Joe Wood Chapter, and is a datacaster (MiLB stringer) with the Eastern League Hartford Yard Goats, the Class AA affiliate of the Rockies. He also works with the Retrosheet Negro Leagues project and serves on SABR's Negro League Committee. His biographies, game stories, and essays have appeared in more than 80 baseball-related publications.

RONALD ELLIOTT, PhD lives in Stillwater, Oklahoma, and is a professor emeritus and former department head in biosystems and agricultural engineering at Oklahoma State University. A member of SABR's Oklahoma Chapter, he has created a statistical database covering the past 75 years of OSU Cowboy baseball. He is a 44-year season ticket holder and was privileged to be in the stands for Robin Ventura's 58-game hitting streak and Pete Incaviglia's 48 home run, 143 RBI season.

CHARLIE GRASSL is a long time SABR member, a graduate of the University of Texas and currently retired from Texas Instruments/Raytheon. Born in San Antonio, Charlie grew up on Texas League baseball. Charlie and his wife Carole now live in Arlington, Texas. At Globe Life Field, he is one of the remaining few who "keep score" at Texas Rangers games. This is his second writing project after contributing to the SABR publication *The Team That Couldn't Hit*.

LESLIE HEAPHY is an associate professor of history at Kent State University at Stark and has been a SABR member since 1989. She has written extensively about the Negro Leagues and Women's baseball. Leslie currently serves as the SABR Women in baseball committee chair and as the president of the Board for the IWBC. She is a lifelong Mets fan!!

ANDREW JETT is a lifelong Texas Rangers fan who graduated from Trinity University with a Bachelor's of Political Science in 2023. Since then, he has volunteered with Retrosheet rectifying discrepancies in play-by-play data of the 1911 and 1910 MLB seasons and worked to deduce play-by-play for Negro Leagues games based on newspaper stories. He currently works at the Dallas Holocaust and Human Rights Museum. This upcoming fall, he will begin a Master's program in Holocaust Studies at Royal Holloway in London.

HERM KRABBENHOFT is a retired chemist (PhD, University of Michigan, 1974) and author of *Leadoff Batters of Major League Baseball* (McFarland, 2001). Among the various baseball research topics he has pioneered are: Ultimate Grand Slam Homers, Consecutive Games On Base Safely (CGOBS) Streaks, Quasi-Cycles, Imperfect Perfectos, Downtown Golden Sombreros, and Pitcher's Cycles. In addition to *The National Pastime* and the *Baseball Research Journal*, Herm has contributed articles to the newsletters for SABR's 19th Century, Deadball Era, Statistical Analysis, and Baseball Records Committees. Krabbenhoft has received three SABR Baseball Research Awards (1992, 1996, 2013).

STEVE KREVISKY has been a professor of mathematics at Connecticut State Community College, Middlesex Campus, for many years. His students get used to him bringing baseball into classes to make it more interesting for them. He is also President of the Smoky Joe Wood SABR chapter, which has periodic meetings, chapter breakfasts, and trips to local minor league games. He has been attending SABR's annual conventions for many years, going back to his first convention in Chicago in 1986. He has been a frequent presenter, has published articles in the journals, and has also been on seven teams that won the trivia championships over the years! He looks forward to returning to Texas for this year's convention. He is in a simulation/fantasy league, and looks forward to that committee meeting as well as seeing old friends there!

BOB LEMOINE is a high school librarian, teacher, adjunct professor, and union president who would rather just be working in baseball. He has written dozens of SABR bios and game articles, co-edited two SABR nineteenth-century related books, and even wrote his own book: *When the Babe Went Back to Boston: Babe*

Ruth, Judge Fuchs and the Hapless Braves of 1935 (McFarland, 2023). He lives in New Hampshire, but to impress people will often say "the Boston area."

WADE McWHORTER lives in Stillwater, Oklahoma, and is an assistant director of communications for Oklahoma State Athletics who oversees Cowboy Baseball and Cowgirl Soccer. A member of College Sports Communicators and the National Collegiate Baseball Writers Association, the 2025 season will be his 20th as the Cowboy Baseball SID. Over the previous 19 seasons, he has worked 1,093 OSU games (he missed two weeks with the birth of his twins in April 2007), with the Cowboys winning 698 of those and making 16 NCAA Regional appearances. Eighteen of the players he has worked with have gone on to play Major League Baseball.

PAUL ROGERS III is president of the Ernie Banks-Bobby Bragan (Dallas-Fort Worth) SABR Chapter and the co-author of four baseball books, including *The Whiz Kids and the 1950 Pennant* written with his boyhood hero Robin Roberts, and *Lucky Me: My 65 Years in Baseball* authored with Eddie Robinson. He is also co-editor of SABR team histories of the 1951 New York Giants and the 1950 Philadelphia Phillies as well as a frequent contributor to the SABR bio and games projects. His real job is as a law professor at SMU where he was dean of the law school for nine years and has served as the university's faculty athletic representative for 38 years.

JARROD D. SCHENEWARK, PhD was born in Southern California and grew up listening to Vin Scully. He earned a Bachelor of Arts in History from the University of Connecticut. While at Connecticut, he was a member of the university football team. He earned a master's degree from the University of California, Berkeley, working with Dr. Roberta Park and focusing on the history of exercise science and sport. He was awarded a PhD in Kinesiology from the University of Texas at Austin in 2008. His wife is from Boston, and all seven of their children cheer for the Red Sox.

JASON A. SCHWARTZ is a member of the Emil Rothe (Chicago) SABR Chapter and Co-Chair of the SABR Baseball Cards Research Committee. His collection of Henry Aaron baseball cards and memorabilia is currently on display at the Atlanta History Center, and his baseball card-inspired artwork can be found at PNC Park and the Honus Wagner Museum.

BILL STAPLES JR. of Chandler, AZ, joined SABR in 2006 and specializes in Japanese American and Negro Leagues baseball history. Born in Troy, New York, and raised in Texas, he considers himself a "Yankee-Texan" with family ties to both the early NY–NJ League and the Texas Negro Leagues. He attended Plano East Senior High, Austin College (Sherman), and the University of North Texas (Denton), where he played for the "Mean Green" Eagles baseball club. His walk-up song is "Pride and Joy" by Stevie Ray Vaughan & Double Trouble. His favorite Willies are Mays and Nelson. Learn more at billstaplesjr.com.

CECILIA M. TAN joined SABR in 2002 and has not missed a SABR national convention since. She has somehow become SABR's longest-serving Publications Director (since 2011). She has seen every current major league team play a home game except for Milwaukee and Detroit.

WAYNE TOWERS, PhD is a retired Sea World San Diego education specialist and retired college professor and administrator. He also worked as a data analyst for *The Oklahoman and Times* daily newspaper and for multiple business and marketing research firms. His published work includes "World Series Coverage in the 1920s" (Journalism Monographs).

THOMAS E. Van HYNING grew up in Santurce, Puerto Rico, and authored *Puerto Rico's Winter League, The Santurce Crabbers, and The Caribbean Series: Latin America's Annual Baseball Tournament, 1949–2024* by McFarland (January 31, 2025). Tom is active in Arkansas's Robinson-Kell SABR Chapter, SABR's Baseball Records and Latino Research Committees, and is a charter member of SABR's Cool Papa Bell (Mississippi) Chapter. He has written 15 SABR bios, plus *Baseball Research Journal* and *National Pastime* articles. Tom, his wife, and Yorkie are full-time RVers in Alabama, Arkansas, Mississippi, Oklahoma, and Texas.

DAN VANDEMORTEL became a Giants fan in upstate New York and moved to San Francisco to follow the team more closely. He has written extensively on Northern Ireland political and legal affairs. His coverage of baseball cultural-related topics has appeared in *The National Pastime*, the California *Daily Journal*, and other publications. His article "White Circles Drawn in Crayon" (featured in *McFarland Historic Ballparks* 05: The Polo Grounds, 2019) won the 2020 McFarland-SABR Baseball Research Award. Feedback is welcome at giants1971@yahoo.com.

JOSEPH WANCHO resides in Westlake, Ohio. He has been a SABR member since 2005 and he serves as co-chair of the Baseball Index Project. He is an occasional contributor to various SABR research committees.

An Oklahoma native, **DOUG WEDGE** has written three baseball history books, *Pinnacle on the Mound: Cy Young Award Winners Talk Baseball*, *Baseball in Alabama: Tales of Hardball in the Heart of Dixie*, and *The Cy Young Catcher* (with co-author Charlie O'Brien). He lives in Oklahoma City.

JOSH WEST has loved baseball since he was born. He is currently attending the University of North Texas, pursuing his bachelors degree and certifications in both Data Analytics and Actuarial Science. After graduation, he plans on working within the world of sports data, trying to find ways to innovate teams from a statistical standpoint. This is his first time writing for SABR.

STEVE WEST is a freelance writer based in Carrollton, Texas. He has written numerous articles for the BioProject, and this is the third book he has edited for SABR. He has been a SABR member since 2006.